Basing his studies mainly upon texts of the *Iliad* and the *Odyssey*—but also upon the works of many other writers of antiquity and upon our great accumulation of archaeological evidence — Emile Mireaux has produced a picture of everyday life in Homeric Greece that is truly amazing in its immediacy. A whole world of men and women of every class of society, with their cares and anxieties, their hopes and their daily preoccupations, rises from the ashes of the past, lives and moves before our eyes.

This was a world in which man lived in close and constant relation with gods and demi-gods, who could manifest themselves in every shape or form, a world in which everyday incidents could take on a special premonitory meaning. But after explaining Homeric man's relation to his gods, and his conception of the world in a geographical sense, the author goes on to describe in fascinating detail the lives of aristocrats, noblemen, intellectuals, peasants, soldiers, craftsmen, artisans, public servants, beggars, wanderers and exiles. He describes life within the family, the occupations and status of women, the popular festivals and the funeral rites, and the public games. He tells us, too, about houses and furniture, clothes and weapons, decorations and food, work and leisure, sports and pastimes, medicine, soothsaying, vendettas, commerce and carriage, and every conceivable aspect of daily life in the time of Homer.

This is a vivid and evocative reconstruction of a richly complex era in human history.

the author of *Les Poèmes Homériques et l'Histoire Grecque, Les Miracles du Crédit, La Reine Bérénice, Philosophie du Libéralisme,* and *L'Organisation du Crédit dans les Territoires d'Outre-Mer.*

# DAILY LIFE IN THE TIME OF HOMER

**THE MACMILLAN COMPANY**
NEW YORK • CHICAGO
DALLAS • ATLANTA • SAN FRANCISCO
LONDON • MANILA

IN CANADA
**BRETT-MACMILLAN LTD.**
GALT, ONTARIO

EMILE MIREAUX

# DAILY LIFE
# IN THE
# TIME OF HOMER

TRANSLATED FROM THE FRENCH BY
IRIS SELLS

*New York*
THE MACMILLAN COMPANY
1959

© George Allen and Unwin Ltd.   1959

First Printing

The Macmillan Company, New York
Brett-Macmillan Ltd., Galt, Ontario

Printed in the United States of America


Translated from
LA VIE QUOTIDIENNE AU TEMPS D'HOMÈRE
*Librairie Hachette*, Paris, 1954

Library of Congress catalog card number: 59-7966

# TRANSLATOR'S PREFACE

*La Vie quotidienne au temps d'Homère,* which is here now offered in a version for the English-speaking world, was published in Paris, in 1954. It may be regarded as an example of that skill in the analysis and interpretation of the documents, of which the French are past masters. It is cool, objective and at the same time sympathetic; and the reader may well be amazed at the richness, the detail and the complexity of the life which is here evoked. A whole world of men and women, with their cares and anxieties, their fears and their hopes, rises from the ashes of the past, lives and moves before our eyes.

Apart from his judicious use of the findings of archaeology, and his references to recent critical and historical studies, Monsieur Mireaux quotes frequently from Hesiod's *Theogony* and *Works and Days*; and also of course from the Homeric poems themselves. In the version now offered, these passages have been quoted from the following British translations:

*The Odyssey of Homer:* translated by Sir William Marris, Oxford University Press, 1925.

*The Iliad of Homer:* translated by Sir William Marris, Oxford University Press, 1934.

*Hesiod: The Poems and Fragments:* done into English Prose . . . by A. W. Mair, Oxford, at the Clarendon Press, 1908.

The page references to the above passages are given in footnotes, but I have not always, after the first few instances, repeated the names of the translators.

The choice of English forms for Greek proper names, and especially for technical terms, presents a problem that rarely admits of a logical solution. For proper names I have usually preferred the semi-latinized forms, such as Alcinous and Periander, rather than Alkinoos and Periandros. The ending in -os is however traditional for many Aegean islands. English forms are in many instances optional, and two or even three may be correct. One can write Eupatridai, or Eupatridae, or even Eupatrids. Technical terms are sometimes more easily gallicized than anglicized. Thus Monsieur Mireaux writes of 'la fille épiclère' (that is, a daughter who, in the absence of a male heir to her father, was capable of transmitting the heritage to her son); in English one is virtually obliged to write 'epikleros' or 'epicleros'. I usually replace 'kappa' with a 'c'. In all the above there is no strict logic, and it is impossible in practice to follow an absolutely uniform system. Some of the names and many of the terms used in this book are rare, and in this matter I have been greatly assisted by the expert advice of Professor Norman Pratt of Indiana University. My husband, Professor Lytton Sells, has read through the whole of the manuscript; without his assistance, the translation could hardly have been completed.

IRIS SELLS

# ACKNOWLEDGEMENT

The publishers are grateful to the executors of the late Sir William Marris for permission to quote extensively from his translations of *The Iliad* and *The Odyssey*.

# CONTENTS

I- Background and Setting,
II - The Life of Nobleman

# INTRODUCTION

THE object of these introductory pages is to specify what we mean, and what should be understood, by 'the time of Homer', and very briefly to explain the data on which our knowledge is founded.

The Ancients were by no means agreed as to when Homer lived. Herodotus placed him in the first half of the ninth century B.C. The historian Theopompus, it seems, placed him at the beginning of the seventh. Modern critics have subjected the Homeric poems to peregrinations in time at least as extensive; but the limits of their present conjectures go scarcely beyond the eighth century on the one hand and the sixth on the other. Of the main solutions that have been offered, we will confine ourselves to the most recent.

Erich Bethe, one of the masters of the German analytical school, places the final form in which the *Iliad* and the *Odyssey* were written[1] as late as the second half of the sixth century, in the time of Peisistratus. This draft was not, according to Bethe, the work of creative poets but only of poetical revisers who arranged material already in hand. They were drawing from a vast and ancient repertory of epic songs and little epics which had been invented by numerous earlier poets on two popular themes: the wrath of Achilles and the return of Odysseus. Thus the author of the *Iliad* threw into his crucible more than ten of these ancient poems; the author of the *Odyssey* was satisfied with six. These elementary compositions dated[2] for the most part from the two preceding centuries.

Wilamowitz-Moellendorff, who belongs also to the analytical school and has long and rightly been regarded as its leader, suggests a different system but one involving similar dates. He assigns

[1] 'La rédaction définitive de l'*Iliade*', etc. The last draft may not have involved more than a number of minor or verbal changes and a certain amount of smoothing out. But it is all a matter of conjecture. (Translator's note).

[2] The use of the conditional mood in French here and in the above lines implies that it is a matter of conjecture (Translator).

to the eighth century the composition of the *Iliad*. It was, according to him, the work of a great poet whose name was probably Homer. The latter had drawn liberally from an already existing treasure of poetry and legend, but his powerful inventive genius had renewed it. His poem subsequently underwent certain modifications. The original ending disappeared, to be replaced by the two more recent episodes which conclude the text as we have it: namely, the funeral games in honour of Patroclus, and the meeting between Achilles and Priam. As to the *Odyssey*, it was 'arranged' at the beginning of the sixth century, nearly two hundred years after the *Iliad*, thanks to the skilful combination of four earlier poems which may have been written as early as the seventh century B.C.

Victor Bérard, whose verve and learning have done so much in France to animate and renew the study of the *Odyssey*, places its composition at a slightly earlier date. Following in his own way the arguments advanced by Adolf Kirchhoff, he considers that the poem originated, during the first half of the seventh century, from the combination of three earlier poems composed by different men: the *Tales of Odysseus*, the *Journey of Telemachus*, and the *Vengeance of Odysseus*. The first, which was the oldest, may go back to the ninth century; the two others probably date from the eighth.

In the weighty introduction preceding his own edition and excellent translation of the *Iliad*, M. Paul Mazon, who is the chief Homeric scholar in France, concludes by adopting a chronology fairly close to the above. He places about the beginning of the eighth century the composition of the songs that formed the first draft of the poem. He does not exclude its having been composed as far back as the ninth. This first draft, recast, enlarged and developed by its author, was rehandled and amplified by his successors and so, by a fairly long and continuous process of creation, became the epic as we now know it. At what moment did it acquire its virtually final shape? M. Mazon very prudently refrains from specifying. Possibly, towards the beginning of the seventh century.

It was at the same moment — if we are to believe M. Friedrich

Focke, one of the latest commentators of the Odyssean poem —
that is, round about the year 700 B.C., that the *Odyssey* was composed.

In his recent book on *Homer*, M. Fernand Robert, for his part,
ascribes the honour of having created the two great epics to an
'adapter' of genius who lived and wrote during the last third of the
eighth century. What he adapted was a repertory of legends and
traditions of sacerdotal origin, much rather — if we rightly understand M. Robert — than of earlier epics, whether long or short
ones. Homer was a creator and not a compiler.

Finally, we may venture to recall that, a few years before M.
Fernand Robert, we had ourselves in our studies on *Les Poèmes
homériques et l'Histoire grecque*,[1] argued that the *Iliad* and the
*Odyssey* were in fact the conscious, original work of a great poet
whose date we placed about the middle of the seventh century. But
this poet was himself only a 'renewer' of genius, who had inherited and continued the work of a first Homer. Now it was, we
suggest, during the last decades of the preceding century that this
first Homer wrote a first *Iliad* and a first *Odyssey*, markedly
shorter and more compact than those we have, very splendid,
however, and powerful in their simplicity, and, besides, so original
that we may well wonder whether it was not they which opened
the way for the development of epic poetry in Greece.

In any case, to whatever opinion we subscribe, it emerges from
this rapid review of the chronological theories, that the 'time of
Homer' is confined within fairly well-defined limits; and this, for
our purpose, is the point of capital importance.

The 'time of Homer' begins at earliest in the eighth century and
ends at latest in the seventh. One may even cut off a few decades
near the beginning or near the end of this period, and, for our part,
we are somewhat tempted to do so. The essential point, to guide
and justify the enquiry we shall now undertake, is this: it is fairly
apparent that the milestone year, the pivotal year, of the Homeric
age, was about the year 700 before Christ.

[1] (i) *Homère de Chios et les Routes de l'Etain*. Paris, 1948. (ii) *L'Iliade,
l'Odyssée et les Rivalités coloniales*. Paris, 1949.

There is, moreover, something symbolical about this year. It was at about this time, if we may believe the archaeologists, that the eighth Troy was founded; that, in other words, Greek colonists occupied the site of the ancient fortress and that the Greek Ilium, which was later to pose as the heir of the glorious and heroic past, comes into the light of history.

What place then is occupied in Greek history by this 'Homeric age', the daily life of which we shall now try to describe?

Like most periods of history, it was an age of transition. It witnessed great and relatively rapid changes of which the birth of the Greek epic was not perhaps, at least in our view, the most striking.

It begins, politically speaking, at the time when the old monarchies of a religious and patriarchal complexion are disappearing. In Athens, the dynasty of the Medontidae comes to an end in the first quarter of the eighth century. A little later, it is the turn of the Corinthian dynasties. About this time the Neleidae meet with a like fate at Miletus, and the descendants of the founder Procles, on Samos. In a large number of cities the same revolution is carried through, but generally, it appears, in a peaceful manner. In many places the descendants of the old royal families retain a religious and honorary pre-eminence, of which the rank enjoyed by king Alcinous in the land of the Phaeacians gives us a fairly good picture.

Almost everywhere by the end of the eighth century, at least in the majority of the maritime cities, the great aristocratic families have seized the reins of power. This is the situation notably along the Asiatic shore, on Mytilene, Chios and Samos, and in Ephesus and Miletus. In Continental Greece, Athens, Eretria, Megara, Corinth, Sicyon and Chalcis are likewise governed by aristocratic minorities.

The political revolutions were accompanied by economic changes of a most drastic kind. In obedience to the call of the sea, which was omnipresent, the new masters rediscovered the vocation of the Cretan thalassocracies, of the Achaean seamen who, prior to the invasion of the rough Dorian landsmen, had in the course of the second millenium B.C. been navigating the Mediterranean.

In fact the eighth and seventh centuries — what we may call the 'Homeric age' — witnessed an irresistible movement of Hellenic expansion, maritime, commercial and colonial. To the west and as far as Campania the Greeks planted settlements round the coasts of southern Italy and Sicily. To the north-east they encircled the Black Sea with their trading posts. They landed in Africa, at Cyrene, and established themselves permanently in concessions on the Nile delta. We have attempted elsewhere to show how, by opening up new horizons and awakening interests and curiosities hitherto unknown, this economic revolution could, and must have created, on the moral and intellectual plane, an atmosphere that would favour the transformation of the traditional poetry of religious and mythological hymns into the heroic epic poetry, and raise up a Homer.

This moral revolution was soon to be accompanied by social changes. The aristocracy of great landowners who exercised political power was gradually transformed into an oligarchy of industrialists and shipowners, an aristocracy of wealth. And now a reaction began to show itself. The lower classes, which had been oppressed and in some instances dispossessed, began to agitate. They found defenders among the great families who were divided by personal ambition. And the first tyrannies appeared, towards the mid-seventh century, at Sicyon, Corinth and Megara.

Democracy appears on the stage. A new era is dawning. The Homeric age is near its end.

We may now ask what materials we dispose of in this attempt to reconstruct its features.

Of the literary texts we must of course set in the first rank the Homeric poems themselves. These are extremely valuable documents, first because they cannot be replaced: practically all the contemporary writings, whether epic or lyrical, of which there were certainly a great number, have disappeared. Apart from this, the more we study the Homeric poems, the more amazed we become at the minutiae of the descriptions and the technical precision of the vocabulary, both in the field of manual arts and in the domains of law and government. The authors, who were unquestionably men of great imagination, were at the same time realists who knew how to observe and perceive.

As they evoke adventures that took place in a distant and legendary past, it is certainly not difficult to detect on their part a certain love of the archaic. We must nevertheless admit that the world they described was the one which lay before their eyes. It was in this way that when our French 'trouvères' of the eleventh and twelfth centuries evoked a Carolingian hero tale which in itself was legendary, they were describing the feudal life of their own time. Let us then take care not to eliminate from the Homeric narratives and descriptions certain features supposedly too 'modern', under the pretence that these are out of keeping with an archaism that is deliberate and on the whole very superficial. When the bards speak of ivory keys, lamps, candelabra and a few other more or less luxurious accessories, we should consider that this is because they had seen them in the already luxurious dwellings of the nobles and princes of their time.

The works of Hesiod may be included among our sources of information, almost on the same level as the Homeric poems. We situate the poet of Ascra's literary activity in the second half of the seventh century B.C., and consequently at the very end of the 'Homeric age'. It is none the less true that the precise details regarding country life which he gives us in his *Works and Days* possess great documentary value; for if there is a domain in which changes are slow and insensible, it is that of the peasant environment.

As to the many lyric poets who were writing during the first half or towards the middle of the seventh century, they unfortunately cannot be used for our purpose. Of Callinus, Archilochus, Tyrtaeus, Alcman of Sardis, and Thaletas of Gortyn, there remain only fragments which merely inform us of the important place this poetry occupied in the daily or public life of the Greek world in Homer's time.

Fortunately however we dispose of relatively abundant archaeological evidence to illustrate the literary texts. It is mainly a question here of the evidence furnished by the excavations of cemeteries, the tombs being the places that best preserved the daily objects buried with the dead. The most valuable remains come from the old Athenian cemetery of the Dipylon. To these may be added the relics discovered at Corinth, Thera, Delos, Myconos and Aegina, to name only a few sites, and also a considerable range of pottery of various origins — itself a source of historical information — although unfortunately the richest and most eloquent portions of it are of rather later date.

Finally we must add to these direct sources the indirect, and the latter are not always the least valuable. We refer to later texts and institutions which bear witness to, or incidentally inform us about, life in the early centuries of Greek history.

In addition to the properly so-called historical texts, from Herodotus to Plutarch, and the scattered information that scholarship has gleaned among various political, philosophical and even literary writings, special mention should be made of the juridical texts. The most ancient legal systems, as far as they are known to us from quotations or inscriptions — those of Draco and Solon, the laws of Gortyn, not forgetting the hypothetical laws of a Lycurgus — contain provisions that inform us about the oldest periods, whether these provisions confine themselves to codifying ancient customs or endeavour to modify or correct them.

A critical study of the institutions and customs which were for long ages perpetuated in the most conservative cities, and notably at Sparta, may throw great light upon the ancient family and social structure of the Greek world. In this field the analysis which M. Henri Jeanmaire has effected in the light of comparative ethnography have proved particularly fruitful: we shall frequently refer to them in the following pages.

By such means as we have described — even if there remain gaps as in a broken vase that one tries to piece together by collecting the scattered fragments — one may try to bring back to life that distant past towards which the magic of poetry draws us by an invincible charm.

# CHAPTER I

# THE BACKGROUND AND SETTING

## HOMER'S WORLD

I T is a commonplace to say that in the last four centuries our vision of the universe has been profoundly modified. Our speculations now extend to embrace the infinite; and, whether we are aware of it or no, our daily life has taken its tone and colour from this tremendous revolution in our outlook. We have only to open our eyes to the cosmic scene for the dolorous cry of Pascal to echo in our hearts and awaken a similar sensation of anguish; from which the humblest intelligence amongst us is not immune.

At the same time we view this colossal world as organized according to some marvellous scheme with a material structure subject to the norms of reason and in the grip of an inexorable mechanism. In those cases, for example in the domain of the infinitely little, when this inexorable determinism seems to yield slightly, the indeterminacy remains subject to the laws of mathematics, with results calculable according to the law of majorities. How different from this grand and logical interpretation was the world as it appeared to the Greeks of Homer's day!

## THE SMALLNESS OF HOMER'S WORLD

Homer's world appears to us today as something diminutive. Homer imagined the earth as a disc, with a radius of some two thousand kilometres and an area of about twelve and a half million square kilometers; that is, about twenty-three times the size of France.

Greece, naturally, was in the centre of the disc, so that the sanctuary of Delphi, which was regarded as being the centre of Greece, came to be referred to as the 'navel of the world'. The terrestrial world was bounded roughly by the shores of the Atlantic, the Baltic and Caspian Seas, the northern shores of the Indian Ocean and the southern frontiers of Nubia.

The earth's disc was surrounded by a vast river with a mighty current — the very edge of the world. Beyond this verge were the regions that gave access to Erebus, to the world of shades, the underground kingdom of the dead, over whom reigned Hades and Persephone. The upper regions were the domain of the Cimmerians, or rather of the 'Chimerians', the dwellers in eternal winter: hither came Odysseus after his crossing of the Ocean to visit the country of the dead. Homer gives a sinister picture of it in Book XI of the *Odyssey*. The ship had fared on until the sun set 'and all the ways were dark':

> 'So came she to the limits of the world,
> Deep-running Ocean; where the land and city
> Of the Cimmerians are, enwrapped in mist
> And cloud. And never does the shining sun
> Look on them with his rays, not when he climbs
> The starry sky, nor when he turns again
> To earth from heaven; but deadly night is spread
> O'er miserable mortals.'[1]

If we interpret this text aright, it would seem that Homer and the men of his time thought of the sun as a disc, the lighted side of which faced towards the earth's centre while the darkened side was turned to outer space. When he rose in the east from the Ocean, he left in darkness the outer shores of the great circumterrestrial river. In his daily course through the highest zone of the sky he gave light to men and gods — to the celestial gods, at least. Beyond the sphere of his journey extended the domains of perpetual night.

This Ocean, regarded by Homer as the father of the gods, was the source of all waters. From his overflow derived 'all rivers, all the sea, all springs, and all deep wells'. He was a divine being, the spouse of Tethys, to whom however he long denied his

[1] *The Odyssey of Homer*. Translated by Sir William Marris. London, 1925, p. 181.

bed; essentially he was a force of nature, a primitive element.

The disc of the earth whose boundary he shaped was divided into three zones. To the north-west, whence blew Boreas bringing winter's storms, extended the domain of winter, where the sun's rays fell only slantingly. Thus the Homeric pole of darkness and cold was situated on the southern shores of our North Sea, a distant, mysterious region to Homer's contemporaries, though in no wise a region of terror. Their descendants, who knew at least by report of the existence of the long summer days of the northern countries, were quite ready to imagine it as a refuge of light, inhabited by the just and happy Hyperboreans. This idea is not Homeric. All the same, the author of the *Iliad* had already envisaged these northern plains, glimpsed by sailors who had made the voyage round the Black Sea,[1] as populated by a simple and happy race who drank the milk of their mares — the Hippemulgi, first poetic pseudonym of the Scythian nomads — and the Abii, who like their Hyperborean descendants, were also numbered among the most righteous of mortals.

In the opposite direction, to the south-east and beyond the lands of Egypt — already by this time known to the Greek traders and pirates carried thither by the Etesian winds — were the burning lands of Nubia, home of the impeccable Ethiopians. The latter, with faces burned by the almost vertical rays of the sun, were according to the *Odyssey* the inhabitants of the ends of the earth. The gods were regular visitants there, drawn thither by the liberal banquets offered them by the pious inhabitants. But beyond all these again to the extreme south, the *Iliad* pictures a race of dwarf pygmies, who dwelt on the very shores of Ocean; and to them every winter came the migrating cranes from the north, to make war on them in the bad seasons.

Between these two extremes, the Mediterranean zone extends from east to west, and here the seasons also alternate, but temperately, following the regular changes of the sun's course in the heavens.

---

[1] 'Periplous', usually a circular voyage, of which Hanno's periplous of Africa was perhaps the most famous (Translator).

Greece, once again, is situated exactly at the centre of this microcosm.

In a vertical direction, the world's dimensions are in proportion to those of the earth's disc. Above the earth is Uranus, the brazen vault of heaven, on which the stars appear scattered. It constitutes the upper limit of the realm traversed by the sun and all the stars. This is the region of the ether. Lying between the ether and the earth is a layer of air, the cloudy atmosphere. It is on the upper limits of the atmosphere that the gods choose in general to make their abode, seating themselves for preference on the mountain tops in order to contemplate the spectacle of earth. Thus Homer places the home of the gods on Mount Olympus.

Below the earth is the domain of Tartarus, a region lying beneath the foundations of earth and sea. This is the realm of darkness and thick mist, the prison house of the vanquished Titans. It is surrounded by a wall of brass and locked by gates made in the workshop of Poseidon. In Hesiod's *Theogony* Tartarus is represented as an immense abyss, and to reach the bottom of this abyss involves a journey lasting a whole year, without rest or truce from storms and whirlwinds. Into this dire spot it was, according to the *Iliad*, that Zeus threatened to cast the gods rebellious to his will (though one must note that this myth occurs only in later additions).

Between the two extremes of the clear ether and the shadowy Tartarus lies the middle realm peopled by the gods, the heavenly gods and the gods of the underworld, man and the beasts, the living and the dead. Thus the surface of earth and sea combined divides this realm into two equal parts, on the one hand the region of mountains and air, where the clouds and winds disport themselves; and, on the other, the deep places of the sea and earth, the realm of Hades peopled by the dead leading their strange vegetative existence.

Hesiod endeavoured to give some idea of the thickness of this intermediate layer, the scene of the human and divine drama, by imagining a brass anvil cast down from the heavens, which had to fall for nine days and nights before reaching the earth at dawn of the tenth day; and, starting from earth, another nine days and nights to arrive at the threshold of Tartarus.

The cohesion and equilibrium of the world structure are secured by means of gigantic pillars, situated apparently on the Ocean verges; rooted deep in earth and maintaining aloft the heavenly vault. It is these pillars which preserve the relative positions of earth and sky, according to Homer. They are kept in place by Atlas, whose name seems formerly to have denoted a divinity of the pillar, and who appears as the father of Calypso, in the *Odyssey*.

The world is thus conceived of as a vast edifice, vaulted and mounted on columns, half of it lying underground. It is filled with matter, solid and fluid, the ether being its subtlest constituent. We may note as a feature of this conception the absence of the idea of space, a notion which has since been made familiar to us by the geometer and the mathematician. The notion of space does not occur in Homer and his contemporaries, for whom extension was the only possible sort of being. Thus the world of Homer is not *in* space; what we call space today is identified with what Homer thought of as extension. For Homer there was no infinity, there was only the incomplete. We must in fact await Democritus in the fifth century before the idea of empty and unlimited space emerges clearly as a concept in Greek and human thought.

### THE HOMERIC WORLD IS A LIVING WORLD

This closed and finite world of Homer, so tiny that its diameter is scarcely the tenth part of the circumference of our globe, differs from our idea of it in another and distinctive way.

Our universe is a mechanical one, governed by the fixed laws of mathematics. The world of the Homeric Greeks is in its substance a living thing. This is not to say that it is the equivalent of an organism endowed with life. But all its material components embody a certain aspect of life, of a more or less obvious or inscrutable type. Uranus is not only a vault of brass, he is also a divine being to whom Hesiod later was to give a place in his genealogical system; but even before Hesiod the gods invoked him together with Gaia, the Earth, and the waters of the infernal Styx, as witness to the supreme oath. The Ocean god cohabits with Tethys; an uneasy union this, however, and one long rent by dissensions, which Hera, in the *Iliad*, makes a feint of trying to resolve. Hades is the underworld home of the dead, but he is also the god who with Persephone presides over its destinies.

A typical example of this interpenetration of matter and divinity occurs in the *Hymn to the Delian Apollo*. The composition of this hymn probably belongs in date to the earliest parts of the Homeric epic; in it occurs the recital of Leto's voyage round the Aegean. Leto is seeking an asylum where she can give birth to her son Apollo. She wanders from one Aegean isle to another, but she makes her prayer for a sanctuary for the divine child, not to the inhabitants but to the very earth itself. Meeting everywhere with refusals, she arrives at last at Delos, where she again prays for asylum. The island hesitates in fear lest the god to be born will despise his arid lands and in anger drown the island under the sea. Leto reassures the island by taking the great oath of the gods, and thus Apollo first sees the world on Delos. It is clear that every corner of the earth appears as a being endowed with personality, emotion, and will-power, just as are men, animals and plants, and gods no less.

The world in effect is a society of living entities, who inhabit earth, sea and sky, and are at the same time indistinguishable from them. Are these creatures of divine origin? The answer is, yes, in a certain measure, but the degree of their divinity is a variable and indeterminate quantity, for all are not immortal. Moreover, it is a society organized as a hierarchy very similar to the human groups, similar inasmuch as it is equally disorderly and turbulent; torn by dissensions, passions, jealousy and competition. At a later stage we see Hesiod endeavouring to reduce it to order under the sovereign authority of Zeus, with his awards of 'honours', that is to say, of domains and fiefs distributed in his capacity of guardian of order and justice.

Man in the Homeric age, at least thinking man, has his being in intimate and constant contact with this divine or semi-divine society. To tread the earth underfoot, to bathe in waters, is tantamount to having this contact; thus when Odysseus arrives at the mouth of the little stream on the island of the Phaeacians, he prays it to give him welcome.

Man has the sentiment or perception of visitations by the gods, even the greatest of them. Should he hap on a stranger by the way, a well-featured stranger, it is perhaps a god; so Odysseus, on his first encounter with Nausicaa, thus addresses her:

> 'Queen, I entreat thee: art thou of the gods
> Or mortal?'[1]

by this not intending merely an elegant compliment, but a real expression of wonder. The divine ministrants can in truth manifest themselves in many guises, however unexpected. One could enumerate the many forms assumed by Athena for example, in the *Odyssey* alone. Having entered the house of Odysseus and shewn herself to Telemachus as Mentes, prince of the Taphians, she flies away at the conclusion of her task in the shape of a sea bird. Returning in the assumed form of old Mentor to conduct the son of Odysseus to Pylos, again she takes to flight, after her encounter with Nestor, in the form of a bird, an osprey on this occasion. In Phaeacia, she enters the chamber by the side of the sleeping Nausicaa like a soft 'breath of wind', and then appears as a young virgin, one of the princess's friends. Further on, when acting as guide to Odysseus in the city of the Phaeacians, she appears transformed into a little child bearing an ewer; and on Ithaca she welcomes him in the form of a young shepherd. In the house of Eumaeus she is a tall and beautiful woman. In the manor, while the massacre of the suitors is going on, she assumes the form of Mentor again; and makes a final appearance at the battle as a swallow perched on a beam.

All mortals naturally are not on as familiar terms with the gods as the heroes of epic. But anyone is liable to encounter a deity of greater or lesser stature, at the turn of the road or on the edge of a wood, in the mists of dawn or nightfall, or on the threshold of his

[1] *Odyssey*, VI, p. 105.

own house. He will be well advised to recognize the god as such immediately, so as to proffer a timely request or offer some sacrifice; following the example of the wise Nestor, when he realized he was entertaining Athena, the companion of Telemachus, in the form of the aged Mentor.

As a rule, of course, the gods (apart from the gods of the hearth, and of the fields, woods and waters) have no direct and permanent relations with men. But this does not prevent their being extremely interested in their behaviour and their destinies. They establish relationships in different ways, as guides and counsellors and as the bearers of warnings; although they may also deceive men and give them delusions. Many natural events are in reality signs employed by the gods, if one can but recognize and interpret them aright. One class of men is particularly so gifted, that of the soothsayers; and momentarily the same inspiration may be vouchsafed to other men and women with this special gift of perception.

The language of the gods may take different forms. They may make their communication through the thunder, the winds, meteors and other portents, even a bird in flight. But they can and do employ also special emissaries to convey their message to man.

Most often these appear in the form of dreams. Homer thinks of dreams as of living creatures, taking on different forms either of men or of animals, and acting as the familiars of the god who is desirous of conveying a message. The dream which Zeus sends to Agamemnon at the beginning of Book II of the *Iliad*, falsely promising him victory, appears to the king of kings in the garb of Nestor. Sleeping Penelope is reassured about the fate of her son by a visitation from her sister Iphthimé. Sometimes the dreams are of a symbolic character, requiring to be interpreted by one of the actors in them. An instance of this is the dream of Penelope which she recounts to Odysseus,[1] in which an eagle kills her geese, foreshadowing the massacre of the suitors; and it is the eagle who, assuming the power of speech, explains the symbolism of the dream to her, from his perch on the roof. The movements of birds indeed

[1] *Odyssey*, XIX, 535-53.

are given an equal place with dreams, as interpreters of the gods, always in situations of grave or decisive moment.

Homer's universe thus appears as full of an infinite number of hidden, mysterious beings who reside in the natural objects which are their servants; these beings can be either benevolent or dangerous, and in any case it is never worth risking a slight or an offence where they are concerned. For they are very prone to be offended, even by actions in themselves at first sight quite innocent and natural. Hesiod has a number of recommendations on the subject, some of them rather picturesque and amusing.[1] Thus it is a good idea, morning and night, to offer libations to Zeus and the other gods; but, he adds, 'take care not to carry these out in the morning without washing your hands first'. The sun takes offence at a natural function carried out to his face; nor will 'the pious and well-advised man' perform this function haphazardly at night, but will be careful to hide it against a wall; for it is the hour when the 'blessed' are at large. Rivers seem to be particularly sensitive, and the wise man will not attempt a crossing of one before washing and making a prayer, with his eyes turned to the water. Above all he will be careful not to sully the clear mouth of a river by bathing in it, or, what is worse, increase its flow. This last act is particularly odious when a spring is in question. The fire on the hearth, too, is divine, and a man should seat himself before it with all due decency.

One must allow that many of the gods, with their sometimes surprising exigencies, have in fact deserved to be made the objects of man's worship by the many, willing services they render him. Thus the countryside was littered with small and homely altars, like the one set up by the spring which flows by the entry to the town of Ithaca: it is before this altar that Eumaeus the swineherd is wont in passing to invoke the nymphs of the spring, that they may look with favour on the hoped-for return of the king.

Upon the stage of this dual-faced world a double-faced tragedy is enacted, human and divine, inextricably mixed; in which the humblest events or the most humdrum incidents may have the

[1] *Works and Days*, 724 et seq.

significance of premonitions, revelations or unexpected reprisals. In the strictly technical sense of the word, Homer's universe is full of enchantment.

## FATE AND DESTINY

But it is not a world governed by pure caprice. Homer and his hearers have the profound consciousness of a fundamental law maintaining the world's organization. They call the law Fate, *Moira*, fortune, lot, or destiny. More exactly it is the system of regulations which control the unfolding of all life; the life of men, of things, and of gods. This system secures that the world is a stable one.

It is *Moira* who allots to men their place and function in society, giving them the role of servant or master, peasant, artisan or warrior. Once for all, fate has fixed the rhythm of human life, its inexorable development from childhood to adolescence, to maturity, old age and death. To each man she apportions his share of years, days and hours. It is the destiny of Achilles to die young and glorious; his divine mother knows it is and that she cannot change it. Zeus himself, anxious to save his own son Sarpedon about to die under the blows dealt by Patroclus, makes the gesture of yielding to fate, lest he trouble the ordained course of the world. His part must be confined to maintaining the balance on which the fate of men is weighed, and to reading the decrees thereon pronounced, and to bowing to them; so does he when the hour of Hector's death is striking. Athena expounds this law of Fate to Telemachus when she says that the gods may help mortals during their lifetime, but:

> Death is the law for all: the gods themselves
> Cannot avert it from the man they cherish
> When baneful Moira has pronounced his doom.

So, gods as well as nature are in the hands of Fate. This is how Homer and his contemporaries account for the idea of a natural law which is imposed on the world in spite of the presence of accidents and cataclysms. Fate ensures the regular evolutions of the sun and stars, the dawn, the succession of night and day, the seasons, the rhythm of the flow of rivers and winds in their season. The general framework of the world has been traced out by Fate for all time.

But this framework, though absolute in a general sense, permits to all living creatures, to men and gods, in their infinite numbers, a measure of liberty. It is natural to see how this concession is made to the gods, whose free will seems to be at one with the unpredictable caprices of nature — added to the privilege of interfering in human affairs, for good or evil. Achilles is at pains to explain to Priam how Zeus possesses two jars, one filled with pleasant gifts and the other with gifts of a sinister sort. Maybe, drawing from the two jars at random, he will hand out to certain mortals a mixture of the good and the bad. Or he may serve out only misfortunes. But there is no instance of his ever having crowned a man with pure felicity.

The freedom enjoyed by the gods, whether beneficent or maleficent, is not absolute, for gods need men to carry on life in the framework of Destiny, no less than men need gods. The latter would founder without their offerings, their ceremonies, rites and sacrifices, just as would mortal men if deprived of light, heat, harvest and all the sources of fruitfulness. The perennial ordering of the world is ensured, first by the laws of Fate; but also, operating under them, by a continuous process of exchange and reciprocity, amounting to an indefinite renewal of debts and credits. From one aspect, the order and continuity are the result of a sort of contract between free individuals, which is ceaselessly renewed.

For men too have their share of free will, and use it for good or ill, and even at times in defiance of the will of the gods. Aegisthus, for example, the murderer of Agamemnon, who ascended the throne of Argos by acts of adultery and assassination, had been duly cautioned by the gods not to stoop to these crimes; and so drew down upon himself the punishment he might have avoided. Zeus in this connection states that men 'in their folly may draw upon themselves misfortunes which were not part of their destiny'. Man, as we see, thus plays a certain part in moulding the destiny of the world, and also his own in some measure.

Life in Homer's time appears thus as an act of collaboration in permanency; and it can be, as in any society, a happy or an uneasy partnership. Although subject to the inexorable law of Fate, this collaboration does not exclude individual acts of excess, of *hubris*, those acts by which a man sets himself apart by his singular and often criminal passions. But the framework remains in its entirety, by virtue of a superior sort of solidarity; and as such it is essential to the preservation of world-equilibrium. The behaviour and appearance of this world from day to day, which it is our task to describe now, would lose in significance and tone if we were to lose sight of this fundamental intuition. It is this which holds up the light to its progress, playing the role which, in our western thought and consciousness, is played by the Christian and scientific way of thinking about life and destiny.

# CHAPTER II

# THE MANOR HOUSE

HOMERIC society was an aristocratic society. If our dates are correct, Homeric poetry saw the light and developed in the historical environment which took shape after the decline and fall of most of the traditional monarchies. These monarchies were the self-styled heirs of the heroic age and some of them, notably in Asia, claimed descent from the Achaean heroes, Agamemnon, Menelaus and Nestor; while others, as successors of the Dorian invasion, claimed to descend from Heracles. By the middle of the eighth century they had all foundered.

The aristocracy which seized power at this moment in most of the Greek cities was called the kingly class and consisted of the old families whose influence and wealth had been for long principally based on their possession of vast landed estates; in addition to their share of the public receipts as city magistrates and to the exploitation of certain prosperous sanctuaries. After taking over the reins of government from the ancient dynasties, the aristocracy continued to expand its activities, adding to the prestige of noble birth that of an aristocracy of wealth.

In the first place it derived its wealth from the success of its industrial undertakings. The older classes of artisans were left to pursue their traditional employments, the potters continuing to make their earthen vases, and the smelters the household utensils, tripods and copper and iron receptacles; and so also the iron-forgers continued to produce agricultural tools and some of the swords; while the carpenters went on making furniture and wooden frames. The aristocracy, leaving these artisans to their several trades, set up the great industries for mass production, particularly of weapons of war but also of many smaller manufactured articles, products of the vast foundries that were built to different from what he imagined to be the princely dwellings of the heroic age; and, to be precise, they must have furnished him with his models.

The plural form, *domata*, dwelling places, which he employs has its own significance. For the house is an elaborate arrangement of courtyards, living-rooms, stables, storehouses and sheds. With its various dependencies, the house appears in fact to constitute a city in itself, more or less self-contained. Here are carried on the various homely tasks, of crushing corn and barley, flour-sifting, bread-making, and the spinning and weaving of linen and wool. A small world finds a home within its precincts. Fifty of Priam's sons reside in his palace with their wives, in addition to his twelve daughters and their husbands; although here we must make an allowance for poetic licence. Nevertheless, the domestic require-ments of the household must have necessitated the employment of a large staff, male and female, mostly female, under the super-vision of a couple of stewardesses. The men for the most part slept outside in dependencies, bringing in fodder and provisions at regular intervals, when they would receive their orders, and make their reports, requests and complaints.

The manorial house was surrounded on all sides by a high wall, armed with spikes, as a deterrent against intruders. The single entrance was through a gateway of massive structure, with folding doors. In Odysseus' house this gateway was flanked on the outside by an enormous manure heap, and we are told that it was on this heap that the old dog Argos was taking his siesta, stiff in joint and covered with ticks, when he recognized Odysseus — the first being on the island to do so — and so died.

On passing through this gateway one enters a large courtyard, the court of honour. This was surrounded on three sides with buildings, among them the sleeping-rooms for the sons of the family, with their wives, if married. The sons-in-law of the master of the house were also accommodated here when they were his guests. In the palace of Priam Homer enumerates sixty-two rooms, fifty for Priam's sons and twelve for his married daughters. They were situated on the side of the court opposite the doorway. The arrangement was always of this sort, whatever the number of rooms. In the house of Odysseus there was but one, occupied by his only son, Telemachus. It was a lofty building, isolated from the other apartments. Again, the sons of Nestor at Pylos, to the number of six, each had his own sleeping-apartment, or *thalamos*.

After crossing the great court, the visitor reaches a portico, supported by pillars, which forms the entrance to the main buildings. This is the gate of honour. It is divided into two parts, one passing into the other, and here separated by a wall with many doorways. The first section is the portico, properly so-called, and beyond it is the vestibule, or *prodomos*, a little rectangular space, the door of which leads directly to the hall of honour, or *megaron*. This vestibule plays no insignificant role in the epic; and here it was that distinguished guests were often entertained at night.

But to go back to the great courtyard, we may recall that in the house of Alcinous, there was to one side of the yard an orchard six acres in extent, in which were planted vines, pears, figs, apples, grenadines and olives, all growing in the very heart of the city. Here two springs gushed up from the earth and one of them, flowing across the yard and passing beneath the great doorway, led to a covered fountain used by the inhabitants of the city.

Set against the inner portico was a highly polished stone chair, where the lord of the house was wont to take his seat, surrounded by his sons and intimates; and here he would discuss with them the affairs of the household and demesne, and take decisions when exceptional circumstances required them. Thus did Nestor before the sacrifice to Athena, who had honoured his house with her presence the day before. For in the courtyard stood an altar, no doubt similar to those which have been discovered in the ruins of the Mycenaean palaces, and notably in the one at Tiryns. The altar that stood in the court of Odysseus' house was dedicated to Zeus the Protector, and on this altar Laertes and Odysseus are reported to have burned the flesh of many oxen.[1]

Another noteworthy edifice to be found in the courtyard arose not far from the encircling great wall of the house. This was the

[1] *Odyssey*, XXII, 333–6.

*tholos*, a round vaulted building mounted on columns. It was from a rope stretched round this edifice that Telemachus caused to be hanged the twelve unfaithful servants whom Odysseus had condemned to death. It was a sepulchral building, thought to represent the house of Hades, the realm of the dead. Perhaps it can be regarded as a sort of family vault, as this appears to have been its original purpose. In Homer's time it seems to have become the counterpart of the altar dedicated to the heavenly deities, and it was specially devoted to the cult of the ancestors.[1]

We may note that there is no mention in Homer of other porticoes round the court, apart from the one described, unlike those which have been found in the Achaean palaces of some centuries earlier.

To continue: the visitor, having passed through the gate of honour (the *aithousai*) — which, be it noted in passing, was always constructed to face towards the sun, in the east or the south — now enters the hall of honour or *megaron*, which deserves a description to itself and to which we will return later; for the court of honour, with the *megaron*, formed the very heart of the dwelling. Around their three remaining sides were all the subsidiary buildings, arranged about smaller courtyards without any particular plan; but all serving as annexes or dependencies.

On three sides of the *megaron*, but well separated from it, were the women's quarters, housing the servants and concubines. There might be as many as fifty women, as in the houses both of Alcinous and Odysseus. These quarters were known collectively as the *megara*, but the name does not imply any resemblance to the hall of honour. The women occupied chambers called *thalamoi*, apparently on the ground floor, and here they did all their spinning and weaving, ground corn, cooked, ate together and slept.[2]

In the women's quarter the master of the house had his sleeping chamber or *thalamos*, where his wife shared his couch; but he might invite instead, according to the whim of the moment, some concubine selected from among the women servants. This cham-

---

[1] *Odyssey*, XXII, 442, 459, 465–7.
[2] In Odysseus' house was a mill were twelve women worked.

ber was also on the ground floor. Odysseus relates that he built his own room about the trunk of an olive tree, cutting and shaping it to form the base of his bed. Adjoining the bedchamber was the bathroom, fitted up with tubs, and here the servants washed the master and his guests, and anointed them with sweet oils. In the case of a guest of distinction, this office might be performed by a daughter of the house.

For the greater convenience of the master, and perhaps also from considerations of prudence, the sleeping chamber of his wife was separate from the other women's quarters. Penelope's room was on a terrace above the *megaron*; and here were other rooms for the servants, apparently two in number, who were specially employed in the mistress's service. Smaller adjacent rooms were used for storing articles of value and one of them was made secure by bars, or an interior latchet opening only with a special key. Here were the coffers of clothes, and articles in bronze and gold; including the famous bow of Odysseus, the quiver and arrows, and the iron axes used to test the strength and skill of the candidates for the queen's favour.

The women's quarters, as we have seen, were all grouped round the *megaron*. The storehouse was generally situated to the north and west of the enclosure. This was a building of great size, doing duty for cellar and lumber room. Homer describes the storehouse of Odysseus as having a high-pitched roof and a massive folding door, from which one went down into the building; no doubt the level was below the ground to ensure protection of the foodstuffs against the great heats. Along the walls were placed the jars[1] containing oil, wine, and finely ground grain and flour, all tightly sealed. Here were also stored supplies of metals, such as gold and bronze, and pieces of cloth which were kept in coffers. The area covered must have been considerable, and was probably divided by partitions against which the jars were leaned, accessible by separate little corridors. When one considers the quantity of wine,

[1] The jar, or *pithos*, was an earthenware vase as high as a man, tapering downwards. It was almost completely buried to preserve the contents. The cover was made of limestone or shale.

oil and cereal required to last from harvest time to the following year, one can see it had to be pretty big to supply a household of perhaps nearly a hundred persons.

The supervision of the stores and their distribution were the responsibility of one of the two stewardesses who slept there. Only the stewardess and the master and mistress knew where the best and the oldest wines were stored. It was from such a secret reserve known only to Maron, the priest of Apollo at Ismarus, that this Maron took the twelve amphorae which he gave to Odysseus. This was the vintage that the hero used to intoxicate the Cyclops.

The manor house was a shelter, however, not only for men and provisions. It also housed a miscellaneous collection of livestock, oxen, she-mules, pack mules and horses. The stables, sheds and storehouses for fodder were grouped around the court of honour, which gave access to the outside world. Here slept the servants who looked after the animals and also had the care of the carriages and other vehicles. In these buildings it is natural to suppose that the sleeping quarters of the senior domestics or higher officers were to be found, those of the heralds, cupbearers, gentlemen carvers, and messengers — the 'fleet servants' whose duty it was to bear despatches and take orders.

## THE MEGARON

After this rapid tour of the house, we now return to the *megaron*, the ceremonial hall, situated in the middle of this maze of buildings and courtyards, where the lord of the house dines with his family, receives his guests and holds his great banquets.

Access to the *megaron* is by a simple doorway, reached through the gate of honour and the vestibule, with a threshold of stone framed by doorposts in cypress wood and slightly raised above the level of the chamber. Odysseus leaps to this elevation, bow in hand, when he proceeds to the slaying of the suitors, commanding from this vantage-point his victims and their possible egresses.

The *megaron* was rectangular in shape and approximately eleven by thirteen yards in area. On three sides it was surrounded by walls completely lacking in windows or doorways. On each side of the principal entrance were two smaller doors. One of these led to an outside staircase ascending to the terraced roof where we saw that the mistress of the house had her sleeping-chamber. This is the staircase which Penelope descends to enter the great hall. The other small door or postern was reached by a few steps. It led into a narrow passage inside the wall, and thence to the women's quarters and outside offices.

The ceiling of the great hall was supported by four wooden columns which traced out a rectangle five and a half by six and a half yards in the centre. Their position and equilibrium were secured by large smooth beams into which the pillars were fitted top and bottom, thus forming a quadrilateral bracing the whole structure. Interlacing joists made it doubly secure.

In the centre of the *megaron* was the hearth, a little round structure slightly raised above the floor and about two or three yards across. A wood fire burned upon it, scattering white ash over the smooth surface. It was on such a hearth that Odysseus sate himself after his entry into the great hall of Alcinous and his appeal to the queen Areté, where she sat with her back against a column, working at her distaff of purple wools in the midst of the lords of Phaeacia.

The smoke from the fire escaped by the roof, in the middle of which was an opening covered by a lantern to keep out the rain. The ceiling must have been fairly low, seeing that it was through this opening that the goatherd Melantheus was able to escape, hoisting himself up from the hall, and making off in search of arms for the suitors whom Odysseus was engaged in slaying.

The *megaron* was the room where meetings were held and where the family took its meals, occupations hardly distinguishable from each other. The lord of the manor and his lady took their places at the foot of the columns facing the hearth, and here also were placed any guests of honour. Here Leto placed her son Apollo, when he burst into the palace of Zeus where the gods were sitting assembled, as we read at the beginning of the *Hymn to the Delian Apollo*. Here the cupbearer Pontonous installed the bard Demodocus, as he prepared to sing during the banquet at which Alcinous entertained the Phaeacians.

Guests and others present were seated against the walls or between the columns. The *megaron* could accommodate up to fifty persons. For men of quality who would not go about without arms, or at the least without a sword or lance, there were arms-racks arranged around the columns for the lances; and the armour of the master, including his helmet, shield and breastplate — at any rate the armour which he normally carried — was always kept in the great hall. The reserves of weapons and armour were usually kept in the store-room, part of which was used as an arsenal. Thus, before their combat with the suitors, Odysseus and Telemachus go to some trouble to clear away all the weapons in the *megaron*.

During the day the *megaron* was lighted from the lantern in the roof and by the great doorway, which remained open. At night the principal source of light was the central hearth; but resinous torches might also be burning. In the palace of Alcinous these torches were fixed into the hands of gilded statues of youths, set on plinths. Or the light might sometimes be produced from standards such as are referred to in the *Odyssey*, consisting of containers mounted on feet and which were fed with dry sticks. Oil lamps were used in going from one room to another and in the passage-ways. Athena employs such a lamp, fashioned in gold naturally, when she lights Odysseus and Telemachus engaged in carrying off the weapons from the *megaron* by night. These different methods of illumination were common, and had long, no doubt, been employed in Homer's time by the Greeks of the eighth and seventh centuries. They all appear rather primitive and certainly produced a good deal of smoke, for we know that the arms of Odysseus, after they had been left long uncared for in the *megaron*, were corroded with smoke.

Finally we must note the floor which was covered with flag-stones, and washed and swept daily by servants. After the massacre of the suitors, the blood and other debris had to be removed with rakes and shovels.

## DECORATION AND FURNISHINGS

The account we have sketched above will have impressed the
reader as giving the idea of a somewhat crude kind of dwelling;
but in fact we were following rather closely the characteristics of
Odysseus' manor, which could be regarded as typical of the rural
regions of Homeric Greece and, no doubt, of the majority of
seigniorial houses.

There were more luxurious dwellings. Greece, after four centuries of comparative barbarism following the Dorian invasion,
had rediscovered from the eighth century onward her ancient
vocation as a great trading country. In certain privileged homes,
the aristocracy who had seized power took the opportunity of
amassing wealth with great rapidity. A taste for luxury became not
uncommon, even if it sometimes showed itself in rather violent
and flamboyant guise.

This change was observed by the epic writers of the second
half of the eighth century, particularly in some of the Asiatic cities
associated with famous sanctuaries like those of Ephesus and
Colophon, or at Miletus the city of shipowners; and, in Greece
proper, at Chalcis, Eretria, Corinth and Sicyon, and again further
south, at Argos where a new era of prosperity and supremacy had
been inaugurated; and finally, in Sparta. Sparta, be it noted, was
far from having always been the city of austerity of classical tradition. Before the outbreak of the second Messenian war, in the
middle of the seventh century, Sparta was a rendezvous of poets
and artists. By reason of her situation, Egypt and the East were
easily accessible when the Etesian winds were blowing, and the
*Odyssey* has a description of how Menelaus brought back great
wealth from these countries. Moreover, to Sparta was due the
foundation of Tarentum, which was a privileged port of call on
the north-west trade routes.

We need not be surprised therefore to come across many references, undoubtedly a little embellished, to this recently acquired
and marvellous wealth. Homer so describes the houses of Menelaus at Sparta and of Alcinous in Phaeacia — by Phaeacia meaning

Corcyra, a colony of Corinth founded by the aristocrat Chersi-
crates, a native of the city of the isthmus. This colony made such
progress that it was able, by the first third of the seventh century,
to cast off the metropolitan yoke and assert its independence.

When Telemachus and Peisistratus enter the *megaron* of Menelaus, they are dazzled by the brilliance of the decoration on the
walls and furniture: decoration in gold, electron (an alloy of gold
and silver), bronze, silver and ivory. More marvellous still are the
details we read of the great hall of Alcinous. The two lateral walls
are covered with bronze, the upper portions being overlaid with a
blue enamel frieze. The doors are plated with gold, and the threshold is of bronze, while the lintels and doorposts are inlaid with
silver. Two gold and silver dogs guard the entrance of this magnificent doorway, and we have already mentioned the golden
youths who hold the torches that light the hall.

These poetic flights must have had their foundation in reality.
The wall-plating in the princely houses accords well enough with
our knowledge of the craftsmanship of the Greek decorators and
metallurgists of the seventh century, and even of the closing years
of the eighth, if we may rely on some of the pieces preserved in the
sanctuaries and described by Pausanias. We refer particularly to
the storied coffer of Cypselus and to the monumental shrine dedicated by Myron of Sicyon after his victory in the horse race at
Olympia in 648 B.C. As for the statues, we may naturally suppose
these to have been in wood overlaid with precious metals, analogous to the statue of Zeus in beaten gold (allowing for the difference in size) which was dedicated by Cypselus, tyrant of Corinth,
about the middle of the seventh century and which Strabo mentions as having seen at Olympia.

Nevertheless the furnishings of houses were not on the whole
of a very high standard. The sole furniture of the *megaron* consisted of seven chairs of different sorts: 'thrones' which were like
armchairs with high backs and moveable footrests (*threnus*). A
piece of cloth was arranged on the throne before anyone sat down,
doubtless for reasons of niceness in a room so charged with
smoke. These thrones were reserved for the most distinguished

persons present as well as for the lord of the house; they were placed along the walls or at the foot of the columns surrounding the hearth. The sons of the house reclined on a sort of chaise longue (*klismos*), covered with worked cloth, and these were sufficiently raised for meals to be taken at the height of the table. When Telemachus receives Athena, who has appeared in the form of Mentes, prince of the Taphians, he causes his guest to be seated on a throne and himself reclines on a *klismos*. The mistress of the house was entitled also to a sort of more comfortable divan (*klisiè*) with various decorations; Penelope's was covered with ivory and silver. The *klisiè* had a fixed step or stool attached by which the lady was able to mount easily and seat herself in a dignified fashion, for the *klisiè*, like the *klismos*, was well raised above the floor. For the general household and staff there were simple chairs, without backs and covered with leather; and also benches. This sort of chair would also be found in the bedrooms.

The furniture of the *megaron* did not include a permanent table. Servants appeared at meal-times, bearing small tables, very light and highly polished, which they set before the guests. Upon the tables were placed a cup and a basket of bread. The gentleman carver then set out the wooden platters — or they might be metal plates — with cut pieces of meat. The fingers, naturally, were used for eating.

The furniture in the bedrooms, apart from a few light chairs, amounted to little more than the bed and perhaps a few coffers, although these last were more often locked away in a special room. The bed itself was of the simplest, consisting of a frame which could be easily moved about and which stood on rather short feet. The lower part of the space inside the frame was held together by wooden stays. We have seen that Odysseus made his own bed a fixture by employing the stump of an olive tree which had been cut down and which served as a pedestal for the wooden stays. Interlacing strips of leather were generally stretched on top of the wood, and above these again was a stuff mattress, dyed purple for the beds of the distinguished occupants. A linen sheet might be placed for them to slip under, such as is described in the bed made up for Odysseus on the ship taking him from Phaeacia to Ithaca. On the very top were disposed coverings and woollen mantles. Many of the beds were richly decorated. Odysseus' bed, which was indeed no ordinary bed, was incrusted with gold, silver and ivory.

## DOORS AND FASTENINGS

The great houses to which Homer introduces us in his poetry must have contained, at the lowest estimate, a hundred rooms of various kinds, sleeping-chambers, store-rooms, stables and offices. Some of these rooms might have a hearth and lantern roof, for when Nausicaa retires at night the servant comes to light the fire in her room. Most of the rooms however were lit only through the doorways, as a result of which the doors were generally large and lofty. They were double doors, each leaf set in a solid wood frame, except in the ceremonial halls where the threshold might be of stone or bronze. These doors were left open all day to admit the light, whatever the weather. The only doors kept shut were those of the coach-houses, sheds and storage rooms.

The great majority of the doors were fastened in a very simple manner. In general they were secured by inside latches of wood or metal worked by leather straps. In order to close the door after him, a person had to bring one of the straps to the other side through a hole in the door, drawing it towards him, and then attach it to a wooden or metal knob (*koroné*), which secured it against any loose play. To enter the room it was only necessary to unloose the straps and let them go in the opposite direction. This simple and ingenious system obviously made the room secure only at night, when one drew in the straps to the inside of the room; a precaution scarcely needed by persons of distinction, because male or female domestics watched, or slept, outside their doors. Nausicaa's door, for instance, was guarded by two chambermaids, and we may recall that one of the stewardesses always slept in the store-room as an additional precaution.

A passage in the *Odyssey* throws light on an exception to the system observed above. When Penelope, at the beginning of

Book XXI, goes to seek the bow of Odysseus in the store-room where all the most precious articles were kept, she opens the door with a key, a bronze key which has an 'ingenious curve' and an ivory handle. The habit of locking up the more secret rooms by a mechanism requiring the use of a key was already common in classical times. In the *Hymn to Hermes*, which is certainly of later date, we have a description of Apollo who, in the course of ransacking the house of the thieving young god and his mother Maia, takes possession of a key that gives access to three secret rooms. The reference to a key in the *Odyssey* could not fail of awakening doubts in the minds of those who see in Homeric poetry only the reflection of a primitive civilization and its archaic customs.

Here is the text in question. Its singularity calls for comment:

> . . . at once she quickly loosed the strap
> From the door-handle, and thrust in the key
> And with nice aim shot back the bolts.[1] And even
> As grazing in the mead a bull will bellow,
> So rumbled the good doors at the key's push
> And opened to her quickly.[2]

The text is limpidly clear and enlightens us unmistakably as to the manner in which the key was used and the primitive way the lock was manipulated. Doors with keys have no bolts, only a latch, for the Greek word *ocheus* has the meaning both of bar and of bolt. The fallen latch is kept in place by a strap attached to a knob and this holds it firmly in the latch but does not permit of its being raised. It is the key which raises the latch as it turns in the hole, once the straps are undone. Then one pushes against the door, with the key still held in the vertical position; and it is this which causes the poet to say that the door is pushed open by the key.

The system was obviously very simple, and there is no reason to

[1] M. Mireaux translates this part: 'Puis [elle] introduit la clef, *soulève le loquet* et pousse devant elle' (Translator).

[2] Trans. Marris, p. 370. In view of M. Mireaux' interpretation, which is almost certainly correct, it would be better to read: 'And with nice aim *she raised the latch*' (Translator).

suppose that this is an addition to the text made by a later writer.[1]
The arrangement simply ensured added security, because of the
shape of the key which was curved in such a way as exactly to
enter and pass through the hole in the door. Penelope's key,
described above as being in bronze, with an ivory haft, was an
elaborate object appropriate to the securing of rich and rare
treasures; but it has a further value for us as a symbol, a decided
indication that Homeric civilization was no primitive affair.

The seigniorial house which we have rapidly described no
doubt included many traditional features, some of them, like the
*megaron*, dating back to Achaean times. The general arrangement
of the house bears the stamp of a regime still in essence patriarchal.
It still remains a feudal residence, obviously the case with a house
like that of Odysseus. But the palaces of Alcinous and Menelaus
are beginning to assume another character, as houses of city
dwellers and even very wealthy ones.

The manor house is clearly the symbol of an age of progress
and change, and bears witness to the emergence of Greece from
the chrysalid stage of development.

[1] In Book XIV of the *Iliad*, Hera retires into a locked room to make her
toilet; and she also uses a 'secret key' (verse 168). No further explanation is
given.

# CHAPTER III

## THE LIFE OF A NOBLEMAN[1]

THE kind of life led by the Homeric heroes, if not exactly primitive, was relatively very simple. The absence of comfort as we know it, and in particular the poor lighting arrangements, meant that they were singularly at the mercy of the seasons and of the natural variations of daylight.

Life in the great house was very busy at the height of the season, apart from the hottest days, when Sirius, Orion's dog — the dog star — made his reappearance at dawn. This occurred during the latter part of our July. It was the period, according to Hesiod, when goats waxed fat, when wine had its richest flavour, and women grew soft and languorous; but when the men were good for nothing. The dog star got into their heads and knees, and the heat burned up their skins. But apart from a few weeks of this, when they could do little but rest in the cooler shade, life was spent in the open air from early spring until December, and was filled with activities of all sorts: inspection of the farm, journeys, hunting and other excursions.

This only came to an end when the harvest was at last brought in, and then people crept back into their houses. The north wind swept the countryside, blowing down from the mountains of Thrace; rushing down the valleys and roaring through the forests. Beneath these storms men walked like bending reeds. The nights became long and tedious; and they were the scene of heavy feasting. The stored up foodstuffs were now heavily drawn upon; for, as Hesiod remarks, one must eat more in winter to combat the

---

[1] 'La Vie du Seigneur.' In this chapter we are concerned primarily with the head of the clan, or 'king' as he was still called; and also, in some measure, with the *gennetes* or clansmen who were his near or distant relatives (Translator).

effects of the cold and of the enforced idleness, breeding soft ways. But this period of confinement to the house was of short duration and was over in two or three months.

Whatever the season, life in the manor house began at daybreak nor was it interrupted until evening had passed into night. The master of the house, no less than his family — all were up and about 'as soon as the daughter of morning, rosy-fingered dawn, appeared', according to the formula so charmingly repeated throughout the Homeric poems.

### THE CARE OF THE BODY, CLOTHING AND ORNAMENTS

For one's morning toilet, no doubt some hasty ablutions were made before one took the first meal of the day, the *ariston*, which generally consisted of what remained over from supper.

In general Homer never spares us any picturesque details, but he has nothing to say about the morning toilet. Probably this is because very little time was devoted to it. It was in the evening, after the day's work and before supper, that attention to one's toilet was usual. In the whole of Homer there is only one exception to this rule, and this is when Telemachus is described as going to bed without a bath, after he had passed the day feasting and conversing with Nestor and his sons at Pylos, where he had disembarked that morning. This omission is repaired early next morning when the young man receives the necessary attentions from the hands of pretty Polycasta, the youngest of the old king's daughters, as such special treatment was usual in the case of a man of quality.

The principal ablutions were, then, regularly performed at the close of day. For this purpose there was a special room in the women's quarters, furnished with highly polished stone bathtubs. The servants sprinkled their master with warm water which they brought in cauldrons; then they rubbed him all over, and finally made a light application of fine oil, which might be perfumed. Particular care was taken to wash and dry the long hair and beard. Odysseus observes this care when he bathes in the stream out of sight of Nausicaa and her women. The combing, or rather disentangling, of the hair was done with the fingers; for the comb, as known to classical writers, is never mentioned by Homer, who portrays even Hera herself as using this primitive method of combing her hair before plaiting it.

The wearing of long hair and a well-trimmed beard was the mark and prerogative of the noble and warrior classes. The hair seems usually to have been fair, possibly another noble characteristic. Nevertheless there is an exception to this rule in the description of Odysseus who, after his bath in the stream, appears with his face framed in long dark curls 'of the colour of the hyacinth'.[1] In the more recent parts of the *Odyssey* these curls reappear as fair, so that perhaps the fashion had changed in the course of the century. Perhaps also the fair hair of great chieftains was a matter of ritual, and due to some artifice, because Odysseus' beard remains black.[2]

There was no great distinction between the clothing of men and women. The *chiton* or straight tunic was the chief garment. The length of the tunic varied according to time and place. The Ionians wore characteristically long tunics, as referred to in the *Hymn to the Delian Apollo*, and certain Athenians remained faithful to this tradition into the fifth century. But most of the continental Greeks only wore the long tunic in cold weather, as Hesiod recommends,[3] or on sea voyages: witness the garment which Odysseus describes as the gift of his host in Crete before his departure for Troy.[4] Above the *chiton* there might be worn a *pharos*, either for use inside the house or in good weather. The *pharos* was a loose vestment in fine cloth, which was thrown over the shoulders and draped round the waist, where it was confined by a belt. In fact, it was a sort of cloak; but it was more especially worn by women. The men normally wore a cape above their

---

[1] '... then Athene, child
  Of Zeus, made him more tall and strong to see,
  And loosed his locks like curly hyacinths'
    (*Odyssey*, VI, vv. 229–31. Trans. Marris, p. 108).

[2] *Odyssey*, XVI, v. 176.  [3] *Works and Days*, v. 537.
[4] *Odyssey*, XIX, v. 242.

tunics, which could be longer or shorter, single or double, and was called the *chlaina*.

The headdress consisted of a bonnet of leather, or it might be of felt, the *cyné*; sometimes provided with a brim to protect the head against sun and rain. The usual footwear was the sandal, consisting of a simple leather sole, fastened by straps and tied at the ankles. The Greeks of our period were, nevertheless, acquainted with the high leather boot, worn in bad weather or when travelling. Hesiod calls this a sandal, but only by poetic licence, for he states that it was made of ox-hide and was generally lined with felt soles. We can get a fairly good idea of these boots from illustrations of a later date, where they appear as open in front, with a tongue and two straps at the instep and the calf.

The clothing as described was very simple, but rich ornaments often accompanied it. Homeric lords liked to make a parade of their wealth, and they could best convince and impress their inferiors by the display of numerous and costly jewels. However, there is only one example in the whole of Homer of this love of jewellery and personal display, and it occurs in the passage describing the golden buckle with its double pin which fastened the purple cape of Odysseus, when he left for the Trojan war. It represented a dog holding a spotted fawn between its two front paws.[1]

We could not attribute much importance to this one instance of the taste for rich jewellery at that time, had we not the evidence of the archaeologists to show how far it could in fact go. Thus, when the tomb of a wealthy lord, who lived on the isle of Aegina about the year 800, was discovered at the end of the last century, it yielded up a veritable treasure trove.[2] Here briefly is a list of the articles found in it.

First, a goblet of gold, rose-patterned in *repoussé* at the base, with the sides covered with spiral designs. Secondly, four gold pendants. The finest of them represents the upright figure of a man holding a swan or a goose by the neck, one on each side of him; his feet rest on a base which is attached to the lower part of

[1] *Odyssey*, XIX, vv. 225–321.
[2] A. Evans in *Journal of Hellenic Studies*, Vol. XIII (1893).

the ornament by two doves with outspread wings; five little gold discs hang from the base by thin gold chains. There are other pendants with doves as ornaments, one of them consisting of a chain of gold discs.

To these more important objects must be added five necklaces in gold and cornelian; a gold bracelet; five finger rings with gems inset; a diadem; fifty-four little flat discs in embossed gold, each with four holes along the edges, from which it would appear that they were intended to be sewn on to some article of clothing.

Finally, there are five circular pieces of gold without decoration. As four of them weigh approximately 132·7 grains,[1] the weight of the earlier gold stater, the inference is that these little ingots may have been small coins, perhaps the gold talent to which Homer refers and which has given rise to much speculation.

This rich collection of jewels, which obviously bears traces of the decorative Mycenaean tradition, points to a positive passion for ornaments. One must allow that Homer's Greeks often seem to rate the richness of their attire above its elegance. This is not to say that there was no ideal of masculine beauty. On the contrary Homer's accounts convey a pretty good notion of what he regarded as the 'godlike' man. The essential features were powerful feet, massive thighs, muscular arms and a broad chest and shoulders. This type persisted in archaic Greek sculpture until the fifth century; and we may take it as our model for the nobleman of Homer's age, whose daily life and behaviour we are now concerned to describe.

When we come to the Homeric women, we must recall that here also it is their stature that the poet praises in the first instance, their commanding appearance, noble gait and bearing. It was taken for granted that they had 'beautiful' feet, meaning 'large'; that they should have large hands (as Penelope's are described), white arms, rounded cheeks, curly and luxuriant hair, and throats nobly modelled; and there is a phrase constantly occurring in Homer which likens their chests to deep gulfs. Homer and his contemporaries seem in fact to have valued the external marks of femininity.

[1] 8·6 grams. The fifth piece weighs 7·5 grams.

## THE 'KING' OF THE 'GENOS'

The lord, or 'king' to call him by his usual title, although increasingly occupied with public business and, in common with his peers, the other kings, with the affairs of the city; and in spite of the growing demands of his interests as industrialist, merchant or shipowner, remained none the less the natural and statutory head of a large, complex family: a sort of vast clan — at least at the beginning of our period — called the *genos*. The relation of the *genos* to the patrician *gens* of Rome is that of a twin brother.

We have now to ask what manner of man was this lord, and how he conducted himself as head of the clan.

The question of the nature and status of the *genos* in ancient Greece, particularly in Homeric Greece, has been much debated, above all since the publication of Fustel de Coulanges' *Cité antique*. Without entering into those juridical and political considerations which would be irrelevant, we can affirm that the artificial and schematic conception which still prevailed fifty years ago and which saw in the *genos* the unit of society in the Homeric city, must now be abandoned.[1] An impartial reading of the texts of Homer and Hesiod makes amply clear that the Greek city was in no sense of the word, and never had been, a simple aggregate of clans. Side by side with the inhabitants of aristocratic birth, the city included a substantial proportion of free men of every condition, who were not attached to any *genos*. The composition of the clan, however, is known to us less from the Homeric poems themselves than from later texts in which we find allusions to traditions and institutions going back to the era of aristocratic preponderance.

The *genos* was essentially a family group, whose members all claimed descent through the male line from a common ancestor; they all bore the same name, that of the putative ancestor, or possibly the name indicating his function; and all were devotees of the cult of this common hero-ancestor.

[1] Cf. Gustave Glotz, *La Solidarité de la Famille*, 1904; and *Histoire grecque*, Vol. I, 1925.

The members of the clan, the *gennetes*, constituted a privileged class, *de facto* and *de jure*, in the city: it was a true nobility which was known at different times and places under different names. Homer, who was writing for all the Greeks, simply uses the general term, *aristoi* or *aristeis*, meaning 'the best'. At Athens they were called *Eupatridae* (the well-born); at Chalcis, *Hippobotes* (breeders of horses); at Ephesus, Erythrae and Chios they were called *Basileides* (the royal ones); at Samos and Syracuse, *Geomoroi* (the landowners); at Corinth, they assumed somewhat late in history a collective name, *Bacchiads* (descendants of Bacchis) perhaps in order to stress the equality of all the clans.

Whence, we may ask, was derived this position of privilege? According to the penetrating and probably definitive studies of A. M. Hocart on the caste system,[1] it had its roots in the most distant past of the Indo-European races themselves. The *gené* were families which had for long enjoyed an hereditary vocation, either as royal heads of the city or as heads of its various sections (the tribes and phratries), or as occupying under the king certain great offices, such as those of commander-in-chief (polemarch), regent (archon), registrars of the courts (thesmothetes), or as heralds, or carvers after sacrifices; or again as guardians of the sacred rites at national sanctuaries, like the Eumolpidae at Eleusis. All these prerogatives explain why the chiefs of the clans quite naturally substituted themselves for the king, after dethroning him, and why for a long period they retained a monopoly of the magisterial offices.

Thus, contrary to the traditional view, the city was in no sense a political and economic aggregate of clans. The soil of Greece was never divided into great demesnes, the collective and undivided property of independent *gené* which subsequently associated in larger political communities: on the contrary, it was by an inverse process that the *gené* came into being; and it was the communities that assigned to the members of the *gené*, on an hereditary basis, their higher religious and political functions.

Lands and property were allocated, or rather donated, to the

[1] A. M. Hocart, *Les Castes* (French translation), 1938.

*gené* to permit the clans and their members to fulfil these avocations as was fitting. From this method of apportionment the property was known as *chrema*, or *chremata*, in the plural; a word that implies the idea of allocation, of something provided in order to meet certain ends; or again it was called *temenos*, the portion reserved to a chieftain or a god. The estates so bestowed were held collectively by the *genos*, in the sense that they could not be alienated from the clan either by gift or inheritance. Hence the venerable rule, still formulated in the classical period, that in the event of inheritance, the *chremata* must remain within the *genos*. In one case only could the property be alienated, and this was when, by the proscription or banishment of the owner, it was confiscated to the benefit of the community whose title was in this case supreme. Even so, the members of the *genos* had the right to redeem it: this is stated in a very ancient law of Argos which has been preserved on a bronze tablet, probably dating from the seventh century.[1]

But these provisions did not preclude the partition of the *chremata*; on the contrary, we have Homer's testimony of a rich Cretan nobleman, the supposed father of Odysseus, whose property at his death was divided among his legitimate sons — according to the imaginary story which Odysseus relates to Eumaeus.[2] So that if the principle of indivisibility of the *chremata* ever existed, it had already disappeared in Homeric times, and this in spite of the political supremacy of the noble clans which, it seems, ought rather to have favoured it.

And, *a fortiori*, there could have been no question of it in respect of acquired goods, or *ctemata*: such goods might be either moveable or landed property. We have two characteristic examples of the latter case in the *Odyssey*. In the first, the property is one which old Laertes, the father of Odysseus, has 'acquired' by his labours and is now living on. It is situated at some distance outside the town, which leads one to suppose that it derived from an act of appropriation, and subsequent cultivation, of a piece of

---

[1] *American Journal of Archaeology*, Vol. V (1901), p. 159.
[2] *Odyssey*, XIV, vv. 208–9.

pasture land in the outlying country, which was the common property of all members of the city. And, in another place, it is his acquired properties (*ctemata*) that Alcinous proposes to offer Odysseus, with a house, in order to prevail on him to stay in Phaeacia and espouse Nausicaa.[1]

It is clear that it is not in the capacity of head of an economic system that the chief of a clan appears to us; but rather as judge, and as the religious and political protector of the clan in its dealings with civic institutions. It may be pertinent at this point to enquire whence he derived this authority and how he was appointed, as a preliminary to examining the functions he exercised.

The general rule was simple and formal: the head of the *genos* was the eldest male in the most direct male line, the head of the senior branch of the family. This primacy of the elder is definitely proclaimed by Homer:

> '. . . And, thou knowest, always
> The Erinyes wait to serve the elder born',[2]

as Iris reminds Poseidon when he wants to rebel against an order of Zeus. There were, however, cases where the head of the *genos* might be led to renounce his right and abandon his authority. Thus old Laertes has handed over his office to his son Odysseus and has withdrawn to a little property some way off. He has retained the respect of his family but is no longer consulted regarding the business of the *genos* and is morally incapable of intervening, even in his son's absence. Homer tells us nothing about the reasons for this abdication. But we know that certain physical infirmities or defects might suffice to create an incapacity for conducting the religious ceremonies which were among the prerogatives of the head of the clan. In fact, the chief of a *genos* on whom certain public functions had devolved by hereditary succession, and who had become incapable of exercising them for physical or religious reasons, might *ipso facto* be compelled to abandon his eminent position. And finally a criminal act committed by the chief against another member of the *genos*, an act which in conse-

[1] *Odyssey*, XXIV, vv. 205–7; and VII, vv. 313–14.
[2] *Iliad*, XV, v. 204, p. 332.

quence was not subject to legal action, or even a simple denial of justice by the chief, might arouse within the clan such reprobation and moral pressure that the chief would be forced to abdicate.

We have a famous and dramatic example of this in the case of Periander, tyrant of Corinth, a case which arose barely fifty years after the age of the Homeric poems. Periander had killed his wife Melissa. One of her sons, Lycophron, was informed of the deed by his maternal grandfather. He then refused ever to speak to his father. The latter in exasperation drove him from the house, put him under an interdict and finally exiled him to Corcyra, a Corinthian colony. After a time, Lycophron was begged to return; but he remained inexorable and declared he would never go back to Corinth as long as his father was living there. Overwhelmed by this, Periander ended by giving way and asked Lycophron to succeed him, while he himself would go into exile and reside in Corcyra. It is true that the Corcyreans then killed Lycophron in order to prevent Periander from settling among them. But the mutual attitudes of father and son, and the father's final decision, are none the less revealing.

The right of primogeniture was not therefore enough to make a man chief of the *genos*. He also needed the consent, or at least the tacit consent, of the other members of the clan, and even sometimes perhaps the assent of the city. When Telemachus comes of age, in his father's absence, and desires to enter into possession of his property and prerogatives in opposition to the usurping suitors, we see him bring the matter before the popular assembly, in Book II of the *Odyssey*.

When the king of the *genos* has been once installed — and the title of king is official — he wields considerable powers.

First, he is the religious leader of the *gennetes*. He is not only responsible for the cult of the ancestors, but, in the name of the clan, when occasion arises, he also offers sacrifices to the great deities. These sacrifices are not offered in the city temples but in the great court of the manor. The third book of the *Odyssey* gives a detailed description of one of them, a sacrifice celebrated by Nestor in honour of Athena. Here we see the old king officiating on behalf of the *genos* just as the city magistrate officiates in the temples or sacred enclosures on behalf of the whole people. He provides the victim and has its horns gilded in his presence; he then assigns their several duties to his sons, who are assessors. Two of them lead the animal by its horns, another holds in one hand the basket of barley, in the other the jar for libations, the fourth handles the axe to strike down the victim, the fifth opens its throat and the sixth gathers the blood in a receptacle. After which, the animal is cut up and roasted on the altar, according to the ritual, the pieces of flesh being held in position with long five-pronged forks. Nestor in the meantime has distributed the lustral water and the barley, has thrown a few hairs from the victim's head into the sacrificial fire, has supervised the roasting of the first pieces of flesh, namely the thighs that have been wrapped round with fat; and he has poured the ritual libation of dark wine. He is the priest of the *genos*.

He is also its judge. Crimes and offences committed inside the clan do not, in fact, fall under the jurisdiction of the city magistrates. On the other hand they are not all brought before the king of the *genos*. Offences committed in the house by the daughters, the servants or the servingmen, or by the male children who, on account of their age, are still subject to paternal authority, are punished by the father himself, who in the case of a serious offence has the right of life and death over the guilty. Misconduct by the daughter is punished with death or expulsion. Odysseus causes to be hanged, without trial, those servant-maids who had fornicated with the suitors and flouted the authority of Penelope and the housekeeper. The goatherd Melantheus, who had openly rebelled against his masters, is punished by mutilation. The wife, in case of adultery, may be put to death or expelled; but the sanction for mere rebellion is only the whip. The murder of a husband by a wife naturally involves her execution by the new head of the family. Orestes, on coming of age, wins great glory by killing his mother Clytaemnestra.

In spite of its limits and exceptions, the 'king's' judicial authority was fairly extensive. He intervened whenever there was a question of punishing the free adult males of the clan. There were not many punishable crimes, but their occurrence was not infrequent. First came murder or attempted murder; quarrels frequently arose in fact between brothers born of different mothers and excited by mutual jealousy. Then there was the violation by a young son of a half-sister or a servant; intercourse with servants was reserved for the head of the family. Finally there was incest: a son might seduce his father's concubine (Phoenix[1] had done this in order to avenge his neglected mother); or a guilty relationship might arise between the son of a first marriage and the young wife of a father who had married again (this was the crime that Hippolytus was accused of). Theft, however, did not exist; such a thing was purposeless because of the rule of mutual aid, which united all members of the clan, and because of the imperative duty of generosity and hospitality which was imposed on the 'king' in respect of all the *gennetes*.

When he had to judge these cases, and even offences committed by his own sons, the clan chief did not sit alone. The accused was confined to a room in the manor. The members of the *genos* were convened and there was junketing for several days as was the custom at all meetings of the clan, whether for funerals, marriages or court cases. Some palavering was also needed, to secure agreement, as decisions had to be unanimous; and in fact it was a question of depriving the *genos* of one of its active members who was an element of strength and prestige. After this the 'king' pronounced sentence.

This might amount to expulsion from the *genos*, that is, death in theory. Expulsion was effected in the form of a manhunt, amid cries of 'Strike! Thrust!' — a pursuit accompanied with blows and stoning. In practice this pursuit was generally a pretence, because the *genos* was loth to shed the blood of one of its members. The condemned fugitive betook himself elsewhere, he left the city and led a life that was usually lamentable. Sometimes the penalty was milder: it might take the form of *atimia* within the *genos*, that is, deprivation of civil rights. In such cases, the condemned man was

[1] In the *Iliad*. Phoenix had taken refuge, after this, at the court of Peleus where he became governor, or tutor, to the young Achilles (Translator).

not driven out, but forced to live isolated in some corner of the domain, and reduced to dependence on charity. The suicide, who was held guilty of shedding the blood of the clan, was treated like the living. His body was denied burial; sometimes he was mutilated by the severing of a hand.

Observe also that the king was not free to refrain from proceeding against one of his own sons, for example, if the latter were involved. Thus the hero Tydeus had killed his cousins in defending his father Oeneus, and the latter had neglected to punish the crime. Oeneus' brother, Agrios, then intervened along with his family, forced Tydeus to flee and Oeneus to abdicate. Which shows how a denial of justice might lead to the dethronement of the king-judge. The history of a *genos* was not without its dramas.[1]

Lastly, these 'kings', priests and judges both, were the natural representatives of the clans in their dealings with the city authorities. From their ranks were recruited the magistrates who had replaced the ancient dynasties or usurped their powers, and also the Council of the Ancients who, after formerly assisting the kings of the city, now sat side by side with the magistrates.

## THE WEALTH OF THE NOBILITY

The prestige and authority of the 'king' of a clan derived first from his birth and the importance of his kinsfolk, but more and more as time went on, they depended on his wealth, which enabled him to live in the style befitting a great lord.

Wealth consisted of landed property in the first instance. This however was not very great. We can form some idea of it by recalling that in the Athenian vocabulary the men who had access to the higher magisterial posts, that is in fact the heads of the clans of Eupatridae, were called the *pentacosiomedimnoi*, which meant that they harvested at least five hundred *medimnoi* of grain every year. Now as at the beginning of the sixth century, before Solon's reforms, the *medimnos* was equivalent to about two bushels,[2] this

---

[1] We shall see in Chapter VIII below what were the relations between this interfamily justice and the exigencies of vengeance for blood.

[2] '74 litres.'

figure represents an annual harvest of about one hundred and twenty-seven quarters.[1] This was a minimum. One may calculate that the average return from the land of a *pentacosiomedimnos* probably varied between one hundred and thirty and one hundred and seventy-two quarters.[2] In view of the indifferent yield of the soil in Greece, and of the practice of letting land lie fallow and only cultivating it every other year, this return corresponds to properties of barely two hundred and two hundred and fifty acres[3] respectively, of arable land.

These were respectable estates but not more. The difficulty was to maintain them from generation to generation, on account of the division that took place among the heirs. How did one contrive to maintain them? First of all, obviously, by limiting the number of legitimate births, because as Homer tells us,[4] on the father's death, the sons of concubines only received a house and small plot of land. Odysseus was an only son, like his father Laertes, and he himself had only one child, Telemachus.

The heads of a more numerous family had, however, one resource, which was the emigration of the younger sons. The eighth and seventh centuries were a period of intense colonization, when the Greeks were swarming overseas. The younger sons were sent to distant lands, to the cities planted in barbarian territory where each of them could found a new *genos* and play the part of political chieftain. We should not forget that Alcinous and the Phaeacian lords were the sons of these emigrants.

But this was not the only resource. The great nobles might, in case of need, enlarge their landed properties by acquisitions: first, within the *genos* itself, by purchasing the property of a relative who had fallen on evil days or who wished to seek his fortune elsewhere; and then, outside the lands belonging to the *genos*, by

---

[1] '370 hectolitres.'

[2] '400 et 500 hectolitres' = approximately the measures given above, or 1100 and 1375 bushels, respectively.

[3] '80 à 100 hectares.' I have judged it better to translate this and the above into English measures (Translator).

[4] *Odyssey*, XIV, v. 210.

encroaching on the fallow or the waste lands that were the common property of the city, whether by purchase from the community or by mere occupation of the ground. No doubt, as we have seen, old Laertes had proceeded on these lines, and so had Alcinous.

In this way the heads of great families contrived without too much difficulty to maintain or reconstitute their demesne. But to compass their ends, what diplomacy and vigilance and perseverance they had to employ! We can be sure that this was one of their main anxieties, and we can be convinced that the judicial powers they disposed of, inside the *genos*, and which enabled them to exclude the holders or heirs of some property they coveted, must have been in their hands a singularly effective weapon to prevent the frittering away of the patrimony. We are justified in guessing that a good many sordid calculations lay behind the brilliant tapestry of legend and epic song.

A property of two hundred or two hundred and fifty acres was certainly not enough to enable Homer's aristocrats to cut a magnificent figure. They needed other resources: we shall see what these were. But landed property was the sign and legal token of their princely dignity and their position in the city. It was therefore a matter of tradition that they should give their principal care to it. They personally supervised the major operations of farming. One of the scenes on Achilles' buckler shows us the ceremony of harvest on a 'royal' demesne. Labourers are mowing while children pick up the loose sheaves and carry them to the binders. Meanwhile, under an oak tree, people are preparing the meal for the harvesters; the heralds have sacrificed an ox, while the maids are making bread. The 'king' is presiding in silence, sceptre in hand; his heart is full of joy.[1] When seed time comes round, it is he who will pronounce the invocation to Hades and Persephone, the gods of the nether world and of fertility, an invocation which Hesiod tells us must precede the burying of the seed in the furrows. But it must be repeated that the main wealth of the great lords did not derive from agriculture. It lay especially in moveable property.

[1] *Iliad*, XVIII, vv. 550–60.

It consisted, first, in immense herds. These herds were not kept in the manor, the stables of which only sheltered such draught animals as horses, she-mules, he-mules, and the oxen used for ploughing and carting. The herds lived in the meadows, moors, waste lands and forests which were the common property of the city and on which the lords had erected shelters for the animals and their keepers, shepherds, neatherds, swineherds and goatherds. We have a picture of this in the rustic dwelling of faithful Eumaeus, the divine swineherd.

The *Odyssey* provides us with a rough but impressive census of Odysseus' herds. On the mainland opposite Ithaca he owned twelve herds of cows, twelve flocks of sheep, twelve herds of goats and twelve of swine. On the island itself his herdsmen looked after eleven herds of goats and Eumaeus, chief of the swineherds, twelve of swine. How much stock did that represent? We can form some notion of it from the inventory of the pigsties which had been confided to Eumaeus. He had charge of six hundred sows which had all littered: this meant several thousands of pigs. The herd of males only numbered three hundred and sixty; but it had been considerably reduced by the exigencies of the suitors. Odysseus' livestock therefore numbered, at a low figure, about thirty thousand head of animals.[1] One could be a rich lord without possessing so many.

Odysseus' fortune was that of a landsman. But other sources of wealth had already made their appearance. Industry and maritime trade were now enriching the cities of the Asiatic coast and also the cities of continental Greece which were well placed on the great trade routes: Chalcis, Cymé, Eretria, Aegina, Corinth, Megara and Sicyon, to name only the principal places. Money was coming into common use, although Homer, with an eye to poetical archaism, only mentions it under the vague designation of 'talent'. The old landed aristocracy was the first to profit from this

---

[1] *Odyssey*, XIV, vv. 13–20, 100–8. A part of these herds lived on the coast of Epirus, opposite the island. The latter was not the traditional Ithaca, but Leucadia. See, apropos of this, in our book on *Les Poèmes homériques et l'Histoire grecque*, Vol. II, the chapter on Ithaca and Pylos.

commercial expansion because, at least at the outset, this class alone disposed of sufficient capital and of the necessary slave labour, in public or private slaves. Hence its economic situation was consolidated; but this was very momentary, because the development of moveable wealth was soon to lead to the formation of a class of *nouveaux riches*, recruited from among the enterprising younger sons and bastards of the great families. This class was to demand its share of power and to seek support for its claims in the discontent of the little artisans who were being threatened or ruined by the competition of the great factories operated by slave labour. Hence the appearance, towards the middle of the seventh century, of the first tyrannies of a demagogic character.

In the meantime, and as long as the nobility retained control of political power, the 'kings' accumulated these new advantages together with those of landed property and also with the traditional perquisites that accompany political power. The latter were not negligible and one must be careful not to forget them in any inventory of a noble's wealth. Hesiod indeed treats 'kings' as 'eaters of presents' ('bribe-devouring'). Was there a reproach in his mind? Perhaps merely regret. It must be observed that the author of the *Iliad* mentions an example of such 'presents' without the least reproof and as something legitimate and perfectly natural. In describing a trial scene which was depicted on the shield of Achilles, he notes that two gold talents had been laid in the midst of the tribunal.

> ... to be given to him
> Who should among them judge most righteously.[1]

The custom of giving 'gratifications'[2] is no doubt as old as the organization of human justice. In any case the 'kings' of Homeric Greece did not turn up their noses at it.

And lastly, this account would be incomplete if we did not in-

[1] *Iliad*, XVIII. Trans. Marris, p. 427.

[2] In seventeenth-century France they were known as 'épices' — the word Monsieur Mireaux uses here (Translator).

clude the practice of wealthy marriages which became more and more frequent with the expansion of moveable riches: a practice that Theognis, a little later, was to stigmatize with indignation when he says that 'a well-born man does not refuse to take to wife the daughter of a villein, if she brings him many possessions'. Homer had already recorded one of these rich marriages;[1] contracted, it is true, by a noble bastard. But were the legitimate sons much more disdainful?

### THE NOBLEMAN'S ENTOURAGE: MESSMATES AND COMPANIONS

There existed in the manor, side by side with the children and the crowd of servants, a superior class of 'domestics' in the old sense of the term. This class deserves special mention because it brings out the feudal character of aristocratic life.

This staff of *therapontes,* 'servers' or, to be more accurate, 'sergeants', comprised in the first place the heralds whose business it was to convene an assembly in the 'king's' name, to see that meetings were decently managed, and sometimes to honour a distinguished guest by serving as his cupbearer. Next came the gentlemen of the table, carvers and servers of meat, and cupbearers. There were also the charioteers and, lastly, a number of 'fleet sergeants' or couriers. From among this class were selected the governors of noble children, men who supervised their meals when they were little and who later trained them in games and exercises. Phoenix had fulfilled this office for the young Achilles.

They were free men, and even of noble birth. They included foreigners, sometimes men of rank who had been forced to leave their country or who had been confided by their parents to the care of a friendly lord. It was under these conditions that Phoenix and Patroclus had been received into the manor of Peleus.

They rendered, of their free will, honourable service to the lord. They followed him in war and, if occasion arose, on his travels. They were at his side in all the important events of life, at marriages, funerals and court trials. They took part in pursuing

[1] *Odyssey,* XIV, v. 211.

blood vengeance, and they themselves had to be avenged by the same right as the members of the *genos*. They were bound to their patron by a close personal bond, which placed them in the clan almost on the level of the *gennetes*. This bond was religious in character: the domestics attached to the king-priest of the *genos* were not substantially different from the assistants, heralds, carvers of victims and other officers, whom we meet with around the king-priest of the city.

They were called *ètai*, which could be translated by the Old French word 'compains'. They were in fact the lord's messmates; they shared his meals. In war they became *hetairoi* or companions. They fought in closest proximity to the lord, and he in turn had to defend or avenge them as a first duty. Achilles has no rest until he has avenged Patroclus, his 'companion'. Odysseus' greatest desire, Homer tells us at the beginning of the *Odyssey*, is to bring his companions back home. It was his desire and also his duty, just as the companions first duty was fidelity. Faithful (*pistos*) was the natural epithet for the companion. One loves one's 'faithful companion' as one's own parents, Homer again tells us.

This system of civil and military companionship[1] was one of the most characteristic features of seigniorial life in Homer's time. It was closely related to the Germanic system described by Tacitus and to the 'antrustiones'[2] of the Merovingian monarchy. It was the foundation of those sentiments of honour and fidelity which are the binding-force in all feudal hierarchies.

The lord of Homer's time lived in the midst of his companions, to whom he was often humanly and sentimentally nearer than to the host of cousins who formed his clan. Between companions there was no rivalry or real dissent, nor could there be. The despair of Achilles when Patroclus is killed is not a poetic hyperbole, but a true expression of the deepest feeling and the closest bond that could unite men in the society of Homer's time.

---

[1] I wonder whether the 'clients' of the old patrician *gentes* in Rome were not the Homeric 'companions' under another name (Author's note).

[2] Low Latin 'Antrustiones', from Germanic *an* (in) + *trust*, i.e. those whom the king could trust in (Littré) (Translator's note).

Seen in this light, the last books of the *Iliad* no doubt afford a decisive revelation of the social psychology of that aristocratic world to the very heart of which Homer's poetry introduces us.

## THE LORD'S AMUSEMENTS: HUNTING

The principal virtues of this nobility, as also of the class of 'companions' so closely bound to it, were naturally the military virtues. They displayed them on the battlefield where they advanced in their war chariots in front of the infantry phalanx. We will not follow them there. In time of peace they displayed and cultivated these qualities in the pastime which has always and everywhere been the prerogative of the nobility, namely the hunting of wild beasts, a test of endurance, audacity and courage.

Wild animals were not rare in the forests of continental Greece and of the Asiatic seaboard, especially of the Troad which was dominated by the wooded heights of Ida. Countless are the epic similes borrowed from the life and character of wild beasts. Of these four species are regularly evoked: lions, panthers, wolves and boars.

It has been questioned whether the lion had not already become extinct in continental Greece. It had probably disappeared from the Peloponnese; but there must have remained lions in the mountains of central and northern Greece; for otherwise one could scarcely understand the insistence with which they are cited as examples, or the remarkably exact details which are given regarding their habits and behaviour. In any case there were lions in Asia. Asia was also the habitat of the panther. Paris wears a panther's skin when he goes to fight. There must still have been panthers in northern Greece. Wolf and wild boar were found everywhere, especially the boar, which ravaged the farm lands. People also hunted the hare, the stag and the 'wild goat';[1] but these were trials of skill and not of valour. The hare and wild goat were hunted with bow and arrow.

The quarry that called for great courage were the lion, the

---

[1] Probably the moufflon which now survives only on the islands (Cyprus, Corsica and Sardinia) and also the chamois which is still widely distributed in the Balkans.

panther and the boar. The wolf can scarcely have been hunted at all. We read nothing about it; and this can be understood, for the wolf runs away and Homer's Greeks had no means of pursuing him. They did not yet practise horsemanship, which was only to come into general use towards the end of the seventh century after the Cimmerian horsemen's invasion of Asia Minor. Against wolves, it was for the herdsmen to defend themselves and their charges as well as they could.

Against lions and panthers, too, for that matter. But lions and panthers were also a quarry that could tempt the courage of a noble who had only spear and sword with which to fight them.

Hunting the panther was the more dangerous. Alerted by the barking dogs whom he despises, he does not retreat. He emerges from the thicket and confronts the huntsman. Now it is a question as to who will strike first. Even when stricken and pierced through with the javelin, he does not recoil but fights to the death.[1] One needs a stout heart to contend at close quarters with an animal as supple, as aggressive and as well-armed.

Lion-hunting really presented fewer risks, unless the animal had cubs. The dogs were of little help, because the most valiant dog does not tackle the lion but remains barking at a respectful distance. The lion was hunted by means of a battue to which 'everyone' was summoned. Roused by the beaters, the animal comes out of his den and at first moves away 'disdainfully' and without haste. A bolder huntsman approaches and strikes him with the javelin. Now the wounded animal stops and gathers himself together. With foaming jaws wide open, he roars, beats his flanks with his tail and springs straight upon one of the pursuers. This is the critical moment when it is necessary to strike a death blow.[2]

Panthers and lions were comparatively rare game. The most usual kind of hunt and also, as we should say, the most 'sporting', was that of the boar. We have a detailed account of a hunt at which Odysseus had received a deep wound in the thigh, leaving

[1] *Iliad*, XXI, vv. 573-8.
[2] *Iliad*, XX, 164-73.

the great scar which occasioned his recognition by old Eurycleia, at the time when she was washing his feet.[1] As a young man he had gone to pay a visit to his maternal grandfather, Autolycus, who lived at the foot of Parnassus. After the hearty salutations and the hearty meal that was offered on his arrival, Autolycus' sons, the very next morning, took their nephew to hunt in the mountains. They set off at the first gleam of dawn. Climbing the slopes of Parnassus under cover of the woods, they reached the higher ground by the time the sun had risen. At the opening of a ravine the dogs picked up a trail and were followed by the beaters. Odysseus and his uncles took up their position at the other end of the glen so as to intercept the animal when it was started. On a thick litter of leaves in the heart of a dense thicket an enormous solitary boar was lying, sheltered from winds and mist, from rain and sun. The animal had heard the dogs and the din made by the trackers. He sprang to his feet and burst from cover with bristling hair and blazing eyes. Odysseus leapt forward brandishing his spear. The animal charged him and tore off with his tusk a piece of flesh on the boy's thigh. At the same time Odysseus struck him in the right spot, the joint of the shoulder, and transfixed him through the heart. The boar fell dead. The hunter's wound was dressed and the party returned to the manor.

All hunters did not possess the dash or the sangfroid of Odysseus. Sometimes, if he were merely wounded or noticed a wavering in the line of armed hunters, the boar would turn, charge the dogs and beaters, and scatter them far and wide.[2]

Like all nobles with a vocation for hunting, Homer's heroes had a passion for dogs. There existed hunting dogs who lived in the manor and were quite distinct from the practically savage mastiffs who guarded the flocks. The former were what in France are still called 'running dogs'.[3] Telemachus takes two of them with him when he leaves the manor and goes to the town assembly. Odys-

---

[1] *Odyssey*, XIX, 428–58.
[2] *Iliad*, XVII, 281–3 and 725–6.
[3] 'Chiens courants.' They may possibly have been greyhounds (Translator).

seus furtively wipes a tear from his face when his old dog Argus (the 'runner'), lying on the dunghill, dies after he has seen him; and Eumaeus recalls with emotion the qualities that distinguished Argus when, twenty years before, he had accompanied his master on the hunt: his speed, his strength and his fine nose.

The possession of a well-selected and well-trained pack was a privilege and mark of nobility.

### TRAVEL AND THE DUTIES OF HOSPITALITY

Homer's aristocrats are very fond of travel. Like Odysseus, Nestor or Menelaus, they love relating their adventures, real or imaginary, in distant lands; and Greek audiences were never tired of questioning and listening to travellers. The stories they told were the reward of hospitality, and much of its charm. After landing on Ithaca, Odysseus, who is distrustful or desirous of concealing his identity, knows that he must satisfy the expectation of those he meets and those who entertain him, of Athena whom he does not recognize, and of Eumaeus and Penelope, with stories as wonderful and dramatic as he can make them.

Travel and voyages not only furnished a knowledge of many men, and their cities, and their minds, as Homer says at the beginning of the *Odyssey*; but they also, and perhaps especially, served to establish far and wide bonds of hospitality which were indispensable. Homeric Greece appears to have been covered with a vast network of great families who were united by the mutual and imperious obligations of hospitality.

Moreover, it was only the existence of this network that made travel possible in an age when there were as yet no hostelries. And travel, whatever its real object, should always serve to refresh and renew, from generation to generation, relationships which were sometimes very ancient. When Athena takes on the form of Mentes, prince of the Taphians, in order to comfort and counsel Telemachus, she — or rather he — does not fail to remind his host that their two families have always been in the habit of receiving each other in their homes; and he appeals, in support, to the testimony of old Laertes.

This hospitality was governed by immutable laws. When a stranger of good appearance presented himself, a member of the family went to receive him, relieved him of the lance which a man of quality always carried, grasped his right hand and led him to the *megaron*. There he was seated on a throne facing the hearth. A maid came with an ewer and basin for him to wash his hands, and then set a polished table before him. On this the stewardess placed a cup and basket of bread; a gentleman carver brought a plate of meat, and the cupbearer or herald filled the cup. It was only after this first meal that the visitor was questioned as to his name, family and country, and the object of his journey. If, as is the case with Odysseus on the evening when he arrives in the palace of Alcinous, the visitor eludes the question, his hosts are careful not to insist. Enquiries will be renewed later, perhaps next day, in more favourable circumstances. The guest shares in the family life as long as he abides there. A bed is made up for him in the vestibule which gives access to the *megaron*. When he leaves, he is given presents appropriate to his dignity, and, as the parting cup is offered him, a libation is poured and the gods are invoked. Should he have need of it, he is lent the means of pursuing his journey, by chariot or ship. Sometimes he is accompanied on his way by a son of the family, as Nestor arranges for Telemachus, or by a servant.

It may be that the visitor is an unknown man, unconnected with his host's family; perhaps he has fled his own country, or been shipwrecked, like Odysseus; he may even be an enemy, like Priam in the tent of Achilles. In this case he comes as a suppliant, he embraces the knees of the mistress or master of the house, makes his request and sits in the ashes of the hearth; after which the ceremonial of hospitality is followed in the traditional fashion.

A lord or a young gentleman might have the most varied reasons for travelling. There were, first of all, family visits, such as that which Autolycus, Odysseus' maternal grandfather, pays to Ithaca on the occasion of the birth of his grandson — a circumstance which gave him the honour of choosing a name for the child; or the visit which Odysseus when a boy paid his grandfather, so as in some sort to return the latter's visit and also to receive the gifts which had been promised him; it was when hunting on this occasion that he received the great wound in his thigh. Then, too, princes had to undertake diplomatic missions. Odysseus as a young man was sent by his father and the elders of Ithaca as an envoy to Messene, in the southern Peloponnese, to require reparation for the theft of three hundred sheep with their shepherds, stolen by Messenian pirates. Odysseus and Menelaus later go on an embassy to Troy to demand the return of Helen, and are entertained by Antenor. Sometimes a great man decided to visit a distant sanctuary to consult an oracle on some important matter; an example of this is the journey which Odysseus is alleged to have taken to Dodona to seek advice from the oak of Zeus regarding the conduct he was to observe on his return to Ithaca. Sometimes, again, one travelled on business. Thus the sham Mentes, prince of the Taphians, is supposed to be going to Temesa, on the shores of the Tyrrhenian Sea to exchange his cargo of iron for Etrurian bronze. And finally there were journeys to gather information, like the one which Telemachus undertakes on the advice of Athena, when he goes to Pylos and Sparta to seek news of his father.

Homeric Greece seems indeed to have been traversed in every direction by travellers of note, who met and exchanged presents. On his mission to Messenia, Odysseus meets in that country Iphitus, son of Eurytus, king of Oechalia: this young man had come to look for twelve mares which had strayed. From Iphitus, Odysseus receives as a gift the famous bow with which, later on, he massacres the suitors.

Many of these journeys involved a sea crossing. The kind of vessel used was a small ship with oars and a sail, which, in a good wind, could make about five knots. It carried a crew of twenty rowers. When one landed, these men remained near the boat which had been hauled up on the beach, and awaited the return of the travellers who now pursued their journey by land. Thus Telemachus' crew remain at Pylos, while he himself proceeds to

Lacedaemon. One had therefore to be very amply provisioned. Telemachus, who foresaw a twelve days' journey, took with him twelve amphorae of black wine and twenty 'measures' of wheaten flour in leathern sacks. Now the amphora and the 'measure' had capacities of about 4·4 gallons and nearly one bushel respectively.[1] This makes a ration of one and three quarter pints of 'black' wine (that is, nearly four and a half pints of diluted wine)[2] and about six and a half pounds[3] of flour. The flour ration seems enormous. But, when the ship cast anchor, flour, a rare commodity, must have served as a sort of currency to barter for the good fresh meat supplied by the people on the spot.

The travelling car was the same as the war chariot. It was a light, rustic affair on which two men could stand upright. The main part of it was a body of which the base consisted of a wooden frame a little over six feet wide — broader than it was long — and which was rounded in front. Over this frame were stretched solid leather thongs which made a fairly elastic floor, good enough to deaden the shocks and jolts. A double barrier surrounded three sides of the car, to prevent one's falling forward or sideways over the wheels. You climbed on to the car or got off behind. A fairly short pole was attached to the body, and this was supported by an axle seven cubits long.[4] The wheels were mounted on this axle when one was ready to start. These wheels comprised a hub in which were fixed eight spokes supporting a rim; the rim consisted of four strips of wood cut in the direction of the grain, warped in the fire and bent in a circle, and encased one within the other — the whole wheel being consolidated by means of a ring of metal which had been first expanded in the fire and which then, as it cooled, clamped itself tightly round the rim. The whole carriage

[1] 'Vingt et trente-cinq litres environ respectivement' = about 35 pints and 77 pounds.

A 'litre' = 1·76 pints, a hectolitre = 2·75 bushels, or one bushel = 37 litres (c. 80 pounds) (Translator).

[2] Black wine was undrinkable. It was diluted in the proportion of three parts of water to two of wine (Author's note).

[3] 'Trois litres' = about 6·6 pounds (5·28 pints) (Translator).

[4] Rather over 9 feet.

did not stand very high, as the wheels were only about three feet in diameter.[1]

The car was drawn by two horses. The harness consisted of a fairly long, light yoke in box wood, of which the rounded ends rested on the horses' backs. To harness up, one began by fixing the yoke on to the pole which was furnished with a peg or pin on its front portion. When the yoke was placed on the pole, a fixed ring, attached to the rear of the central part of the yoke, was slipped round the pin; and this arrangement prevented the yoke from moving forward or backward. The yoke was then fastened to the pole by a leather strap nine cubits (about $12\frac{1}{2}$ feet) long. For this purpose a hump had been contrived on the middle portion of the yoke; the strap was passed three times round the hump and knotted underneath. The horses pulled on the whole harness with breast-bands resting against their chests, the ends of which were knotted to rings fixed on the rear part of the yoke. It was an ingenious but complicated and rather primitive arrangement; but it explains the Homeric image which shows the horses tossing the yoke as they trot. The latter must have been provided with thick padding to prevent the animals from being galled.[2]

In an equipage of this kind, Telemachus and Peisistratus made, from sunrise to sundown, stages of about fifty miles a day, from Pylos to Pherae, where they stayed with Alpheus' grandson, and from Pherae to Sparta. These stages were evidently interrupted by several stops to allow horses and travellers to rest, eat and drink. This was good going, at an average speed of five miles an hour, remarkable going when one considers the poor state of the tracks, the equipment, and the gear.

We are here, of course, considering the performance of epic heroes; besides, the fatigue of travel was greatly compensated for by the generous hospitality that awaited the pilgrims on their arrival.

[1] 'Trois empans de diamètre.' 74 centimetres, to which must be added a few centimetres for the metal circle: say about 80 centimetres altogether (Author's note).

[2] For the disposition of the car and the harness, see especially *Iliad*, V, vv. 720 et seq.; XXIV, 265 et seq., etc., and Hesiod, *Works and Days*.

## BANQUETS AND FESTIVITIES

Everything in this patrician society appears to have furnished a pretext for banquets and festivities; even rapine and injustice could serve as excuse. The gilded youth of Ithaca and the neighbouring islands instal themselves in the house of Odysseus who is presumed dead, to court Penelope, presumed to be a widow; they behave in the fashion of regular suitors who have been invited by the master, they banquet and junket all day long, and pillage the goods of the absent lord.

It was, besides, a kind of 'noblesse oblige' frequently to invite to the house kinsfolk, neighbours, friends and men of the same rank. Any pretext would serve: a domestic ceremony, a public festival, the visit of a distinguished guest. Such parties, when frequently given, established the prestige of a real lord, and were the source of a moral claim over the guests as a whole. Generosity was a form of investment. It opened the way for gratitude and for access to public office. One had to be rich and magnificent to play a part in civic life. At the end of the seventh century Solon, who was heir of one of the noblest families in Athens, began by restoring his fortune in maritime trade before he aspired to public life and to figuring as a political leader.

Even in the normal way, a great deal of food was consumed in the manor house. There were three meals in the day, consisting basically of bread and meat, washed down with plenty of wine. The *ariston* was taken in the morning, *deipnon* towards noon, and *dorpon* at the end of the day. When it was a question of ceremonial banquets only the second and third counted, and they constituted, so to speak, a single festivity in two acts, separated by games, songs, dances and other forms of enjoyment.

Meals were cooked in the courtyards of the women's quarters, and here too the girdle cakes were prepared every day. The meat was cooked in cauldrons standing on tripods, but the noble portions, such as the back and thighs, were roasted or grilled on glowing embers; and this cooking was usually done in the open air, although in bad weather the fire was lit in a building with a lantern roof. Prior to this, of course, the beasts brought in from the fields had been killed, skinned, singed and cut up by the gentleman carvers, or sometimes by a member of the family.

On the occasion of a ceremonial banquet the animals were usually killed in the court of honour, and the act took the form of a genuine sacrifice in honour of some god. Whenever a beast was killed, someone reserved a few hairs from its head and threw them into the fire, while invoking the favour of the immortals. Eumaeus does this when he entertains Odysseus, disguised as a beggar, in his cabin: it was in fact an immemorial custom which survived also in current language: to kill an animal was to 'sacrifice' it.

On these exceptional occasions a part of the cooking, and notably that of the noble portions, was also done in the court of honour. And, as the multitude of guests precluded their being all received in the *megaron*, which could hold only about fifty persons, the men of lower rank remained in the peristyle and the great court. Only persons of quality had a right to a seat and a polished table set before them; the others sat on skins spread on the ground.

The ritual was always the same. Maids came in, each with a basin and ewer, and poured water over the guests' hands. Next, someone set a basket of bread and a cup before each guest. The cups were of metal, sometimes even of gold or silver; some of them were works of art like the cup with two handles,[1] adorned with doves, which Nestor uses in Book XI of the *Iliad*, the shape of which recalls a cup that has been found in a tomb at Mycenae. The carvers then brought the meat, already cut up, on wooden or metal platters, while the cupbearer or the heralds mixed the wine and water in great 'craters' — large two-handled jugs, with feet — and from these the cups were filled. Everyone ate with his fingers. Sometimes, out of deference for a guest of quality, the master of the house or some great man present would take a choice morsel in his hand, carry and present it to the guest he wished to honour. While the meal was going on, beggars moved about seeking portions of meat and crusts of bread.

[1] It appears to have had 'tessara ouata', i.e. *four* 'ears' or handles (Translator).

'The rage of thirst and hunger satisfied' — to quote the Homeric formula — the amusements began. The first and most popular was the poetical recitation. A local bard was regularly invited to attend feasts. In Ithaca, his name was Phemius; in Phaeacia, Demodocus. If we may believe the author of the *Odyssey*, himself a bard and no doubt inclined to exalt the dignity of his brotherhood, the singer was received with distinguished marks of courtesy. For the feast he gives in honour of Odysseus, Alcinous sends a herald to bring the 'divine' bard, blind Demodocus. On his arrival at the palace he is set on a throne at the foot of a column in the *megaron*. Odysseus presents him with a choice morsel. After the meal, he gets up and, accompanying himself on the *cithara*, recites amid general silence episodes from the song of the Achaeans. These memories cause Odysseus' tears to flow, and his emotion betrays him.

Other diversions follow. Some guests sit on skins on the ground, playing at counters, a game that was perhaps like our draughts. In the court of honour others vie in strength and skill by throwing the discus or hurling the javelin. Menelaus amuses the company he has invited to the weddings of his son and daughter by engaging two jugglers who amaze the guests by their acrobatics. The suitors of Penelope, on a night of mirth, take it into their heads to force the sham beggar Odysseus and the professional beggar Irus to settle their quarrel by a boxing match. But the favourite and most distinguished pastime was the dance, an essential part of a young nobleman's education. It was still imbued with religious feeling. There was no banquet or festivity in the manor without a formal period of dancing when the young men would compete in efforts of virtuosity. These dances were executed in the court of honour, amid a crowd of onlookers all standing and beating time with their hands. They were naturally accompanied, too, with music and merry singing. After which the guests fell once more to feasting and only desisted at sunset.

All this took place in an atmosphere of joy; but it sometimes ended in a tumult. Though people rarely got drunk, the wine often excited them, and men of violent temper sometimes lost control of themselves. Thus, in a fit of anger, the suitor Antinous hurls his stool at Odysseus when the latter is begging. Sometimes there was a quarrel like the one which broke out between Odysseus and Achilles during a 'rich banquet of the gods' — an episode which the minstrel Demodocus recalls in one of his songs.

★   ★   ★   ★

Taken as a whole, the life of the nobility in Homer's time reveals to us a class still rough, and even brutal and violent in its pleasures, affections and resentments. A sometimes munificent generosity went hand in hand with a passionate love of wealth. Family ties were strong and close, marked at times by a quiet and sincere tenderness as in the home of Alcinous. The poet incarnates them in feminine figures which are noble, touching or charming; as in Areté, Penelope and Nausicaa. But there were also frequent dramas of passion, pride or instinct; there were rivalries between wives and concubines, and between brothers; sons would sometimes rebel against their fathers. Apart from this, the life of the nobility went far beyond the limits of the family. It not only comprised the vast body of kinsfolk who constituted the *genos*, but also included the circles of 'companions', bound to their lord by ties of fidelity which are sometimes moving to read about. Often, owing to the traditional and unavoidable obligations of hospitality, this life stretched to the very confines of the Hellenic world.

And what constitutes its main and attractive originality is that, in spite of its apparent roughness, and although it was involved in a family structure that was still rigid and selfish, this life could rise to a veritable 'gentleness', in the old and noble sense of the term,[1] owing to its touching insistence on the sentiments of loyalty and friendship.

[1] 'La véritable "gentillesse" humaine.'

# CHAPTER IV

# THE RELIGIOUS AND INTELLECTUAL PROFESSIONS

HOMERIC society did not include a middle class. There is hardly at this time to be discerned even the rudiments of a class which was to play a considerable part in the Hellenic world two centuries later. By then, there had arisen a class of 'metics', or aliens resident in the big industrial centres. Homer merely tells us of a man of noble but illegitimate birth who had amassed a fortune in commerce and piracy. We know also that Hesiod's father ran a coastwise trade at Cymé in Aeolis, which proved his ruin. But all important business was still in the hands of the aristocracy.

If there existed no middle class in the strict sense of the word, we have none the less to take account of a class on the fringe of the nobility, consisting of specialists of an intellectual order. It corresponded roughly to what are today called the liberal professions, and its members drew profit, honour and even sometimes wealth from the practice of their art.

These specialists were intimately associated with religious observances. More accurately, they were regarded as deriving their very faculties, knowledge and aptitudes from the gods themselves. Usually these gifts were inherited and the practice of them was a family privilege; although it could also happen that an individual might receive the grace of inspiration. Hesiod seems to have been thus inspired.

The experts in this intellectual domain were, naturally, the priests; then the soothsayers, the doctors and the poets, or, as Homer calls them, the bards. Later on we shall see their affinities, or the affinities of some of them, with the class of public workers or *demiourgoi*.[1]

The existence of this class appears to go back, like the aristocracy, to the social structure of the earliest Indo-European times. Comparative studies seem to confirm the existence, within its inmost structure — side by side with the families of royal status, the ancestors of the Homeric nobility — of a class of experts versed in divine lore, whose duty it was to counsel, guide and assist the 'kings' in the exercise of their functions. They were guardians of ritual and of the forms and language of the sacramental songs; preservers of the motions and rhythms exacted for the due observance of ceremonial; interpreters of the signs and often obscure sayings by which the gods manifested their decrees, desires or warnings; and, lastly, they were the custodians of the science of precedents in all domains. But their members are not properly to be called 'officers' of the 'kings', as this style was only applicable to members of the 'royal' families; they were rather the king's aids, assessors or 'assistants', whose infallible memory took the place of archives for the leaders of the tribe or the city. They were the ancestors of the Brahmins of India, the Magi of Persia and the Druids of the Celtic world, as also of the Roman *flamines*, a name which is the exact homologue of the Indian Brahmins.

Among the Greek tribes, certain families in this class were sometimes elevated to 'royal' dignity. This appears to have been the case with the Eumolpidae of Eleusis, who were probably descended from a line of singers, as their name indicates. We shall see later what happened to the others; but nothing could be more misleading than to imagine them as members of a closed group. The social structure of the races of Greece, as also of Italy, always retained a certain suppleness. The earliest formed classes never became castes but remained accessible and absorptive.

Thus the social frontiers of the intellectual professions in Homer's world are not easily definable. They were often flexible

[1] See Chapter VII below. The author explains that they were not ordinary manual workers but exercised some kind of official or semi-official function (Translator).

and indeterminate. Machaon, the famous doctor to the Achaean army before Troy, was at the same time a soldier. As the son of Asclepios, he was almost on an equality with the families of royal blood. So the soothsayer Theoclymenus, who was descended from Melampus and came to Pylos to seek asylum with Telemachus,[1] also belonged to a line that could have taken its place beside the *gené* of the nobility, but for the fact that, from the nature of their calling, the families of soothsayers were obliged to break up and travel the world in exercise of their profession. By contrast, Hesiod, the bard-interpreter of the Muses of Helicon, was only a small landowner in the Boeotian town of Ascra.

In spite of such circumstances, this group of professions had its own social individuality and a way of living sufficiently distinctive.

### THE PRIESTS

To understand the position of the priest in Homeric society we must lay aside all modern notions of his vocation.

There was no permanent or regular cult of the gods, and it was not the priest's function to celebrate any such cult. The principal ceremony was the one connected with sacrifices, and there were only a few that fell at regular dates during the year; now these were celebrated by the city, or by groups, or even individuals, in their own names and for their own purposes. In all these ceremonies the person officiating was not the priest, but a magistrate, a head of a clan or tribe, or an individual.

The role of the priest was to be present, to assist in, and to organize the ritual. He was especially responsible for its exact conduct, because a knowledge of the liturgy was his speciality and was often an ancestral calling. Generally, it devolved on him to execute some of the more important functions, such as the slaying of the victim, its subsequent flaying and the separation of its entrails. He also dissected the flesh and supervised the ritual which attended the cooking of it, although he might have helpers in these duties, the *mageiroi*, or 'butcher-cooks', attached to the

---

[1] This was on the occasion of Telemachus' return from Sparta, when on his way back home. (See *Odyssey*, XV, vv. 223–60 — Translator).

sanctuary. Lastly he made the arrangements for the sacrificial repast. Two essential rites fell to his share: that of consigning the victim to death and of initiating the dedication; and that of pronouncing the right formulae for the prayer accompanying the sacrifice, which was the object of the ceremony. The presence of the priest was in fact required, not to serve as minister of the god, but as minister of the person officiating, and indispensable as such.

In the Homeric vocabulary two words exactly describe his role. He is the *hiereus*, the sacrificer, who makes the offering acceptable to the gods; and he is the *areter* who offers the prayer on behalf of the suppliant. He is the symbolic intermediary between man and the divine, because he has the ear of the gods.

A passage in Homer furnishes a perfect illustration. It is the account of the sacrifice offered in the name of the Achaean army by Odysseus to Apollo in his temple at Chrysé. It is necessary to appease the god who, at the request of his priest Chryses, has unloosed a plague on the army; because Agamemnon had insulted the priest by refusing to give up his daughter Chryseis.

Odysseus, with the Achaean delegation, disembarks a hundred head of cattle, and this tremendous sacrifice is about to be offered up to the god. Odysseus addresses the priest as follows:

> 'O Chryses, Agamemnon king of men
> Has sent me forth to bring thy daughter back;
> And in the Danai's name to sacrifice
> A holy hecatomb to Phoebus, that
> We may propitiate the king who now
> Has brought upon the Argives grief and pain'.
>     With that he placed her in his arms; and he
> Took his dear child rejoicing. Hastily
> Around the well-built altar to the god
> They set out the brave offering in a ring;
> Then washed their hands and took the barley groats
> To throw; and Chryses lifting up his hands
> Prayed for them earnestly:
>     'Lord of the silver bow, give ear, that hast
> Chryse and holy Cilla in thy keeping
> And guardest Tenedos with thy strong arm:

E'en as before thou heardest when I prayed,
And honouredst me, and sentest great affliction
Upon the Achaean people, so too now
Accomplish this my prayer, and here and now
Avert the hideous havoc from the Danai.'
    So said he praying, and Apollo heard him.
Then having prayed and thrown the barley grains,
They raised the victims' heads and cut their throats
And skinned them and cut portions from the thighs,
Wrapped them in fat, and laid raw meat on them;
And these the old man burned upon the billets,
And poured the red wine on them, while beside him
The young men held in hand five-pointed forks.
And when the thigh-pieces were wholly burned,
And they had tasted of the inner meat,
They cut the rest up small and spitted it
And broiled it carefully, and drew off all.
Now when their work was done, and they had made
The banquet ready, then they fell to feasting,
And lacked for nothing at the feast they shared.
But when they wanted no more food or drink,
The young men crowned the bowls with wine, and first
Pouring libation-drops into the cups
Served out to each. So all day long they soothed
The god with song, the youths of the Achaeans,
Raising a lovely paean, and extolling
The Archer-god; and he took pleasure listening.[1]

The sacrificial rite, as narrated here in what is probably the oldest description in Greek literature, was the regular ceremonial. But in a cult of many manifestations, which varied according to the sanctuary and the god, the role of sacrificer was not the only duty of the priest. At Eleusis one of his essential functions was to reveal the sacred objects to the initiated in the course of the ceremony of the *epopteia*, or initiation of the second degree. At Ephesus the high priest, later to be known by the Persian name of Megabyxus, went at the head of the annual procession in honour of Artemis, and for this he was apparelled in purple and gold, with all his priestly and royal decorations. It was his task to

---

[1] *Iliad*, I, vv. 442–74. Trans. Marris, pp. 16–18. (Cf. *Odyssey*, III, 447–59, and XII, 359–65, where the same formulae recur in several places).

represent the goddess at games and festivals outside the shrine. At Claros the priest might on occasion assume the duties of prophet.[1]

In addition to his role as minister to the god, the priest was also guardian of his possessions and custodian of the sacred relics.

He was also the steward in charge of the sanctuary and of its upkeep, repair and improvement. This duty was not exacting. At the time in question the sanctuaries were still very simple constructions. We can form some idea of their appearance from the excavations of the shrine of Artemis at Ephesus, which was built towards the end of the eighth century and was subsequently pillaged by the Cimmerian invaders in the middle of the following century. It consisted of an enclosed area of some six hundred square metres,[2] in the shape of a rectangle. In the centre stood the sacred tree, an elm or an oak. On the east side was a structure in the form of a niche where the sacred objects were kept, and on the west stood the sacrificial altar. It has been questioned whether the enclosure did not contain a covered building of some sort, to house the ancient idol of the goddess which at one time hung simply from the sacred tree; whether there did not exist for her any shelter, or *neos*, which could be regarded as the earliest form of the great temples. A small building of this type, made of unbaked bricks and wood, with a roof supported by a colonnade along the axis, is known to have existed in Sparta. It had been erected prior to 700 B.C. in honour of Artemis Orthia.

However that may be, the Homeric poems allude frequently to several such houses of the gods, and these references occur in some of the oldest books. In Book I of the *Iliad*, which dates from an early period, the priest Chryses reminds Apollo in his prayer that he has placed a covering over his gracious *neos*.[3] In another very old section, the twelfth book of the *Odyssey*, Eurylochus exacts a promise from his companions who are about to sacrifice some heifers to Helios, that they will raise in Ithaca a *neos* in

---

[1] Cf. Ch. Picard, *Ephèse et Claros*.

[2] I.e. more than 700 square yards (Translator).

[3] Sir William Marris interprets this passage as 'roofing' the temple (Translator).

honour of the god. In yet another very early portion, Book VI of the *Odyssey*, we are told that Nausithous, the father of Alcinous, built *neoi* in honour of the gods in the city he was founding. In Book VI of the *Iliad*, a more recent portion, the Trojan women repair to the *neos* of Athena, to supplicate the goddess and offer her an embroidered veil; the priestess Theano opens the doors and places the offering on the knees of the image, while the women utter their ritual supplications with arms outstretched to Athena. Theano then offers up a prayer, which is not granted. But no one apparently penetrated into the *neos*, which must still have been no more than a little covered building. Only in special circumstances would the doors be opened, and the appropriate rites would then be performed in front of the *neos*.[1]

The priest, as keeper of the temple, was also the administrator of the god's property. For every divinity who was the object of an official cult became thereby a member of the city or of the social group which worshipped him, and was bound to the group by an alliance or reciprocal contract which followed from the continuous and mutual exchange of services. The divinity was thus entitled to a share of the group's possessions, which was made good by a grant of property; and this ownership might be augmented by public or private donations, or by purchase, or even confiscation of properties, and lastly by fines imposed for the god's benefit.

In the execution of his religious and administrative duties, the priest was assisted by a certain number of deputies or auxiliaries, who were subordinate officers of the priestly class. We have already mentioned the role of the 'butcher-cooks' in the sacrificial rites. But each sanctuary and each cult might have its specialists. At Claros the priest of Apollo was assisted by a prophet, whose pronouncements interpreted the will of the god; and also by a *thespiodos*, or religious poet, who cast these utterances into poetic

---

[1] *Iliad*, I, v. 39 and VI, vv. 297–311; *Odyssey*, VI, v. 10, and XII, vv. 346–7. A *neos* of Apollo at Troy is also mentioned in Book VII, v. 83 of the *Iliad*; but in our opinion this book was not composed earlier than the beginning of the sixth century.

form. At Ephesus we find, in addition to the high priest of Artemis, a college of virgin priestesses who were called the *Melissai*, or bees. As servants of the goddess they took part in dances and processions. Side by side with them was a college of Essenes (perhaps the drones), also bound by vows of chastity and abstinence; they lived in the temple precincts and were in special charge of the ritual banquets. In the Greek colony of Ilium, founded about the year 700, the care of the temple of Athena Ilias was in the hands of two young girls who had to be natives of Locris, in continental Greece, and their duties included the sweeping and sprinkling of the sanctuary. Their heads were shaven like those of slaves, and they went barefoot, wearing a chiton without a girdle. Nor do we need to remind the reader of the place of honour which was occupied by the prophetess of the Pythian Apollo in the temple at Delphi.

Thus we see that, in addition to the titular priests, there were present in Greek sanctuaries a subordinate clergy fairly numerous and diversified.

We may ask, what was the social position and the origin of this religious body, and what was its manner of life?

It was recruited from many different sources. The priesthood was exercised for the most part by men, but women could also serve, even in the highest capacities. Such was the case at the Heraion in Argos; and we have just seen that the temple of Athena at Ilium was administered by a priestess.

It was not impossible for the higher offices in the priesthood to belong to families, the importance of whose functions was great enough to place them in the aristocracy. At Eleusis the priest was a Eumolpid. At Athens the priest of Poseidon-Erechtheus and the priestess of Athena Polias were seconded from the *genos* of the Eteoboutadae; the priest of Zeus Polieus traditionally belonged to the *genos* of the Thaulonidae. These, in the classical era, were families of Eupatridae. It was even the custom for certain inferior duties, involving women, to be reserved for the nobility. In this way the servants of Athena Ilias were selected from among the daughters of a hundred noble families of Locris. The *Arrhephoroi* attached to the temple of Athena were chosen by lot in Athens from the daughters of its most aristocratic houses.

As a general rule, the priestly functions of every rank were exercised by members of honourable families who possessed an hereditary vocation for the ministry. A tradition, which we have no reason to doubt, assigns Orthagoras, the first tyrant of Sicyon, to a family of *mageiroi*, or butcher-cooks, attached to a temple. Birth alone, however, was not sufficient. A good physique was obligatory; no blemish or disability was permissible, and good looks were no negligible qualification. Sometimes the appointment was by election; or it might be left to the god to decide, in other words, one proceeded by the drawing of lots. The investiture took the form of solemn rites peculiar to the occasion, of which sacrifices were of course the most usual. These might be supplemented by some ritual ordeal. The high priest of Artemis at Ephesus was a eunuch, but this was perhaps unique in the Hellenic world and was probably of Eastern origin. At his enthronement the priest wore garments of special colours, generally white, red, or saffron-yellow. His tunic had to be long, and his insignia were the sceptre and keys of the sanctuary. For official occasions he placed on his head a crown of gold, or of leaves twined about a head-band, or sometimes a diadem. His hair was worn long, since only the slaves of the sanctuary had shaven heads.

Whatever their rank, all priests drew their subsistence from the altar-offerings, no mean revenue in many cases. They had the disposal of all temple emoluments and also enjoyed a share of the civic dues. They were lodged and fed free; while a portion of the sacrifices was reserved for their use, in particular the skins and a generous piece of the flesh. Of this privilege they certainly availed themselves, since it was they who carved up the victim. With the sacrifices, moreover, there went certain formal dues, such as the bread, cakes and wine used for the libations. In return, the priests had to supply the wood, oil and honey that were required for the sacrifices. But no strict account was kept of these provisions, and as the sanctuary expenses were well covered by the participants, the priest could usually turn them into an additional source of revenue. So that a well-frequented sanctuary would normally furnish a comfortable living or even considerable wealth.

The priestly class was thereby not only honourable and honoured; it had also a large share of wordly goods, and this material wealth contributed further to its influence and to the respect it enjoyed.

## THE SOOTHSAYERS

Soothsayers, and the interpretation of omens, occupy a prominent place in Homeric poetry. The poet who put together the two great epics of the time was undoubtedly a man with a high opinion of the professional soothsayer. Thus Achilles advises the assembly of warriors afflicted by the plague:

> Come, let us ask some priest or soothsayer,
> Ay, or a dream-expounder, since of Zeus
> Come also dreams, if he can tell us why
> Phoebus Apollo is so greatly angered. . . .[1]

The soothsayer of high rank appears in both poems. In the *Iliad* we have Calchas, who holds this position in the Achaean army; and also Helenus, a son of Priam, Polydamas and Eurydamas. Halitherses of Ithaca, Teiresias and Theoclymenus occur in the *Odyssey*, where also we have a reference to the oracle of Zeus at Dodona.

The soothsayer's art consisted in discovering the thought in the divine mind, made manifest by signs in need of interpretation; or, in cases of inspired knowledge, revealed directly by the gods. It was, indeed, the practice of a direct communion with the mind of the gods.

The gods employed many different signs to convey their messages. Sometimes these would be unnatural manifestations — marvels — like the great light shining from Athena which suddenly illuminates the house of Odysseus when father and son are removing the arms from the *megaron*; or when Zeus hails the departure from Aulis of the Achaean fleet with a sudden thunderbolt; or, again at Aulis, the appearance of a fearful serpent which

[1] *Iliad*, I, p. 3.

devours eight young sparrows with their mother on the nest. In this last event Calchas was able to divine without difficulty that the nine victims symbolized the nine years which the Achaeans were to spend in their vain struggle before the walls of Troy.[1]

These divine auguries often took the form of dreams; but dreams could be deceiving. Through their association with night and darkness, their affinities lay with the underworld. Thus Penelope on two occasions is visited by truthful dreams, of which one is the harbinger of the approaching massacre of the suitors, while the second predicts the safe return of Telemachus her son. But at the beginning of Book II of the *Iliad*, Zeus sends Agamemnon a 'deadly dream', which falsely promises him victory over the Trojans. A dream might then be simply a ruse, or a trap, set by the god. So Penelope reminds Odysseus that dreams are of two kinds, coming to man by two gateways, one of horn and one of ivory. Only the former are favourable and to be trusted. The dreams which pass through the ivory portal are heavy with fate and always lying. How is one to distinguish between them? There are indeed experts, the *oneiropoloi*, who are considered to be good counsellors. But Homer himself distrusts them. He is more than scornful of old Eurydamas, one of these interpreters, for failing to foretell the death of his own two sons who were to fall by the hand of Diomed when fighting before Troy.[2]

Homer places far more confidence in divine messages conveyed by birds, by their manner of flight and behaviour. The species of bird chosen as messenger varied with the god. The most important were the swiftest and strongest, as, for example, all the birds of prey, eagles, falcons and sparrow-hawks. In Book II of the *Odyssey* an assembly of the citizens of Ithaca has been convoked by Telemachus and is sitting in council when two eagles descend from the mountain, hover over the gathering and give a fighting display before disappearing; and this terrible augury is at once interpreted by Halitherses as foretelling the vengeance of Odysseus. Again, when Telemachus and Peisistratus have mounted

---

[1] *Odyssey*, XIX, vv. 36–40; *Iliad*, II, 350–63, and 308–29.
[2] *Odyssey*, IV, 795 et seq.; XIX, 536 et seq.; *Iliad*, V, 148–51.

> ... Therefore shall utter death
> Fall upon all the suitors, every one.[1]

A less pleasant noise might serve as an augury. When, in the *Hymn to Hermes*, the child Hermes hears Apollo say: 'Thou wilt for ever be known as the prince of thieves'; to confirm the prophecy, he emits a rumble from his stomach, and this omen he hastens to make effective with a sneeze.

The ingenuity of professional soothsayers was exercised in devising many other means of discovering the mind of the gods. There was the specialist who examined the entrails of sacrificial victims: this kind of interpreter, the *thyoscoos*, is mentioned by old Priam in the *Iliad*, as an authority. In the *Odyssey*, the first of the suitors who tries to bend the bow of Odysseus is Liodes, a *thyoscoos*. Another method was to call up and consult the dead, as Odysseus calls up Teiresias in the land of the Cimmerians, or Chimerians. The soothsayer Amphiaraos gave posthumous consultations of this kind at Oropus. The *Selloi*, who slept on the earth, were skilled in interpreting the rustlings of the oak tree above their heads, in the sanctuary of Dodona.

Finally, the soothsayer could receive a direct revelation from the god and be transported out of himself, when he would speak in a state of 'enthusiasm'. Such were the prophets attached to certain sanctuaries, like Apollo's prophet at Claros and the Pythia at Delphi. But unattached soothsayers might also possess this gift, for without it they would be incapable of understanding signs and prodigies. At the beginning of the *Iliad*, Calchas needs no particular sign to understand the reason for Apollo's anger.

Sometimes the prophetic gift was associated with a priestly avocation; or it might be the momentary or accidental property of an individual who had no special vocation. When Telemachus is about to leave the palace of Menelaus, Helen, seeing an eagle fly off with one of her geese, is transported and exclaims:

> 'Listen to me, and I will prophesy
> As the immortals put it in my heart',[2]

[1] *Odyssey*, XVII, 539–47, p. 313.
[2] Book XV, p. 262.

and she predicts the return and vengenace of Odysseus. Helenus, Hector's brother, is a good amateur prophet among the Trojans. In most cases, however, the soothsayer was an independent practitioner.

The vocation was usually an hereditary one. In Book XV of the *Odyssey* we read details of the genealogy of Theoclymenus, a descendant of Melampus. His family already numbered four generations of diviners, including Amphiaraos, the hero of the *Thebaid*. According to the legend the daughter and the grandson of Teiresias both inherited his divine gift. The fact is that hundreds of oracles dotted about Greece, often associated with deep earth-fissures or rocky sites, were the affair of families who passed them on as a part of their belongings.

The *modus vivendi* of members of the profession might vary greatly. There were those who did not travel at all, and they were consulted at the spot whence they drew their inspiration. Oropus and Lebadea were places of this kind, the one associated with Amphiaraos and the other with Trophonius. There were official diviners like Halitherses who prophesied spontaneously in the assembly of the citizens of Ithaca; or Calchas who was attached to the staff of the Achaean army and followed it to Aulis and Troy. There were also wandering soothsayers who practised as they travelled from city to city. Melampus, the ancestor of Theoclymenus, after a dispute with king Neleus, had to leave Pylos and retire to Argos, where he became possessor of many ships, married and built himself a house. His grandson was compelled by his father to leave and settle at Hyperesia in Achaea. His great-grandson, Theoclymenus, practised the family profession at Argos until he was obliged to leave in consequence of a murder. Mopsus, the grandson of the Theban Teiresias, was supposed to have founded the oracle of Claros, near Colophon in Asia. All these legendary accounts confirm, at least indirectly, the wandering vocation of the principal diviners in the Homeric world, as they sought further and further afield a public whose appetite for the divine and the marvellous they could most profitably exploit.

Homer states explicitly that there are four types of guests whom a lord may summon from abroad for consultation: the doctor, the bard, the carpenter and the diviner.[1] The profession had its drawbacks however, as when the diviner had to take a decision and pronounce upon some family or civic difficulty — which was the usual case: he would then risk doing damage to somebody's interests, causing discontent or even making enemies among his clients.

Calchas, an old hand at the business, was particularly alive to this danger. We may recall how, before giving his verdict to the assembled warriors regarding the origin of the plague, he first desired Achilles' protection, certain as he was of infuriating Agamemnon, whom he was about to bring to judgment. But this precaution did not save him from being anathematized by the king of kings. Halitherses again, who, at the assembly of the Greeks of Ithaca, takes the risk of predicting the return of Odysseus and the punishment of the suitors, is immediately taken to task by Eurymachus (one of the latter), who gets up and threatens him:

'. . . Go to, old man,
Get home and prophesy unto thy children,
Lest they come haply to some grief hereafter!'

and he adds a little later:

'While we shall lay on thee, old man, a fine
Payment whereof will irk thee, and thou shalt
Be sore distressed.'[2]

The least danger was that of being rebuffed by a friend whom the diviner has displeased. This is what happens to the wise Polydamas. He takes as a bad omen the fight between an eagle and a dragon which occurs in the air above the Trojan army; and Hector reproves him sharply with the words:

'Our one best omen is our country's cause.'[3]

Nevertheless, it was in general a well-paying profession. Diviners could always claim the gratitude of those clients

[1] *Odyssey*, XVII, 382–5.
[2] *Odyssey*, II, pp. 24, 25.
[3] *Iliad*, XII, 200 et seq., pp. 264–6.

whose designs and hopes they had encouraged. They were influential in politics and they certainly knew how to make their profession lucrative. Their clients never came to them empty-handed and their friendly intervention would be well reimbursed. Eurymachus speaks to Halitherses of

> '. . . rousing passionate Telemachus,
> In expectation that he may perchance
> Make some gift to thy house. . . .'[1]

The oracle at Delphi was to garner very great wealth by virtue of its foresight enlightened by a good information service, and also by reason of its venality. The soothsayers of Homer's time were no doubt scarcely less disinterested. Homer himself describes Melampus as having amassed a fine fortune at Argos. In any case, material success could well be regarded as proof of divine collaboration, or, one might even say, of divine complicity.

## DOCTORS AND EXORCISTS

The doctors, like the soothsayers, flattered themselves on having divine affinities; for was not their knowledge also a kind of revelation? To be explicit, they were in fact the inheritors of a past rich in magic and witchcraft.

They play no large part in Homeric poetry, where they occur mostly in the *Iliad*. These 'experts in remedies' appear on the stage when some warrior of high rank is wounded, although they may at the same time be warriors themselves and receive wounds too, as happens to Machaon, the son of Asclepios, one of the best known of them: he is injured in the great battle described in Book XI. Their only strict medical task in such an emergency was to dress and attend to the wound. First, it was opened, made to bleed, and washed with warm water. Then some soothing powders were applied and the wounded member bandaged, the flow of blood being arrested by an incantation pronounced by the doctor. But he had not the monopoly of this simple technique. The uncles of Odysseus give similar treatment to a thigh wound received by

[1] *Odyssey*, II, p. 24.

their nephew during a hunt on Parnassus. In a similar way, Patroclus attends to the wounded Eurypylus with the application of a bitter root, which he crushes in his hands, and which eases the pain, dries the wound and arrests any haemorrhage.

This surgical practice naturally did not exhaust the sum total of medical knowledge of the time. Homer tells us that the military doctors are acquainted with 'many remedies'. But we are given no details of this pharmaceutical science. It was certainly for the most part traditional. We are only told that it was in process of considerable development owing to the more frequent contacts with Egypt, a country

> Where earth, grain-giver, in profusion yields
> Herbs, many that are wholesome in the cup
> And many that are baneful. There each man
> Is a physician, skilled o'er all men else. . . .

Helen has brought back from Egypt a miraculous drug, with sedative effects, which when mixed with wine, has the power

> to lull all pain and anger,
> And bring forgetfulness of every ill.[1]

Although, as regards the general principles of medical knowledge then obtaining, the Homeric texts are silent, one piece of information can be indirectly gleaned from them. The two great doctors Homer refers to, Machaon and Podalirius, are both sons of Asclepios; and Asclepios was the mythical patron of a medical tradition which in one direction was to develop towards the rationalism of Hippocrates; but whose roots belonged to a remote past, going far back to the time of pure magico-religious practices.

Asclepios, who was associated with the powers of the nether world as the serpent-hero, had his cult in the *asclepieia*. These establishments were part hospitals, part sanctuaries, the most celebrated in the classical period being that of Epidaurus. They were administered by doctor-priests, or soothsayer-doctors, who were called Asclepiads, as supposed descendants of Asclepios; and these men passed on from father to son their natural gifts and the

[1] *Odyssey*, IV, 220–32, pp. 59–60.

traditions of the profession, as well as their clientèle of patients and devotees.

These *asclepieia* were widely distributed throughout Greece and were generally established on some site near a grotto, or wood, or sacred spring. Before any consultation took place, there were certain rites to be observed, such as fasting, bathing, ablutions, anointing and other forms of purification. The next step was for the sick man to offer up a sacrifice; and he was then prepared to undergo the decisive treatment known as the 'incubation'. For this he had to spend the night lying on the skin of his victim, under the portico of one of the subsidiary buildings; and here, in silence and darkness, amid the sacred and familiar serpents gliding between the sleepers and uncoiling themselves over the floor of the sanctuary, the patient was visited by dreams and visions, and listened to the words of the god; which visions and sayings were, on the following day, appropriately translated by the Asclepiads into prescriptions.

The sacrifices and payments accompanying these propitiatory ceremonies were obviously a regular source of income to the sanctuary and its ministrants. The gratitude of patients who were cured sometimes took the form of substantial gifts. Thanks were also expressed on votive tablets which gave the symptoms from which the patient had suffered and also the saving remedies; so that every *asclepieion* had a store of medical archives which came in time to contribute materially to the advancement of medical science.

Strictly speaking, it was the god himself who bestowed the gift of healing; it was in any case his natural right and privilege, since all illness, like any other evil, was a result of the anger and jealousy of the gods. The most striking example of this is the plague let loose on the camp of the Achaeans by Apollo, at the beginning of the *Iliad*. It fell later to the pessimistic Hesiod to cast into poetic form the myth which illustrated the moral and theological conceptions underlying this belief, in his story of the jar of Epimetheus and of how Pandora raised the lid and thereby released all the ills that were to affect mortal man.

Certain sicknesses deserve special mention. We refer to maladies of the mind; for the treatment of these is as old a preoccupation as the cure of bodily ills. These maladies of the mind, among them delirium, madness and melancholia, were not merely sent by the gods but indicated their direct intervention, by which act the sick man became possessed of a *daimon*. So Pandarus attributes the warlike frenzy of Diomed to the action of a god.[1] And Helen similarly declares:

> '... and I
> Bewailed the blindness Aphrodite gave me,
> What time she led me from mine own dear land
> To Troy, abandoning alike my daughter
> And my bride-chamber and my lord. . . .'[2]

One could multiply these instances. All mental aberrations denote the seizure by some god of the patient's mind. Agamemnon propounds this theory of divine possession when he confesses his error:

> '... Yet not I
> Am blameworthy, but Zeus and Destiny
> And that Erinyes who in darkness walks;
> They cast fierce madness on my soul that day
> When in the gathering wantonly I robbed
> Achilles of his prize. What could I do?
> God brings all things to issue. Zeus begot
> A fearsome child in Até, that ill power
> Who maddens all men. . . .'[3]

Até, otherwise vertigo, blindness, folly or delirium, never sets foot on earth, but 'descends into the minds of men'.

Madness was indeed pre-eminently the 'sacred malady', as the Greeks called it. In seeking to discover how they treated it, our knowledge is limited to the practices described in a later text, a short treatise on *The Sacred Malady*, which was doubtless a pro-

[1] *Iliad*, V, 185.

[2] *Odyssey*, IV, 260–3, p. 61. (Cf. also what she says to Priam in *Iliad*, III, p. 60, and the bitter reproaches she hurls at Aphrodite later in the same book, pp. 67–8 — Translator).

[3] *Iliad*, XIX, 86–91, p. 435.

duct of the rationalistic school of Hippocrates towards the end of the fifth century. The author of this tract vehemently denounces the magico-religious practices — probably very ancient — which were used as a therapeutic for this disorder of the mind.

The principle underlying the treatment was, first of all, to determine the source of the malady; that is, to discover what god had taken possession of the patient. Howlings, accompanied by convulsive movements of the limbs, indicated the Mother of the gods; cries like the whinnying of a horse denoted the presence of Poseidon, the horse-god; sounds imitating bird-song were indicative of Apollo; foaming at the mouth betrayed the presence of Ares; while delirium at night or sleep-walking were imputed to Hecate, or to some dead hero from the underworld. Once the diagnosis was made, the next step was to reconcile the patient with the deity in question by appeasing the latter's wrath. In the case of a cure, this was obviously the result of a simple homoeopathy which consisted in replacing the obsession, thanks to the use of purifying measures, incantations and regulations involving food and dress, accompanied by the usual rites of initiation and instruction in doctrine — all of which doubtless implied a substantial dose of suggestion. The object evidently was to modify the patient's own personality, as has remained the purpose of all modern psychiatry.

In the late period when this treatise was written, these practices were in the hands of itinerant 'purifiers', preachers and beggars, or wandering clerics, all of whom were of the profession. Their methods were no doubt the outcome of a long tradition of magical healing; so that one may draw the not very risky conclusion that the Homeric world of an earlier age was also overrun by a similar class of exorcists.[1]

They were certainly not the aristocrats of the medical profession; which is probably the reason why Homer has so little to say about them.

[1] The study of the phenomena of 'possession' in ancient Greece has received a new and remarkable impulse from M. H. Jeanmaire in his book on *Dionysos* (Payot, 1951). See particularly the chapter on the divine *mania*.

### BARDS AND CHOIR-MASTERS

Like the prophets, diviners and doctors, the poets, or bards, were men inspired and enlightened by personal contact with the deity.

It is not Homer who sings of the wrath of Achilles, but the 'goddess'. If it is given to him to relate the wanderings of Odysseus, this is because the words come to him from the Muse. 'The god has breathed in me songs of all kinds,' cries Phemius to Odysseus, as he begs for mercy. And Plato in the *Ion*, three centuries later, was still to interpret poetic inspiration as a divine 'possession', even when it was merely a matter of recitation.

The bard followed a vocation that was in its essence religious. Like his congeners, the priests, diviners, prophets and doctors, he belonged by birth to that class of 'assistants' who played an indispensable part in the performance of the rites observed between men and the gods, or between men and the heroes who had been deified. Their ancestors were singers, masters of the art of song, of cadence and of rhythm: all elements which had their allotted place in the observance of the sacred ceremonial. The first bards had been keepers of the rules of sacred prosody, the art which gave its measure to the dance or the rhythmic movements exacted by the ritual with its accompaniment of song or dirge; for this prosody had mystic and unique properties. The bards who had composed or refashioned them, were also entrusted with the guardianship of the hymns used traditionally to accompany the rites which were performed when the exploits of gods and heroes were described; and the recitation of their lives, adventures, trials and triumphs was an inseparable part of the ritual.

Thus the bard was also a member of the élite in the intellectual and religious sphere, and he had clearly defined hereditary duties. We will now try to reconstruct and describe the rank he enjoyed and the part he played in the Homeric world.

The best example of this élite whose members were dedicated to that cult of the speech of the gods which we call poetry, is appropriately to be found among the illustrious Homeridae of Chios. The members of this clan were, with time and as a result of their achievements, to evolve by degrees into a simple confraternity of rhapsodists; and, according to the evidence, they played an important role in the religious ceremonies of the island. The name Homer would appear to be a synonym of 'servitor' — servitor, naturally, of the deity. Thus the Homeridae appear to us as heirs to an ancient line of singers, originally associated more or less closely with a single sanctuary or possibly with several.

At the time we are considering, their profession was already become largely laicized. The romantic epic we still read and admire was in fact born of this process. We have tried to make clear elsewhere[1] how this epic derived from the earlier religious poetry and hymnodies, and the affinities it retained with these origins; but we now see it becoming an autonomous genre, completely separate from them. Its brilliant success had made the composition, and especially the recitation, of epic poetry the chief occupation of the bard.

Henceforth he was to make his living mainly by the exercise of this art. He had certainly not broken entirely with the past; he did not completely neglect the prestige and profit to be had from taking part in the hymnological competitions, for these perpetuated an ancient tradition. We have evidence of the fact in the so-called 'Homeric Hymns', which continued to be composed in honour of the gods, and which perpetuated the forms of pre-Homeric religious poetry. We have, above all, the *Hymn to the Delian Apollo* in which 'the blind singer, dweller on bleak Chios', who was certainly one of the Homeridae, recites his short poem to the choir of young girls in the sanctuary of Delos. Hesiod himself tells us that he once went to Chalcis to take part in a hymn competition in honour of the hero Amphidamas, and how he won the prize, a two-handled tripod which he dedicated to the Muses of Helicon. But such occasions were only incidental.

They do, however, make it clear that the bards did not exercise a sedentary profession. If they were not, strictly speaking, wanderers, as later legends about Homer pretend; if they still had their roots in the family hearth; they were none the less great

[1] *Les Poèmes homériques et l'Histoire grecque*, 2 vols. Paris, Albin Michel.

travellers. The poet who composed the oldest books of the *Iliad*
and the *Odyssey* was certainly acquainted with the plains of Troy,
and must have travelled as far as Corcyra, which he turns into the
isle of the Phaeacians. We have reason to suppose that the member of the Homeridae who subsequently put together the two
great poems, about the middle of the seventh century, frequented
the courts of the tyrants of Corinth and Sicyon, Cypselus and
Orthagoras.

A celebrated bard would be a much sought-after guest. The
great sanctuaries would summon him to take part in their pane-
gyrics and games; the cities, to appear at their festivals; and the
great families, at their private celebrations. To all these his presence added lustre and adornment. The 'divine' bard Demodocus,
who is blind, receives special consideration at the hands of Alcinous and his guests. Phemius, who has taken part in the exactions
of the suitors in the house of Odysseus, escapes the avenging
massacre only by virtue of his calling.

The badge of the profession was the sceptre, the baton of command held by kings and heroes. Like the priests, the bard wore a
long tunic, and officiated standing. At the end of a banquet he
would rise and begin his chant in the midst of the seated guests.
Again, at public festivals, he would sing as an accompaniment to
the dancing in the open air: he would then take his place in the
middle of the arena; or he would recite for the benefit of a circle
of listeners. He would give the words their measure by accompanying himself on the cithara, a three- or four-stringed instrument; the notes of the cithara stressed the rhythm of each verse,
with its succession of longs and shorts, and marked the tonic
accent, which in Greek was almost wholly musical, by gliding up
or down a semitone, according as the accent was acute or grave.
The language of the poet was not that of everyday speech, but a
conventional poetic diction whose form was adapted to meet the
requirements of epic prosody. Thus it abounded in readymade
formulae and conventional epithets which relaxed the strain on
the memory of the singer, and also the strain on the attention of
the audience.

The recitations were of no fixed length. A hymn containing a few hundred lines given in the course of some sacred ceremony would take no more than perhaps thirty or forty minutes of our time. Where it was a question of epic recitations designed for the entertainment of guests taking their ease during the long hours of feasting and rejoicing, we must allow for the patience and well-nigh insatiable curiosity of Greek audiences, for whom a sitting of two or three hours, hardly interrupted by any intervals, was not in the least intimidating. The early epics were shorter and simpler than those which have survived, and cannot have exceeded the above length. But as they became longer and more complex, they evidently had to be spread over several days, like the interminable mystery plays of the Middle Ages. And we cannot but admire the prodigious effort of memory that these recitations exacted from the poet; education and practice were responsible for their skill. A good bard had in his repertory at least a hundred thousand lines, because in our estimate we must include all the epics that have been lost.

When we speak of the poetry of the Homeric age, we are of necessity thinking almost exclusively of the epic poem. We must not forget, however, that this was not the only poetic form in existence. The lyric poem, which like epic was of religious origin, was equally venerable. It had its masters and traditions, which had evolved in a similar way within the sanctuary; and the performances of lyric choirs played a part in social life which vied in importance with the epic recitations, because by their very nature they had the power to awaken strong collective feelings.

The simplest form of the lyric, the 'nome' or canticle, was hardly distinguishable from the liturgical hymn, except that the musical element, the song and its accompaniment on the cithara or the flute, played a greater part. This musical accompaniment was being continually amplified and improved. Terpander of Lesbos revived the seven-stringed cithara which had been forgotten for centuries. The simple, four-holed flute was doubled to give eight notes: an improvement which allowed regular tunes to be played. At the same time the lyric poem became richer and more diversified.

It was laicized, and the first result was the individual poem with its single exponent. The elegy began as a funeral chant, accompanied by the flute; its analogue was the threnody which had a cithara accompaniment. In the hands of Callinus of Ephesus, Archilochus and Tyrtaeus, in the first half of the seventh century, the elegy became freer, more personal, social and political. It still remained sometimes a lament for the loss of someone dear; but more often it went no further than the expression of personal emotions, joyous or melancholy; above all playing a part in the life of the city by its exhortations to the defence of the fatherland, or to harmony and domestic concord. In the hands of Tyrtaeus, it actually contributed to the salvation of Sparta during the troubled days of the second Messenian War.

Choral lyric poetry naturally remained closer to its religious origins. It was really the poetry of the sacred songs, with their accompaniment of music and dancing; it was the joyous paean in honour of Apollo; the lively hyporcheme which was emphasized by mimed dancing;[1] or the *prosodion* chanted at processions; or again the *partheneia* sung by a choir of maidens; and the dithyramb in which the choir made a circle round the singing-master as he celebrated the glory of Dionysus. All these collective displays were designed to 'inspire' the community and lead to the exorcizing of the 'demons' of envy, discord and civil strife.

Nothing could be more revealing in this respect than what happened at Sparta in the first half of the seventh century, between the two Messenian wars. The city was rich and prosperous, but deeply divided. In 676 B.C. the citizens invited the poet Terpander of Lesbos to reorganize the festivals of Apollo Carneius, and at the same time the teaching of music. Ten years later, Thaletas of Gortyn was brought from Crete, under similar conditions, as master of the paean and the hyporcheme, to organize the festival of the *gymnopaidiai*. Alcman of Sardis, renowned for his *partheneia* and a Spartan by adoption, also came and settled at

[1] I have suggested that the mischievous story recited by Demodocus in Book VIII of the *Odyssey*, with dance accompaniment, on the theme of the adultery of Aphrodite and Ares, may be simply a hyporcheme.

the same time in Lacedaemon, to perform the same two functions of poet and reconciler of men with themselves, or reconciler of men with the gods; which, as we have seen, were one and the same thing.

Thus the poets, whom Plato wished to banish from the city, figure here as peacemakers and mediators.

Nevertheless we must not over-idealize them, for we scarcely know them outside the realm of legend. Only two of them, living at the end of our period and contemporaries no doubt of the poet we have called the second Homer, offer any distinguishing features; but these are not without originality. The first was Hesiod the peasant poet, servitor of the Muses of Helicon: a man of piety, obedient to the will of the gods, enamoured of justice; but a bitter misogynist and pessimist, and not much inclined to indulgence in his criticism of human and divine activities. The other was Archilochus who was born on Paros of a good family in the priesthood,[1] because his grandfather was apparently represented at Delphi side by side with a priestess of Demeter. Archilochus is famous for his iambics, a kind of lyric poetry superbly transformed by him from its original religious purpose into a model for satire, unsurpassed in the ancient world. In his satires he is vindictive, ironical and cruel; he tears to pieces the fair Neoboulé (whom he adored and who spurned him) and also her father Lycambes. These were not his only works, for he also composed hymns and elegies. Richly endowed by nature, impetuous and enthusiastic, this artist in words had at bottom an adventurous soul. Spurred on by poverty, perhaps also by a taste for fighting and danger, he followed for awhile the career of a mercenary. It chanced that once, in an unlucky engagement on the coast of Thrace, he took to his heels and lost his shield; and he was the first to make fun of the mishap. Having later returned home, he lost his life in a battle between the men of Naxos and Paros.

If we are to form a true picture of the bards and poets of these olden times, without misrepresenting them and turning them into

---

[1] 'De vocation cléricale' — occupied, at any rate, on an hereditary basis, with the performance of sacred rites (Translator).

lay figures, we should bear in mind that the gift of poetry has always gone hand in hand with some peculiar or whimsical slant in the poet's conception of life.

\*    \*    \*    \*

After this rapid review of the life of the intellectual classes in our period, we must conclude that already it contained the seeds of curiosity, of a taste for liberty and for personal thinking. We shall thus be in a better position to understand how, from such an environment, still in the rut of thousand-year-old traditions, the marvellous flower of Greek thought in the centuries to follow could expand so soon and so gloriously.

# CHAPTER V

## PEASANTS AND SOLDIERS

THE structure of the Homeric states, in spite of the increasing changes brought about by industrial and commercial expansion, remained none the less solidly based on the old rural traditions.

This state of equilibrium was to some extent jeopardized by the rapid rise to wealth of a section of the great aristocratic families: these were now in possession of political power and they continued to control their own class-group, that of the hereditary nobility, within the solid structure of the *gené*. The balance was also disturbed by the increase in population, not always accompanied by an improvement in material conditions, for the increase mainly affected the populace. This section contained many heterogeneous elements, including the free artisans, the agricultural labourers, the smaller landholders, not to mention the members of the servant and slave classes.

Nevertheless, the equilibrium of the state was still assured by the existence of one very important class, which enjoyed material and moral autonomy and was justly proud of the privilege. Its economic independence was based on landownership, for it was a race of peasants. Its social standing was due to the right of taking part in the popular assembly and, in consequence, of holding the rank of citizens. And its prestige was further enhanced by the right of bearing arms, because it was from this class that the phalanx of heavy-armed infantry, which formed the bulk of the army, was recruited. It was therefore a military class.

The mode and conditions of peasant life varied from country to country and from city to city. In general, a preoccupation with land was the dominant interest; but it might happen that military interests so far predominated that the landholder disdained his functions as farmer, as was the case in Sparta and the Cretan cities. Nevertheless, the landed interest remained fundamental, because the peasants lived on their land, and derived their civic rights from its possession.

## THE POSSESSION OF A *Cleros*

The social status of the peasant class was in fact based on the possession of a *cleros*, a 'lot' or portion of land assigned to each family. This enabled it to maintain its rank, to be represented in the civic assembly, to contribute to the collective taxes levied by the city, whether regular religious taxes or exceptional contributions;[1] and finally to supply the army with a fully equipped soldier.

In the Homeric vocabulary the word *cleros* appears actually to designate a unit of property. An *acleros*, a man 'without a lot', might own a servant, but his property did not amount to the value of a *cleros*. A rich family owning numerous lots was called *polycleros*; here it was a question of a noble family whose patrimony would normally be equivalent to several 'lots'. According to Homer, a prince could grant lots to the members of his household, doubtless out of the city's common lands.[2] This was for long the practice in Sparta, in the case of the *neodamodae*, or helots promoted to the rank of citizen on account of their military prowess.

We can form a fairly exact notion of the nature of a *cleros*.

In Sparta it was defined by law. The helots who cultivated it had to make a return to the owner of eighty-two *medimnoi* of grain for his wife and family, the equivalent of one hundred and sixty-five bushels; to which was added a contribution of wine, oil and fruit. As a helot would retain about two-thirds of the harvest[3] for his own use, these figures indicate an area of about seventy-four acres, perhaps rather less.

[1] Thus Alcinous commands the whole body of the citizens to contribute to the gifts offered to Odysseus (*Odyssey*, XIII, 14–15).

[2] *Odyssey*, XI, 490; XIV, 211, and XIV, 63–4.

[3] The helots of Messenia, who were more heavily burdened, had to hand over half of their harvest. The Laconian *medimnos* and the ancient Athenian *medimnos* contained a little over two bushels.

In Athens we know that membership of the class who served at their own expense in the heavy-armed infantry of the hoplites — the so-called 'zeugites' — in other words, the men who owned at least one pair of ploughing-oxen, involved the possession of property which would yield a harvest of two to three hundred *medimnoi* of corn. This would also correspond with the above area of about seventy-four acres, of which roughly sixty-three acres[1] would consist of arable land and eleven or twelve would be enclosed meadows, vineyards or olive groves.

In the strictly historical tradition, therefore, as also in Homer, the *cleros* represented a sort of property qualification, distinguishing a certain social class. The 'lot', at least in principle, was held by the titulary only in order to enable him to fulfil his civic functions; hence it remained under the authority and control of the civic authorities, kings and magistrates, and its status was defined by law and custom.

At the outset, the *cleros* had certainly been indivisible and inalienable. In Sparta, until the fourth century, it was a kind of entailed estate, to which the eldest son succeeded by right but which reverted to the state in the absence of an heir. Aristotle tells us that in most cities the old laws forbade the sale of family 'lots'. This was the case notably at Locri and at Leucadia, two colonies which continued in the natural course of things to observe the laws obtaining in their home countries. At Corinth and Thebes, states Aristotle, the law laid down that the number of families and of landed properties should remain unchanged.[2]

Indivisibility was also at first the rule, and the lot had to be transmitted as a whole to the eldest son; and this necessity of transmission by direct descent seems to have been so strictly enforced that it inspired the very old law regarding a daughter known as *epicleros*. When the owner of a 'lot' died without a male heir, his daughter became *epicleros*, that is, 'eligible to transmit the

---

[1] M. Mireaux writes '300 arpents' and adds that the 'arpent' or 'plèthre' contains 8·7 'ares'. An 'are' equals about 4 square poles, i.e. 119·6 square yards (Translator).

[2] *Politics*, II, 3, 7; 4, 4; 9, 7; VI, 2, 5.

cleros'. She had then to marry her paternal uncle nearest in the line of descent, and therefore the oldest. But the land, though provisionally administered by husband and wife, belonged in advance to the child of the marriage. Thus, by a sort of posthumous adoption, the grandson of the deceased became his son and heir. All collateral relations were thereby excluded from the succession as long as a direct heir was producible, even by this roundabout means. All that the others were entitled to was a general eligibility to inherit, in the event of the complete extinction of the elder branch of the family.

As may be imagined, this eventuality would be greatly to their interest and they would naturally connive to bring it about. It often happened that these marriages between an old man and a young girl would remain childless, especially when the husband already had a son, and thus a possible heir, through his first marriage. In order to put an end to this abuse, Solon promulgated a law at the beginning of the sixth century, requiring the husband of an *epicleros* to fulfil his conjugal duties at least three times monthly. If the lawful husband proved incapable, or unwilling, the woman had the right to bring a suit against him and to choose a more capable partner among the other members of the family.

Nevertheless, by the time this law was put in force, the epiclerate had lost much of its early bearing and significance.[1] In most of the cities, outside Sparta and Crete, the habit of dividing up the *cleros* among the male heirs became progressively the rule, and this was already the case in Homeric times. It seems, however, that the property was not at first divided into equal shares.[2] Moreover, when the patrimony *was* divided, this did not absolve the eldest son, who was still the theoretical holder of the entire 'lot', from his civic and military obligations to the community. He had

---

[1] In the classical period, when the word *cleros* now designated no more than a heritage in landed or immoveable property, the laws governing the epiclerate merely sought to protect the portionless daughter whom it obliged her nearest relative to marry or provide for.

[2] It was only Solon who instituted an equal division of property in Athens, in order to accelerate the splitting up of the estates.

therefore to remain in a position to fulfil them, even if he had to
call upon his younger brothers to assist him.

Such, in any case, is what appears to emerge from Hesiod's
dispute with his brother Perses over the paternal heritage, which
was an estate they had divided. Perses was no doubt the elder
brother, the political head of the family, in which capacity he as-
siduously attended the tribunals and the popular assembly. Hesiod
says this was detrimental to his work, and he makes a bitter
grievance of it. Perses had first summoned his brother before the
tribunal of the 'kings' in order to obtain a revision of the property
arrangement; and moreover he had obtained it. On what pretext,
Hesiod does not tell us, though he complains of the verdict. We
may suppose that Perses pleaded the inadequacy of his means for
the carrying out of his civic duties. We have the more reason to
suppose so, since, while Hesiod was writing the *Works and Days*,
his brother was preparing to make a further petition, and the poet
was replying:

> O Perses, lay thou this to heart, nor let strife that exulteth in evil turn thy
> mind from work, to watch contention and to hearken in the market place.[1]

It seems, moreover, that Perses' claim cannot have been so ill-
founded in law, because Hesiod was very anxious to persuade him
to refrain from going before 'the bribe-devouring princes', which
would cost him dear; and he proposed instead that they should
settle their differences privately by an arrangement in accordance
'with just judgement, even of Zeus'. If our interpretation is correct, this text of Hesiod is an invaluable and singularly vivid document on the inside history of the *cleros*, towards the end of the
Homeric age, at a time when the ancient structure of the family
was beginning to fall into decay.

This decline was a natural and almost inevitable development,
at least in those cities[2] where a rigid social and political discipline,

---

[1] See *Works and Days*, vv. 27 et seq. Trans. Mair, p. 2.

[2] The reader will understand that in these contexts the word 'city' (Greek
*polis*) does not designate the urban agglomeration, but the political community, the body of free citizens who constituted the city state and controlled
its territory (Translator).

like that of Sparta and the cities of Crete, was no longer in force to maintain the traditional framework of society.

## THE CONSERVATION OF THE *Cleros*

The preservation of these 'lots' from which the free military and peasant class drew its strength and pride, was a singularly difficult problem, involving political and domestic issues.

In spite of the rigour of the law and the strength of tradition, the increasing birth-rate was a natural disruptive force, not easily controllable. The preservation of the *cleros* created a problem almost exactly similar to that of maintaining the integrity of an aristocratic demesne; but it had a greater urgency, owing to the relatively restricted area involved. The same means were employed in attempting to solve it.

Emigration was the first of these. The younger members of the military and peasant families who were unable, through lack of resources, to marry and found a home, would set out for distant countries in the suite of some young noble, also destined to emigrate, with the purpose of founding new colonies in 'barbarian' lands. The 'Parthenians' who left Sparta with a scion of the Heracleidae, at the end of the eighth century, to found Tarentum, may well have been a band of single men and women — despite a later legend to the contrary — who were determined to find a home free from traditional restraints.

Another way of solving the problem was to wage a war of conquest. This method had a two-fold efficacy, of a rather grim kind; since by depleting the male members of the population, the victorious survivors were assured of a larger slice of the conquered territory. Such was the object of the Messenian war, begun by Sparta round about 700 B.C., if at least we are to believe the cynical proclamation attributed to king Polydorus at the opening of the campaign: 'Let us go forward to a land not yet divided up' — meaning, obviously, not yet divided among the Spartans.

Birth control was another means employed: less violent but quite as efficacious. It is the method recommended by Hesiod, who advises landowners to limit themselves to one son. Nevertheless, it might happen that several brothers had to live on the same lot. At Sparta, we are told, it became the custom for them to take only one wife; and to this habit may be attributed the fact that women played so important a role in that city of warriors.

The exigencies and vicissitudes of life always ended, however, in bursting asunder the juridical framework by which it had been sought to fix and stabilize it. In many families the issue was inevitable, and the *cleros* became insufficient to support all the members. They were then obliged to run into debt; and not being allowed to sell the land in order to pay the debt, they had to resign themselves to making over the revenues. The *cleros* continued to exist, but was little more than an empty shell. At the time we are concerned with, the evil was only in its infancy, but it was already apparent.

There is a reference to the situation in a passage of Hesiod's *Works and Days*, in which he describes the procedure of transfer:

> That thou mayest acquire the estate of others, but not that thy estate be acquired, invite thy friends to a banquet, exclude thy enemies, and especially call to meat all thy nearest neighbours.[1]

The banquet in question was the ritual feast following a sacrifice, the gods being invoked as witnesses and guarantors of an act as solemn as the cession of a *cleros*, or family lot. The Greek verb, *onein*, which is used to describe the acquisition, is purposely ambiguous, having the dual meaning of 'to buy' and 'to take on lease'; and it exactly defines this singular transaction by which one became master of a lot, inalienable in theory, without becoming its actual proprietor.

This was only the beginning of a change, which was accelerated by economic developments and by the appearance of a new

---

[1] *Works and Days*, vv. 341–3. G. Glotz saw clearly that verse 341 is connected with the two following verses, and not, as in the traditional reading, with the preceding ones. (Cf. *La Solidarité de la Famille*, pp. 196–7.) (Author's note). Mr Mair (p. 13) follows the traditional reading. Glotz's emendation is, however, certainly correct, and I have modified the translation accordingly (Translator).

sort of mobile wealth. In Sparta, where the old juridical structure was to be maintained, the number of 'equals', that is, of proprietors able to maintain their rank as holders of a *cleros*, was to go on steadily diminishing. The total number of lots was not to vary until the fourth century, but they were in fact to be monopolized by a minority of the population. In Athens, under Solon, the land was 'liberated'; and most of the other cities followed this example.

But all this is another story. In the eighth century and during most of the seventh, the class of property-owning peasants and soldiers was still firmly entrenched in its ancestral domains. It remained one of the bastions of the traditional order of things, a bastion which was only just beginning to crumble.

## THE EXPLOITATION OF THE *Cleros*

The ambiguous situation arising from the dual avocations of farmer and soldier could not but have its repercussions on the state of the lands which had been assigned or conceded to the class in question with the object of enabling its members to carry out their political, military, economic and also religious duties to the community. These men would be pre-eminently soldiers, or farmers, according to their circumstances which varied from time to time, and place to place.

In most of the 'cities', agriculture took first place. The holder of a *cleros* was simultaneously its proprietor and working farmer. In a few other places, chiefly in Sparta and Crete, the military avocation had priority, and almost excluded any other: the holder of a *cleros* was first and foremost a soldier, and he would leave the actual farming of his domain to the helots, although even for this the conditions were fixed by common law. It is not without significance that both procedures could coexist in the same 'city'. In Lacedaemonia, for example, the Spartans who held lots in the Eurotas valley, on the 'civic lands' or in Messenia, were purely soldiers; but the *perioeci*[1] who owned land outside the civic territory, in the periphery of the city, remained regular cultivators, while being also subject to military service in the armed infantry.

[1] 'Perioikoi' in Greek orthography.

Both these classes of men served as hoplites in the Lacedaemonian army, at their own expense.

The mode of cultivating those Spartan lots whose holders were simply soldiers is known in most detail. These lots were divided into a certain number of tenures, each of which was cultivated by a family of helots attached to the soil and occupying it on an hereditary basis.

In the Cretan cities, the situation of the military class and the administration of its agricultural interests were very similar to those prevailing in Sparta. The family 'lots' of the citizens were also cultivated by tenants attached to the soil, the 'clarotae', who were the homologues of the helots of Laconia.

Athenaeus, who wrote in the third century A.D., has preserved for us in his *Doctors at Dinner*[1] the text of an old Cretan song which is put into the mouth of one of this class of land-owning soldiers. It sums up, with a certain swagger, the spirit of the organization: 'My wealth consists of a long lance, a sword, and the good buckler that protects my body. With that I plough, with that I harvest, and I gather the sweet wine of the vineyard.'

It may be well imagined that a very different mentality existed among the farmer-proprietors who had the same status as citizens in most of the other Greek states. For them the *cleros* was more than a mere means of subsistence; it became progressively, as Hesiod bears witness, the principal aim and end of life; while their military duties, notwithstanding the pride they took in them, came to be of secondary importance. They cared for their land and farmed it with their own hands, unlike the citizens of Sparta.

In Homeric society, agriculture was a noble calling. When the suitor Eurymachus reproaches Odysseus, who is disguised as a beggar, with idleness, the latter challenges him in the following words:

> 'Eurymachus, I wish we two could have
> A match of work in the spring season, when
> The long days come, at mowing grass; and I

[1] *Deipnosophistae*, which may also be translated as *The Banquet of the Sophists* (Translator).

their chariot and are about to take leave of Helen and Menelaus, in Book XV, another eagle appears and carries off a goose before their eyes; this is a favourable omen which the queen, by an inspiration, translates as predicting the imminent return of the king of Ithaca. When, in the last book of the *Iliad*, old Priam is about to leave his house in order to supplicate Achilles, he calls upon Zeus to give a favourable sign by the approach of an eagle on his right hand. For the eagle is the bird of Zeus and the most imperious of harbingers. When an eagle appears on the left of the suitors, in Book XX of the *Odyssey*, the latter no longer have any mind to kill Telemachus.

When the son of Odysseus, returning from Pylos, disembarks on Ithaca, a falcon is seen to fly on his right hand, engaged in stripping a dove of its feathers. This message, according to the soothsayer Theoclymenus, has been sent from Apollo to advise Telemachus that his own royal family is the most powerful in the island.

Naturally, for these manifestations to have any meaning, they had to coincide with some important event, whether an assembly, a departure or an arrival, or some dramatic turn in a combat. Moreover, any remarkable coincidence could give meaning to an event; it could, in particular, confer the value of a prediction on the words that had been pronounced. This was called a *cledon*, when such an omen was contained in the words spoken. So Odysseus listens to the suitors expressing the hope that *his* wishes may be granted by the gods and declaring that they will dispatch the beggar, Irus, whom he has just overthrown, to the court of the terrible king Echetus; and Odysseus rejoices at this *cledon* because, rightly interpreted, it means that the suitors themselves will be vanquished by him and sent to Hades.[1] A resounding sneeze, made more conspicuous by a burst of laughter, might also confer special significance on the spoken word. Penelope, in conversation with Eumaeus, expresses aloud the wish that Odysseus may return and destroy her persecutors. At this moment Telemachus sneezes violently, and the queen at once bursts into laughter, exclaiming:

[1] *Odyssey*, XVIII, 115-17.

Would have a crescent scythe, and thou another
Just like it, and there should be grass in plenty,
That we might test our labour, without pause
For food right up to dark. Or would again
Oxen there were to drive — the best there are —
Tawny and large, a pair well filled with fodder,
Of equal age and power to bear the yoke,
And strength untired; and that there were a field
Four-acred, and the clod should yield before
The plough; then thou shouldst see if I can cut
A furrow straight before me to the end.'[1]

So we see that even a noble lord did not disdain to be known as a master-farmer on the land.

Nevertheless the full exploitation of a farm of seventy-four acres, even when, as was customary, it was only tilled every other year, required a variously-composed staff of servants.[2] We have textual evidence, unfortunately not very detailed, that there existed in the early centuries of Greek history a class of farm labourers whom Homer and Hesiod call *thetes* and who received 'wages'. Their status was sometimes not unlike that of the Spartan helots or the Cretan *clarotae*. We will return to them later.

One can form some idea of the kind of life led by farmer-proprietors from the sketch Homer gives us, in the last book of the *Odyssey*, of the country domain to which old Laertes has retired. Situated at some distance from the town, it extended round a 'well-built' house, that is, a house built of stone. This dwelling was flanked by stables and outbuildings which housed the servants, or more strictly the slaves, of the establishment. No doubt these offices were built round a closed courtyard, as this, though not mentioned in the Homeric text, was a normal feature of the country house in Greece and elsewhere. The main building included a great hall containing the hearth, and with a lantern above the opening in the middle of the roof. There were also a bath-room and bedrooms, known as *thalamoi*. Homer merely tells us

[1] *Odyssey*, XVIII, 366–75, p. 329.
[2] 'Une main-d'oeuvre d'appoint', i.e. servants and labourers who were 'odd' — unequal or varied as to their status and functions (Translator).

that old Laertes, who is in mourning for the absence of Odysseus, refuses to sleep in a *thalamos* but makes his bed in the hall, beside the ashes of the hearth and among the servants who, during the winter months, take refuge there at night. Over against the house is a large garden for fruit and vegetables, and here flourish vines, figs, pears, apples and olives. It must have been fairly spacious, since Odysseus reminds his father of the promise made in his childhood that he should have ten apple trees, thirteen pear trees, forty fig trees and fifty rows of vines.[1] The whole garden was surrounded by a wall.

Old Laertes takes pleasure in working in this orchard. Odysseus finds him digging at the foot of a tree, clad in rustic fashion and wearing an old tunic, patched and soiled. His legs are encased in skins sewn together, which serve as gaiters; his hands are pro-.tected from scratches by gloves. It is true that the old man, in his grief, deliberately neglects his dress, as a sign of mourning.

We should note, however, that the property to which Laertes has retired is not a 'lot', but an 'acquisition';[2] that it is of modest dimensions, and that he can maintain it with the help simply of his own servants, a very old Sicilian slave-woman who looks after the house, her son, already an aged man, and the latter's sons.

We have only to elaborate this picture in imagination to get a fairly good idea of the life of a rural landholder in the Homeric world; and we can further amplify it with some details taken from Hesiod.

For the author of *Works and Days*, the farmer-proprietor is and should be a worker. He can be a good citizen without sacrificing the care of his property to public affairs, or neglecting it in order to attend the tribunals and appear in the agora, like Perses,

---

[1] This recollection, together with the story of the boar hunt, were the 'signs' that convinced Laertes that the glorious stranger was indeed his long-lost son (Translator).

[2]        'The fine well-ordered farmstead of Laertes,
       Which he had gotten for himself of old
       After much toil for it. . . .' (Trans. Marris, p. 425).

the poet's brother. Hesiod's ideal, as a Boeotian peasant, is at the opposite pole from the Spartan, for to him there is no disgrace attaching to work: the disgrace is in doing nothing. The Immortals favour the man who works.

The proprietor, then, should take a personal share in tilling his land, assisted by his servants and, if need be, by his wife, who should be able to follow the oxen with the plough. He is up with the dawn, for the early morning hours include a third part of the working day. In the season of high summer he will rest only during the short period of great heat, after the harvest has been taken in. Then he may seat himself in the shadow of a rock, near some spring, with a well-raised girdle cake,[1] some goat's milk, a slice of lamb or veal, and a portion of wine which he will mix with the spring water. After a good meal, he will drink his wine and stretch himself in the shade with his face turned to the breeze which brings a breath of cool air from the sea. If, however, he is an enterprising man, this is the moment he will choose for any maritime business, as the sea is calm at this time and the winds favourable.

In spring and summer he will work 'naked', that is to say, clad merely in a short tunic. At the end of autumn he will do well to put on a long tunic and a woollen cloak, which should be woven in the house. He will lay aside his sandals and fasten high boots on his feet, made of ox-hide and lined. In the very cold season, he will also don a cape of goatskins, sewn together with ox gut, and protect his head with a felt bonnet coming down over the ears. Inside the house there will be feasting, and for this purpose he will draw on his stock of provisions to ward off the cold and weakness due to enforced inactivity.

The livestock of the holding include at least one pair of nine-year-old oxen required for the plough, and a few pack or draught animals, mules and asses; not to mention the watchdog. Only a younger son, with a poor share of land, would have to put up with a single ox.

The chattels that make up the farm equipment are of household

[1] Probably a flattish round of barley bread (Translator).

manufacture. They include at least two ploughs: one constructed of a single piece of wood, the other, of stronger make, being constructed of fitted components — namely, the plough beam, the share beam[1] (a piece of curved wood shaped to connect the plough beam with the heelpiece), the heel holding the ploughshare which might be of iron; and finally, the stilt on which the ploughman presses with both hands in order to force the share into the ground and maintain it there. In the house, in addition, there would be a mortar and pestle for crushing grain; mallets for breaking up peat sods; and lastly, an essential piece of gear, a heavy cart with side racks, mounted on two or four wheels, and one or two axle-shafts about seven feet long.

This description of the holding would be incomplete if we failed to mention that the owner was not only an agriculturist but also a stockbreeder. More precisely, he would always possess a few herds, of oxen, cows, goats, sheep and swine. These herds lived and grazed far from the farm and the arable lands, in grazing country and woods, on the common lands lying on the foothills and mountain sides which were the common property of the city. Here each proprietor owned a few makeshift shelters, such as stables provided with litter, scarcely more than enclosures open to the sky and intended for the larger stock; while there were pens for the sheep and shelters for the sows and their young. The animals lived here all the year round, suffering greatly during the coldest period of winter; a few oxen would then always succumb to the cold, Hesiod tells us.

These flocks and herds were watched over and cared for by servants who stayed with them all the year. The shepherd was, in principle, a slave or at most a thes.[2] In those farms, however, where there was a shortage of labour, it might happen that a younger son would guard the animals during the summer. Thus the young Hesiod himself tended the flocks on the slopes of Helicon; and it was here, as he confesses in the prelude to the *Theo-*

[1] See *Works and Days*, vv. 425 et seq. Trans. Mair, p. 16 (Translator).

[2] The 'thes' (plural 'thetes') was a farm labourer, juridically a free man. See Chapter VI below (Translator).

*gony*, that under the influence of the Muses of Helicon he felt the stirrings of his poetic vocation.

### THE TRAINING AND LIFE OF A SOLDIER

We have defined the citizen-landholders as a class of peasants; they were also a class of soldiers. The two occupations, essentially of a public nature were inextricably mixed.

In India, where the peasant caste corresponded to that of the military peasants of the Homeric era, the gods of the farmers, known as the 'Marut', formed the bodyguard of Indra. In the same way, the farmers formed the king's bodyguard in the army.

Each *cleros* had therefore to provide the city with a soldier — a hoplite, or heavy-armed infantryman, who was required to furnish his own equipment. This comprised a cuirass, or rather a coat of mail to cover breast and belly, made up of interlocking metal plates; a round or oval shield; two metal greaves, called 'cnemids', to protect the front part of the legs; a helmet or plated headgear; a javelin, and a sword.

It was usually the head of the family who was required to perform military service. Age or some physical infirmity might prevent his fulfilling this duty himself; in which case he was replaced by a member of the family, most often by one of his sons. When old Priam goes forth at nightfall to make his prayer to Achilles, in the camp of the Achaeans, he meets Hermes on the way. Hermes has taken on the form of a soldier in the Greek army and introduces himself to Priam in these words:

> 'I am a Myrmidon by stock: Polyctor
> Begot me; he is wealthy, and as old
> As thou. Six other sons he hath, and I
> Am seventh, and with my brothers I cast lots,
> And won the chance of serving here. . . .'[1]

If an able-bodied man, liable to be called up, wished to avoid serving, he exposed himself to a heavy fine; or, more precisely, it would appear that he had to pay a considerable sum to indemnify himself. Thus, when the expeditionary force was being assembled

[1] *Iliad*, XXIV, 397–400, p. 552.

to sail for Troy, it was revealed to the Corinthian Euchenor, through his father the soothsayer, that he was fated to die in the war; but that, if he remained in Corinth he would still die, of a grievous malady. In this cruel dilemma, he resigned himself to going forth, in order, as Homer tells us, to escape the malady, but also to avoid paying the heavy indemnity he would have incurred by default; and this in spite of his wealth.[1] Echepelus of Sicyon was more fortunate; he succeeded in obtaining exemption from Agamemnon, but he was obliged to give him in exchange his fleetest mare, one of the finest in all Greece.[2]

The obligation of military service necessarily entailed a form of collective training. Greek writers describe, with a degree of admiration amounting to amazement, the rigorous nature of this training as it was practised in the classical era at Sparta, the military city *par excellence*. The details they give us comprise a great number of features so obviously archaic that they certainly reveal a much earlier state of affairs. Properly to understand them, we need to compare them with certain practices peculiar to so-called primitive societies. In these communities the adult male population, in what one may call its full status, formed itself into one or several groups with secret traditions and practices. These groups had a communal centre to which men alone were admitted, and here they spent part of each day in various distractions and took some of their meals. The young men were not admitted until a certain age, and then only after undergoing a series of initiations which involved training in common and ordeals that were often cruel or revolting.

We can follow the progress of these promotions fairly clearly in the case of the Spartan system of military education. At the age of seven the child was taken from his mother and entered in the first section, the *ila*. At twelve he became a *païs*, and rose by successive promotions to the status of *iran*, which he attained at the age of twenty. During all this time he was subjected to a severe physical and moral training. His intellectual education was very

---

[1] *Iliad*, XIII, 663–70, pp. 298–9.
[2] Ibid., XXIII, 295–8, p. 516.

simple; he learned a little poetry, and also the sacred or warrior songs which accompanied the group dances. And at each degree of his initiation, there were also revealed to him the mythical, legendary or ritual traditions appropriate to his age group. His physical and military training was more severe. Bareheaded and barefoot, wearing only a short tunic, he must sleep on a bed of reeds; every day he performed a march to the sound of the flute; and applied himself to such gymnastic exercises as leaping, running and throwing the discus. Finally he learned the use of arms. Among the ordeals required by the successive initiations, two have remained famous: the flagellation before the altar of Artemis Orthia, and the final one, known as the *crypteia*. After this the youth became an *iran*.

The scholiast on Plato's *Laws*[1] describes the *crypteia* as follows: 'The young man was banished from the town, under obligation of not being seen during this period. He would roam the mountains, sleeping always on the alert to avoid being taken by surprise; he had no servant with him, nor any provisions of any kind. He was sent out naked and solitary, under duress to pass a whole year in this state, to wander on the mountains and live on whatever he could filch or get by other means, and to conceal himself from all the world. If anyone saw him, he was punished.'

Monsieur H. Jeanmaire[2] has offered a very pertinent interpretation of this ordeal, which has its counterpart in many primitive societies. It appears to have been the decisive rite in the young man's initiation, as it embodied the mystical significance of both death and resurrection. During the *crypteia* the novice suffered a symbolic death: he had left his social group, bearing nothing with him, and was cut off from all intercourse with it. He lived as a familiar of elementary spirits of animal form and nature; the centaurs, satyrs and silens who haunt the woods and mountains and have some kinship with the spirits of the dead ancestors. When he reappeared, he was another man; or rather, he was a man. It is

[1] *Laws*, I, 633 B.
[2] 'La Cryptie lacédémonienne', in *Revue des Etudes grecques*, XXVI (1913). See also the book by the same author: *Couroi et Courètes*.

not impossible that, originally, the *cryptos* was under the obligation of killing an enemy before his return. This is at least suggested by a later tradition according to which the *cryptoi* received from the Spartan ephors the mission of liquidating certain helots reputedly dangerous. Having accomplished this bloody deed, the regenerated novice was then eligible to take his place among the warriors.

He assumed this right on his return. At the age of twenty, he sought admission to a table where he would participate in the common repasts, or *phiditia*. These meals were eaten at tables seating fifteen members, all of whom were united in an intimate fellowship. On campaign, they slept under the same tent. Each participant furnished his own score, a monthly ration of about two bushels of flour, eight gallons of wine,[1] about 6 lb. 9 oz. of cheese, 3 lb. 5 oz. of dried figs; and, in money, ten obols to buy the necessary meat. The newly promoted member continued to sit at the same table for forty years, that is, until he was sixty. Up to the age of thirty, he took his two meals in this fashion, and slept in the common shelter. If he married, he could visit his wife only for a short time, at night, after the evening meal. After the age of thirty he would take only one meal in common, in the evening, after which he could pass the night in his own house. It was only now in fact that he became a full citizen; he could participate in the assembly and take his place among his 'equals'.

His house was of the simple, rural type. It closely resembled the house of old Laertes described above; for Sparta was not properly speaking a town, but a simple agglomeration of large villages of a rural aspect.

In Crete the warrior class received a very similar education and led a similar sort of existence to those we have described in Sparta. The future soldier began his physical, and then his military, training at the age of fourteen. At eighteen he attained his majority and was entered as a member of a *hetaireia*, or fraternity, corresponding to the group which in Sparta ate at the same table. In Crete the young man now took part in the public repasts for men, which were provided at the city's expense.

[1] '73 litres de farine, 36 litres de vin.'

This mode of existence was in no way the outcome of the fairly recent legislation which the ancients attributed to Lycurgus. Such was, indeed, the view of later centuries; but it now appears that, on the contrary, we are dealing with a survival from much earlier times. These customs were probably maintained in Sparta and in the Cretan cities owing to the organization there of the agricultural interests, combined with the military requirements, of those cities; and we have just seen how this organization functioned, by releasing the holders of 'lots' from any concern with actual production.

Much new light is shed by this discovery on the traditions and background of Greek life in the age we are considering. But we are also led to enquire how life was organized elsewhere, from the military point of view, for those farmer-proprietors who were obliged to manage their holdings personally, instead of delegating the task to a class of demi-serfs, helots or *clarotae*, as did the Spartans and Cretans.

Homer himself throws no light on this question. Nevertheless we find details in later authors about an institution already in their time fairly flourishing, so that its origins must certainly have gone very far back into the past; and we are thus able to draw conclusions about the state of affairs in the earlier period.

We refer to the *ephebeia* of classical times, the organization of which in Athens is comparatively well known. It existed in many cities, notably in Argos, Megara, Sicyon, Plataea, Thebes, Thespiae, and others. The *ephebeia* was the military training which future citizens of Athens were compelled to undergo in the classical era. At eighteen the sons of citizens were enrolled among the *epheboi* for two years. They received their gymnastic education from the *paidotribai* and their military training from the *didascaloi*. On receiving their arms, they took an oath in the sanctuary of Aglauros, the daughter of Cecrops, on the northern slope of the Acropolis. They swore in particular not to dishonour these sacred arms, not to desert their comrades in battle, to fight for the gods and for their homes; and they took to witness Aglauros, Euryalos, Ares, Thallo, Auxo and Hegemone — all ancient deities, more or less closely associated with the powers of the underworld. These circumstances show that the ceremonial was of great antiquity. In their second year, the youths were posted to garrison duty on the borders of Attica, where they patrolled the mountainous regions of the frontier zone.

This last feature naturally recalls the Spartan *crypteia*, but it was a *crypteia* much modified, adapted, attenuated and in some sort laicized. The institution in classical times could not in any case have been more than vestigial, with its reduction to the purely essential features of an old educational organization which may have had some analogy with the one that the conservative traditions of Sparta had kept alive. Even Homer has a few revealing details for the imagination to work on. Thus he tells us that the centaur Cheiron was a sojourner in the wooded solitudes of Mount Pelion, where he instructed Achilles and Asclepios in the art of medicine. Now Cheiron, learned in the virtue of herbs and in their employment for medical and magical purposes; Cheiron, the dweller among woods and uninhabited mountains, has many of the characters of a master in initiation, a revealer of the mysteries which are discovered to novices towards the age of adolescence, after a period of retreat and isolation has prepared them for the knowledge. And this picture of Achilles and Asclepios as young men, exiled on Mount Pelion in the company of Cheiron, again makes one think of the *crypteia*,[1] and, in consequence, of a moral and military education somewhat similar to that of the young Spartans.

It may be appropriate at this point to recall the episode of the *Doloneia* in Book X of the *Iliad*, although this, to be sure, is of fairly late composition. It has been interpreted, with some degree of likelihood, as a modified and poetized description of one of the ordeals connected with the initiation of the young men who were about to be promoted to warrior rank. We read in this book how Odysseus and Diomed set out on a night foray and surprise Dolon, a Trojan spy, whom they kill. They next invade the camp of the sleeping Thracians, massacre the sleepers and seize the horses of

[1] Cf. H. Jeanmaire, 'Chiron' (in *Mélanges Henri Grégoire*, 1949).

the king, whom they have also slain. In the same way the initiates were often only admitted to the dignity of warriors after they had slain an enemy and seized some booty or other.

The parallelism is even more striking in that the protagonists in the *Doloneia* wear animal disguises for their nocturnal expedition. Odysseus has a headgear with wild boar's tusks for garniture, Diomed is clothed in a lion's skin, and Dolon in a grey wolf's skin. Now the young initiates were grouped in brotherhoods bearing the names of animals, and the initiation ceremonies included animal disguises, the favourite one being that of a wolf.[1] From which it would appear that the education of young citizens of Sparta in the sixth and fifth centuries was the same as that received by the sons of free men in all the Greek cities a few centuries earlier.

One might even point to other possible connections or try to discover other clues and indications. What, for example, was the *lesché*, that covered building, set in a conspicuous position, which was to be found everywhere, in the towns and large villages, on Ithaca and at Ascra? Towards the middle of the seventh century, when Hesiod or the second Homer were writing, the *lesché* was probably no more than a meeting-house where even a beggar in distress might be received. But is it impossible to recognize in these buildings, without going very far back, the houses for men — meeting places, dining- and sleeping-quarters — which played so distinctive a part in the life of the citizen-soldiers of Crete and Laconia?

Thus one is led to believe that the care for agriculture, and the dispersal of a peasantry so firmly rooted to the soil, must have brought about, in most of the cities, at a quite early stage — and no doubt as early as Homeric times — the dissolution of the primitive brotherhoods of youth and soldierly companionship, and the breaking up of their community-centres. Nevertheless, even if the traditions of a life in common and an armed confraternity were growing looser, they were not yet so obsolete that they could not still colour the lives of the rough peasant classes, guiding them

[1] Cf. H. Jeanmaire, *Couroi et Courètes*, pp. 392–9.

and instilling into them the old ideals of honour and pride; for they still knew that their lands were only truly theirs as long as they could defend them, with helmet, buckler and javelin, after an appropriate training and a traditional initiation received at the hands of their elders.

# CHAPTER VI

# THE LOWER CLASSES AND THE
# CULTIVATION OF THE LAND

EVEN in the city states where the owners took a direct part in the cultivation of their land, the bulk of agricultural work was carried out by the class of servants and labourers who made up the mass of the rural population.

Their conditions and way of life differed widely; depending on their juridical status, that is, according as whether they belonged to the class of domestic slaves, or of slaves attached to the soil and leading a separate existence; or to the class of free workmen; or again to the class of vassals of various kinds, *thetes*, *penestai*, *gymnetai*, helots, *clarotai*, and so on, who might be bound by a permanent and personal tie to some lord or proprietor, or simply attached to the soil by legal statute. Conditions varied also according to the kind of cultivation, and according as the land was predominantly agricultural or pastoral.

## LACONIAN AND MESSENIAN HELOTS AND CRETAN
### Clarotai

We may begin with the group which, if not the best known, is at least known in most detail, and also the one which had the most restricted geographical distribution; for it is not met with outside the southern Peloponnese, in Sparta and Messenia, and on the island of Crete.

We have seen how the 'lots' were cultivated in the case of those assigned to the families of the Spartan warriors, on the civic lands in the Eurotas valley.

The 'lot' was completely divided up into a number of holdings. Each of these supported a family of helots who handed it on from

generation to generation, and who had full control of the cultivation of the 'lot', owing nothing to the proprietor but the return
which was fixed by law and unchangeable.

The helot could not leave his holding, but this was not because
he was personally dependent on the owner. It was to the state that
he was bound, and the state alone could grant him freedom; that
is to say, release from bondage to the soil. In the words of ancient
writers, the helots were 'slaves of the community'. Lest we should
be misled by this expression, we must emphasize the fact that the
helot was neither more nor less bound to his holding than the
Spartan to his 'lot'. His private life was subjected to a kind of
discipline far less strict than that which governed the Spartan
soldier. Fundamentally, the great difference in their legal standing
— and it was important — lay simply in the fact that the Spartan
citizen had political privileges, while the helot had none.

Writers of the classical era have handed down a rather gloomy
picture of the life of the helots. They are represented as bowed
beneath the yoke of very severe political restrictions; forbidden to
carry arms or to hold assemblies at night. We are told, moreover,
that the ephors, who were the highest of the civic magistrates,
took advantage of the *crypteia* to induce the young men undergoing this initiation to get rid of any helots who were considered
dangerous.

This may have been a fairly true description of the conditions
prevailing in the fourth century, that is, at a much later date; at a
time in fact when the Spartans who enjoyed full rights of citizenship were no more than a very small minority, with every reason
to regard themselves as being at the mercy of a rebellion of the
masses. It is possible, too, that their uneasiness, before it became
widespread, had had as its object in the first instance, and at a
much earlier date — in the seventh century — the helots of
Messenia, who had been subjugated in war and were consequently far more harshly treated than the helots of Laconia; as we
shall see presently.

We must now attempt to form some idea of the way of life of
the latter. And we must first enquire how many holdings might be

included in the 'lot' of a soldier-citizen of Sparta. At the battle of Plataea, at the beginning of the fifth century, it appears that there were seven helots for every Spartan in the Lacedaemonian army; as they served, on campaign, in the light-armed troops and also as army servants. It has been rather hastily concluded from this fact that each 'lot' must have comprised seven holdings; but we shall see that this is very unlikely.

We know that the tenants of the 'lot' had to supply the proprietor with a fixed annual return of one hundred and sixty-five bushels. It may be admitted that in Laconia this contribution represented about one third of the harvest. The helots of Messenia, who were less well treated — 'burdened like asses', according to Tyrtaeus — returned in effect half of their harvest. Consequently, a 'lot' would yield, taking an average of good and bad years, a total of roughly four hundred and ninety-five bushels of grain. Out of this had to be taken one hundred and sixty-five bushels for the owner, and at least fifty-five for seeding and about twenty-seven for fodder and poultry-feed. The two hundred and forty-eight bushels remaining represented approximately two hundred bushels of flour. This would suffice for the needs of about twenty persons, on the calculation of one litre or about 2 lb. 3 oz.[1] of flour a head per day; since, if Homer's aristocrats were great meat-eaters, the common people, except for the shepherds, were largely consumers of bread and thick soup.[2] A 'lot' therefore could hardly support more than four helot families with an average of five members in each. In default of exact textual information, this is the most plausible conclusion.

Each family worked a holding of about twenty acres. The greater part of the land was devoted to the growing of cereals, barley and wheat. For this purpose about seventeen acres were set aside. Every year half the area was sown with crops, and the

[1] The author gives this and the quantities mentioned above in measures of capacity (litres, decalitres and hectolitres). It seems appropriate to translate the large quantities (for grain) into bushels. One litre makes just over 1¾ pints in liquid measure (Translator).

[2] The *choinix* (about a litre) was considered to be a man's daily ration.

other half lay fallow until the following spring, the time of the first ploughing. From these eight and a half acres the helot harvested about one hundred and twenty-four bushels of grain on an average, a third of the amount going to the proprietor. This harvest represented an average yield of about four hundredweight to the acre,[1] which would seem about the right figure in view of the productive capacity of primitive Greece.

The rest of the holding was parcelled out as a few meadows in the moister areas, and as vineyard and orchard, the latter mainly planted with olives and figs for drying. The helot was under the obligation of furnishing his master with a supply of oil, in addition to dried figs and wine, for the wherewithal of the communal repasts. The contribution of wine, amounting to nearly eight gallons a month, was of first importance.

The livestock of this modest holding amounted to very few animals: an ox, or perhaps two, as a second one would be generally needed if there were no good neighbour around to lend a beast at the critical moment of ploughing; an ass for transporting the contributions of grain, wine, etc., to the city; a few goats and sheep whose milk was used mainly to make cheese; a sow with her young; and a few geese. We must not forget one or two hives which provided honey, necessary for sweetening.

One cannot form any reliable idea of what the helot's house was like, not even by comparison with dwellings we know about. Apart from Eumaeus the swineherd's hut on Ithaca, the characters in epic only frequent the houses of the great. We might simply, if we wish, picture the hut as a building with a simple living-room and hearth, at the back of a courtyard surrounded by stables and a few cabins for the rest of the family; the whole probably roofed with rushes which grew thickly on the banks of the Eurotas.

Despite his inferior status on the social and political plane, from the economic point of view the helot's situation was far from being a poor one. He was bound to his holding, but he could not be evicted from it; and so he enjoyed security. He was obliged to

[1] '10 quintaux a l'hectare', i.e. ten quintals (or hundredweight) to the 'hectare' ( = 2·471 acres) (Translator).

furnish only a fixed return, never crushing, and only heavy in a year of bad harvest. On the other hand he took the whole profit of any excess in a good year. In particular, he had the advantage of any improvements he himself had worked to procure for his holding; and, lastly, he owned all the moveable property — this being no small privilege, as those helots who accompanied the army on campaign had the right to a share of the spoils.

We tend to be so much influenced by the picture of the helot's condition in classical times that it may be we exaggerate the gulf which originally separated him from the citizen-soldier. The helot was not restricted to his role as agriculturist; nor were his activities limited to the boundaries of his holding — too small in any case to support more than five or six people. The problem of younger sons was a present problem for the helot class, as for all classes in Homeric society.

Some of the younger sons would go into the service of the aristocracy or into that of their own landlords. They then became *mothaces*, a sort of domestic retainers living with the master, forming part of his train at assemblies and festivals, and accompanying him to war. It was perhaps from the ranks of these men that the so-called *epeunactoi* were selected, who, we are told, were allowed to marry Spartan women and fill the gaps caused by the depletion of the warrior class in the Messenian wars of the eighth and seventh centuries. From the ranks also of those helots who had been freed from the soil, were recruited the *aphetai*, who were no doubt archers or slingers; and the *desposionautai*, who made up the ships' crews, for the Sparta of Homer's time was a maritime power. And in a general way the helots supplied the army with orderlies and light-armed troops.

It might happen that a helot who had distinguished himself by his valour would be promoted to the dignity of citizenship. He then took his place among the *neodamodai*, or 'new citizens', and very probably received a 'lot' of land. In the classical era these new citizens were considered as of inferior rank; but it is not certain that they were so regarded at the outset.

Thus we see that the life of the helots living on the banks of the

Eurotas was by no means intolerable. But a very different state of affairs prevailed among the helots of Messenia.

In the closing years of the eighth century, the Spartans, feeling their country had become too small for them, crossed the passes of Taygetus under the leadership of king Polydorus and began the conquest of the fair and fertile plains of Messenia, watered by the Pamisus and its tributaries and by the little streams that come down from the massif of Ithome on the west. Legend has it that the conquest took twenty years of brutal conflict.

The conquered territory was divided into lots and portioned out among the victors. The local population, or that part of it which had not fled before the invaders, had been reduced to the severest plight. The Messenian helots were obliged to yield up to the owners of the land the half of their harvest, having themselves to supply the seed for the next year; unlike the Laconian helots, who as we have seen had to make only a fixed contribution, and that a fairly moderate one. The condition of the Messenians was most miserable, so much so that half a century later they rose up against their masters and waged against Sparta a war so long and desperate that it required all the discipline of the Spartan state and all the eloquence of a Tyrtaeus to triumph over the discontent and discouragement which at one time threatened to demoralize the Spartan warriors.

Messenia was subjugated afresh. Yet she was never to cease from being a hotbed of rebellion; and it was doubtless in their dealings with the Messenian helots much rather than with the Laconians that the Spartans employed the ferocious treatment traditionally imputed to them by classical writers.

The organization of country life in the Cretan states closely resembled that of Sparta. The *aphamiotai* there corresponded with the Laconian helots. They were also known as *clarotai*, meaning 'dwellers on the lots'. Side by side with this group, the *mnoïtai* cultivated the communal lands of the city states, under similar conditions.

The life of these small Cretan farmers, bound to the soil but quite free in other respects, appears to have been fairly comfortable, more so even than that of the Laconian helots. They were allowed to acquire moveable property and marry free women. When the owner of the lot died childless, they might even receive a share of the estate. But two privileges were significantly barred from them: the right to bear arms and the right to take part in gymnastic exercises. On the other hand, the Cretan *clarotai*, unlike the Spartan helots, were dispensed from military service; for the Cretan cities on their island had no urge to conquest; and the Cretan peasant was at bottom content with his lot and had no wish to rebel.

### *Thetes* AND LABOURERS

In those states where the owners of lots cultivated their own land, which was the case over the greater part of Greece, there existed according to Homer and Hesiod a class of hired labourers who assisted in farm work and received in return a *misthos*, or wage. These workmen were known by the generic name of *thetes*.

The *thetes* were free men. Lest the modern sense of the word mislead us, we must observe that in Homeric Greece everyone was free who was not the property of some master; which does not mean that the conduct of his life was not limited and regulated by very strict rules, in origin legal, traditional or even contractual, which latter might be inherited. In this sense the Spartan helots were free men, since they owned no master but the law and the city magistrates. From this point of view, their freedom of behaviour was quite as unrestricted, and might even be more so, than that of many Greeks who enjoyed full citizenship. Simply they had no political rights. The *thetes* in other parts of Greece were in a like case; they had no share in the control of civic affairs.

The *thetes* appear to us in Homer and Hesiod as pure mercenaries, who hire themselves out as manual labourers for a piece of work, or for a period of time, sometimes for a year or more.

In the course of the battle of the gods in Book XXI of the *Iliad*, Poseidon reminds Apollo of how, at Zeus' command, they had entered the employ of king Laomedon as *thetes* at an agreed wage, for a year:

> 'I built the sons of Troy the ramparts round
> Their city, broad and beautiful, to keep
> The town impregnable; and, Phoebus, thou
> Didst tend his rolling-gaited crook-horned kine
> On many-folded, wooded Ida's spurs.'[1]

In his *Works and Days* Hesiod recommends that for ploughing a man of forty should be hired, strong and reliable and able to plough a straight furrow. His food would be provided daily in the form of a good loaf or girdle cake, divided by four dents into eight portions.[2] After threshing and before the grape harvest, a *thes* and a woman-servant should be hired, and one should also get a 'dog with sharp teeth'. Their duties would consist in safeguarding the garnered harvest and caring for the livestock during the winter months. The *thes* should, preferably, be a man without a house, or family, of his own, and the woman should have no child to care for. This would reduce the temptation to petty larceny that the hired worker might yield to for the sake of his dependants during the winter months or if out of work.

Wages were paid in kind, but not always with meticulous honesty. Hesiod is emphatic in recommending the employer to treat his hired man fairly.[3] Poseidon recalls to Apollo the memory of their misadventure when, after they had completed their task, they were driven off by the brutal Laomedon without payment, and under threat of being chained up, and sold as slaves, and having their ears cut off.

In this aristocratic society a lonely *thes* was a defenceless person, equally exposed to violence or injustice. But this isolated situation was probably not the rule. The *thes* 'without a family' and the servant 'without a child', of whom Hesiod speaks, must have been young men or young women obliged to leave their homes on account of straitened circumstances.

---

[1] *Iliad*, XXI, 446–9, p. 481.
[2] See trans. Mair, p. 16 (Translator).
[3] He also says of the dog: 'Spare not his food' (Trans. Mair, p. 22).

In the mass, however, the *thetes* seem to have made up a class of workers bound to the soil and enjoying a status established by custom if not by law — and perhaps sometimes legal — related, with local variations, to that of the Laconian helots. This status gave them guarantees and some sort of security and conditions which, if rather mean, were not intolerable. We have Achilles' declaration to Odysseus, during the latter's visit to the nether world, that he would choose the life of a *thes*, a hired labourer, rather than enjoy royal rank in the kingdom of the dead.[1]

Both Homer and Hesiod are unfortunately silent about the general conditions governing the life of the *thetes*. Nevertheless various later documents, which allude to a much earlier state of affairs, are susceptible of yielding us information on this point, the more precious for its brevity.

At the time Solon was legislating, at the beginning of the sixth century, that is, scarcely a century later than our period, we know that there existed in Athens a class of workers on the soil called *hectemorioi*, or men of the sixth part, who obviously belonged to the class of the *thetes*. These *hectemorioi* worked on the land for the owners and received as wages a sixth part of the harvests.

Their position has been a subject of much discussion. One hypothesis would make of them former landowners who had fallen into debt and who, being unable to pay, had consequently fallen by law, with their wives and children, into the power of their creditors. They continued to work on their land but, in order to redeem themselves, had to surrender to their creditors five-sixths of the harvest. This hypothesis must be rejected, for two reasons.

First of all, any landowner who had mortgaged property which was theoretically inalienable could liquidate his debt by a procedure that was currently practised; this consisted in surrendering to the creditor the yield of the whole or part of his property, in other words the produce of its cultivation.[2] If this concession was

---

[1] *Odyssey*, XI, 489–91.

[2] This surrender, or concession, was generally made in the form of a sale with the right of repurchase, the vendor preserving a right of redemption, which symbolized the inalienable nature of the estate.

not sufficient to free him from his debts, the latter must have been relatively enormous, greater in fact than the capitalized value of the yield of the estate.

Secondly — and this reason is decisive — a debt, or dues, equal to five-sixths of the harvest is absolutely unthinkable from all we know about the economic conditions of agriculture in modern times, and still more so in the ancient world. No case of agricultural exploitation or management has ever existed in which the nett return is equal to five-sixths of the gross revenue. Had this been so, all the *hectemorioi*[1] would have died of hunger after the first year.

We must conclude that the 'men of the sixth part' in Athens were not, and never could have been, former landowners who had been ruined and enslaved.

The more plausible solution of this minor problem, and the one most in accord with the texts, appears to be as follows:

The *hectemorioi* were *thetes* attached to a property by a contract founded on custom. They were under obligation to work for the owner, and received, as wages, the sixth part of the harvest.[2] An Athenian *cleros* which produced, on an average, four hundred and ninety-five bushels of grain would bring an annual yield of about eighty-two or eighty-three bushels to the *hectemorioi* concerned, enough to support two families, or three at most. Each of these families had in addition, almost certainly, the enjoyment or concession of a parcel of land on which they would have built a small house, with a little garden, where some vegetables grew (beans and lentils) and some trees, and where a few geese would be reared. After the garnering of the harvests, they had the use of the common lands for their small herd of pigs, goats or sheep.

It was this parcel of land, regarded as a concession, that united the *hectemorios* and the owner of the domain and in some ways lent colour to the theory of the owner-debtor. Any 'concession'

[1] There also exists the form 'hectemoros' (plural -oi), which is perhaps less common (Translator).

[2] Aristotle writes in *The Constitution of Athens*, II, 2: 'It was for such wages that they worked on the lands of the well-to-do.'

which has been received and accepted is, in fact, by customary law everywhere regarded as the source of an obligation to compensate in some way, an obligation transmitted through successive generations until annulled by the yielding up of the concession or its abolition by law. An abolition of this kind was apparently enacted under Solon, at the beginning of the sixth century.

We can thus, conjecturally, form a reasonable picture of the way of life of the Athenian *thetes*. And we possess some information, if equally meagre, about another class of *thetes*, the *penēstai*[1] of Thessaly.

The *penēstai* have sometimes been assimilated to the helots. The probability is that they enjoyed a position intermediate between that of the Laconian helots and the Athenian *hectemorioi*. They were free men who provided the army with its contingent of light-armed troops, and the navy with crews for the ships. Writing in the fourth century, Theopompus affirms that they could not be punished unless judged and convicted; nor expelled from their holdings; and that this had always been so. He states that the *penēstai* had to cultivate the lands of the citizens, and make certain contributions. Whence one may conclude that their holdings must have been large enough to furnish them with means of subsistence and permit of their discharging their other obligations, doubtless not heavy. In short, their situation seems to have been comparable with that of our free copyholders[2] of the Middle Ages, who had to make returns in kind and in statute labour.[3] The latter was doubtless the more onerous burden, and these men are reputed to have been rather turbulent.

Analogous categories of workers existed in all the city states. We know little more than their names. Of these the best known and most expressive name was that of the *thetes* of Argolis, who were called *gymnētai*, meaning men 'without weapons'. For the right to bear arms, that is, the superior arms of the hoplite, or mailed foot-soldier, was in the whole of Homeric Greece a privi-

---

[1] The first e is an epsilon, the second an ēta (Translator).

[2] 'Nos censiers libres', i.e. in France.

[3] 'Soumis au "champart" et à la corvée.'

lege of the nobility and of the citizen-soldiers. The bearing of arms, particularly lance and sword, on all solemn occasions of civic life, was the distinguishing feature which, more than any other, marked the separation of classes in Homer's time.

## SLAVE LABOUR: SERVANTS AND SHEPHERDS

The *thetes*, or free wage-labourers, did not constitute the bulk of the rural labour-force in the majority of city-states. The 'servants', that is, the slaves, generally made up the greater part of this. Old Laertes who, though of royal lineage, cultivated only a small domain, had about a dozen slaves in his service, including old Dolius who with his six sons and their mother, a Sicilian, who attended to the house. The servingman (*dmos*) and the female servant (*dmoe*) might be indifferently employed in the house or in the fields. The work of the house was naturally carried out by the women, who ground the corn, sifted the flour, baked the girdle cakes, made the soup, spun, wove, sewed and embroidered, under the supervision of the mistress or, in 'royal' houses, of the stewardess. They ministered, at the same time, to the pleasures of the master. But they also went into the fields; and in the harvest scene on the shield of Achilles we see them preparing the meal for the harvesters.

The men-servants had little to do inside the house beyond what was needed for the care of beasts of burden and draught animals; for the fashioning and upkeep of their tools, the bringing in of the harvest, of litter or bedding for the stables, and the preparation of wine. They were out in the fields by dawn and did not return until the evening. After the last meal of the day they slept in outbuildings constructed round the courtyard. In winter only they were allowed to sleep on the ground in the main hall, for the sake of warmth from the hearth. The master, as in the case of Laertes, sometimes slept among them for the same reason.

The majority of the men-servants did not, however, live on the demesne proper. In Homer's Greece it was less agriculture than stockraising which provided the main source of wealth; as we saw when going into the question of the wealth of the nobility. This held good for all landowners; and in the majority of states, the nucleus of cultivated farms was always surrounded by a spacious area of common lands where every citizen enjoyed the right of pasturing his stock.

The flocks and herds were kept by servingmen who brought in to the master the animals required for slaughter; this might occur either daily, as we read in the *Odyssey*, if there was a large household to provide for; or at intervals, for a more modest one. In return, the manor house or the farm provided flour and wine for the servants; and the latter naturally had no scruples about slaughtering an odd animal or two for their own use; as was the case with Eumaeus when he wished to receive with due honour the guest sent him by the gods; who turned out to be none other than Odysseus, disguised as a beggar and unrecognized by Eumaeus.

The charming and picturesque episode of Odysseus' sojourn in the house of the 'divine swineherd' in Books XIV and XV of the *Odyssey* gives us an inside view of the life of the herdsmen: a class of slaves who yet led beyond the outer margin of the cultivated lands, the almost unfettered existence of nomads.

The permanent shelters to which the stock were brought in at night for milking, for the suckling of the young animals and for protection against wild beasts, were situated in combes or ravines protected from the wind; near a spring or beside a stream, or not far from a larger watercourse, which would supply water for the drinking troughs. Eumaeus' pigsties were built under the shelter of the Raven's Rock, near the fount of Arethusa.[1] The sheepfolds depicted by Hephaestus on the shield of Achilles were situated in a 'pleasant dell', while the byres for the oxen were beside 'a murmuring river, by the shivering reeds'.[2]

These shelters were very rudimentary. The byres, with the straw litter for manure were merely enclosures or pens open to the sky. The ten pigsties watched over by Eumaeus were arranged

[1] *Odyssey*, XIII, 408.
[2] *Iliad*, XVIII, 588 and 576-7, p. 430. The sheepfold of Polyphemus, in Book IX of the *Odyssey*, was in a huge cavern.

round a vast circular enclosure, shut in by a high stone wall. This was topped with large thorns and strengthened on the outside with a line of stakes. Each contained fifty sows with their young. The boars were kept outside; but all were guarded by four dogs nearly as savage as wild beasts.

The shepherds' houses were scarcely more elaborate. They consisted of cabins or frail huts which, according to Hesiod, needed repairing each summer. The house of Eumaeus was a little less modest than the common run, with its porch or vestibule and a larger room containing a hearth. The furniture was of the most rustic kind, comprising a table for cutting up meat, and trusses of thick brushwood to sit on. At nightfall sheep- and goatskins were spread before the fire to serve as bedding, and the shepherd slept on these, wrapped in his cloak.

In the wooded solitude of the mountains the herdsmen and shepherds lived in small groups. Each herd was entrusted to several herdsmen who were under a headman responsible to the owner. In the *Odyssey* we make acquaintance not only with the worthy Eumaeus, the master-swineherd, but also with the wicked Melantheus, master-goatherd, and the faithful Philoetius, master-neatherd, all of them sharing responsibility for the numerous herds and flocks of Odysseus. Eumaeus has under his control four young boys, to whom he has added a personal servant, acquired at his own expense.

The life of these little communities was of the roughest. Often they slept under the stars; for after dark they had to be on their guard against marauding visits from other shepherds near by, who might, with their dogs, attempt to carry off some of the stock.[1] Eumaeus, after making Odysseus comfortable for the night, goes off on the lookout for such a foray, wrapped in his long cape and goatskin and armed with a sword and well-sharpened javelin. The flocks had also to be defended against wild beasts, wolves, panthers and lions. On the shield of Achilles we see a representation of four herdsmen endeavouring, with their dogs, to beat off two lions who have just brought down a bull.

[1] *Odyssey*, XIV, 531.

These were not the only risks. The worst and most to be feared was the danger from warriors in neighbouring states, and from pirates who might have come from afar. For a goodly herd always made fine booty; and the shepherds could also be added. While Odysseus was still a young man, a band of Messenian pirates landed on Ithaca and carried off three hundred sheep with their shepherds.

Finally, to add a note of gloom to the picture, we observe that no women accompanied the shepherds. It may, however, be appropriate to add a further touch, a lighter one, in the bucolic manner. Hesiod tells us that it was as a shepherd that he received his first lessons from the Muses of Helicon.

The herdsmen in Homer are adepts on the flute; and we might conclude from this that songs, music and, notably, flute-playing were already in his time amusements dear to the shepherds, so that the tradition of poetic and musical contests, which Theocritus and Virgil have handed down to us, may perhaps go back to the Homeric age.

The role of shepherds and herdsmen in the economic scheme was first and foremost the supplying of fresh meat to the inhabitants of the cities and the plain. But we must not forget the making of cheese, mainly from goats' and sheeps' milk. We are not likely to overlook the description in the *Odyssey*, given in some detail, of one of these cheese dairies, the one belonging to Polyphemus.

It is in the grotto of the Cyclops. When Odysseus and his companions enter the cavern, they make a rough inventory of its contents: wattle frames or trays on which the cheeses are fermenting and hardening, jugs full of whey, baskets which allow the curd to drip, bowls, and wooden pails into which the animals are milked.

The processes of cheesemaking in Homer's time are fairly well known. The flocks went out to pasture early in the morning, after feeding their young. The latter remained at home to free the ewes from further suckling during the day. At nightfall the flocks returned. The mother ewes with full teats, noisily claimed their young; the latter responded from the folds, and there was a regular uproar.[1] The ewes were then milked before being allowed to return to the folds, but of course not completely. A small part of the milk was set aside for use at meals and the rest was made into cheese.

In the latter process, the milk was curdled as rapidly as possible. The curds were placed in rushen baskets to drip, after which they were kneaded and pressed. The solid portions thus obtained were finally placed on wattle trays, in a protected spot, to complete the processes of fermentation and drying. This method produced a cheese of firm consistency. The more delicate, softer sorts do not seem to have been made by Homer's shepherds.

We may enquire as to the origin of this relatively numerous slave population. Certain of its members, though not the majority, were born on the demesne itself. Dolius, Laertes' old retainer, had seven sons by his wife, a woman from Sicily. Six of these worked for Laertes himself. The seventh had become head goatherd — the faithless Melantheus, who had gone over to the side of the suitors. His sister, Melantho, grew up in the manor house of Odysseus and became a servant there; but she too behaved very badly.

Other servants, principally women, were born of free parents. They had been distinguished by some lord, on account of their beauty, and purchased at a good price; for a father had the right to sell his children. Eurycleia, whose ancestry, as a sign of good birth, is frequently insisted on by Homer, had been bought by Laertes at an enormous figure, no less than twenty oxen. 'He honoured her as much as his wife', we are told; but he never dared make her his concubine, for fear of scenes with his wife Anticleia. She became Odysseus' nurse, and later Telemachus' also; and she finished up as stewardess of the manor.

The most fruitful sources of slave labour were war and piracy.

In war it was the custom to kill the grown men. Few prisoners were taken, save in the case of men of noble birth for whom a heavy ransom might be extracted. Lycaon, a son of Priam, was sold by Achilles for a hundred head of oxen, and his purchaser did extremely well, as Lycaon was ransomed for thrice that amount.

[1] *Iliad*, IV, 433-5.

Doubtless it was felt that prisoners of war would make poor slaves, for, with their skill with weapons, they might prove more danger-ous than useful. On the other hand, when a town was captured, the women and children were usually spared, as they constituted a splendid booty, one that could be easily traded in the already existent slave markets. The isle of Chios early specialized in the traffic of wine and slaves.

A surer way of acquiring slaves was through piracy, which kept the markets well provided. The Phoenician mariners had a solidly based reputation in such dealings. Eumaeus tells Odysseus how some Phoenician merchants who had landed at Syros seized him when a child, aided by a Sidonian slave-woman of his father's. In the northern Aegean the men of Lemnos regularly raided the coast of Thrace for slaves. In the west, the principal traffickers were the Taphians and Teleboeans. No man of spirit would hesi-tate to make a profitable raid, for booty, when he had the chance. Odysseus tells Alcinous without a blush how, when driven by the wind on to the Thracian coast at Ismarus, he had picked up a goodly cargo of women, after sacking the town and killing the warriors, when a counter-attack forced him to take to sea again.

Thus we see that slavery was rooted in deeds of violence. But once he was introduced into his captor's house, the condition of the slave was not too bad. He became part of the family, by a sort of inferior act of adoption, which gave him the rank of associate as much as of subordinate. Young slaves who grew up in a household were well treated. Eumaeus, who had been brought up in Laertes' family, calls Odysseus his 'honoured brother'. He had remained at the manor until he was twenty, when he was sent into the fields, provided with new clothing, tunic, cloak and sandals. When talking to Odysseus, he praises the kindness of Anticleia:

> '... Yet servants greatly long
> To talk before their mistress, and to learn
> Of what goes on, and eat and drink, and then
> To carry off some trifle to the farm,
> Such things as always warm a servant's heart.'[1]

[1] *Odyssey*. XV. Trans. Marris, p. 269.

Melantho, the daughter of Dolius, who was born in the manor house, was spoiled and loaded with gifts by Penelope, but showed no gratitude.

Fidelity and affection were often, however, the reward of good treatment. When Odysseus reveals his identity to Eumaeus and the neatherd Philoetius, they embrace him, kissing his forehead and shoulders. The servingwomen who have remained faithful do likewise, and so do old Dolius and the six sons who worked for Laertes.

It is true that disobedience and disloyalty could be punished without mercy; for the master had power of life and death over his slave. Odysseus, after his victory, has the goatherd Melantheus savagely mutilated, on the spot, and he hangs the twelve serving-women who have flouted the authority of Penelope and the stewardess, and fornicated with the suitors.

Such drastic treatment, however, was only called for in exceptional circumstances, and one needed to be rich and powerful to afford it. A slave was a pretty valuable person; his price on an average was the equivalent of four oxen.

## WORK IN THE FIELDS

We must now try to describe the work in the fields, as it was pursued by the master and his servants.

The Farmer's Year began sixty days after the winter solstice, towards the end of our month of February, when Arcturus, the most brilliant star in Bootes, rises towards midnight — 'at the night's climax', as Hesiod states with precision. This was the right moment for pruning the vines, before the sap has risen. The appropriate day of the month for beginning this task, as indeed for all the others, had to be chosen with care. The fifth was particularly unfavourable, whereas the eighth and the ninth were specially propitious. After pruning the vines, one had to dig or loosen the soil round their roots. The first days of spring, as soon as the soil was soft enough, saw the first ploughing of the fields which had lain fallow for ten months, since the last harvest. This first ploughing was for the purpose of 'breaking up' the earth, as the peasants in southern France continue to say, so as to prevent its drying and completely hardening in the great heat of the coming summer.

The second half of spring, when the Pleiades rise and set approximately with the sun, brought the hay season and the harvest. The hay was mown with the scythe. Barley and wheat were harvested with a sickle, where the land was uneven or difficult. In the open fields on the plain, however, the scythe also was used, as appears from Homer's description of the shield of Achilles. The harvesters laid the swathes in the furrows, and children then gathered them up in their arms and carried them to the binders to be trussed into sheaves. The sheaves of corn, and also the hay, were built into ricks to complete the drying.

Haymaking and harvesting were finished, and the workers then rested awhile. For now the first heats of summer had arrived, when 'men are good for nothing'; and so they reposed in the shade, eating a little meat, and drinking what cooling draughts they could.

The respite was a short one; for the appearance of Sirius in the morning twilight, a month after the summer solstice, gave warning that the grain was now well dried and the time for threshing had arrived. The sheaves were carried to a round threshing-floor of well-beaten and flattened earth, near the house and in a place exposed to the wind. The sheaves were laid out, and the servants beat and trampled them, and turned them about so as to release the grain from the husks. Then they waited for a wind to arise, when they winnowed the threshed corn by raising it as high as possible in huge wooden shovels and letting it fall again. The wind carried off the husks and straw, while the heavier grain fell back to earth.

It remained only to take it into the store-room where it was poured into great jars called *pithoi*, almost as high as a man; these they sank deep in the ground. When full, the jars were carefully sealed with stone or wooden lids. At the same time the straw and hay were brought into the granary; by now, they were well dried by exposure in ricks and secure from any chance of fermentation during the winter.

The end of summer is in sight, and now the grapes are ripe on the vines where they cluster heavily. The vine harvest begins, and it is a veritable festival. Girls and boys pile the grapes into wicker baskets which porters then carry to the house down the path that leads from the vineyard. In the midst of the harvesters a child is singing, accompanying himself on the cithara, while others keep time with cries and dances, leaping[1] merrily along. This was no doubt a survival of old magical rites, designed to favour a successful harvest.

Grape harvest came late for a hot country like Greece: it took place, according to Hesiod, when Orion and Sirius rose in the middle of the night and Arcturus in the morning; that is, about the first half of our month of October. The Greeks required their grapes to be completely mature, and even a little over-ripe, to make the rich wine which they only drank when much diluted.

Hesiod[2] gives a full description of the method of preparing this wine. The grapes which had been gathered were first exposed for six days and nights in a sunny spot, in order to dry out part of the water. They were then crushed and left to ferment for five days only, in a vat in the shade. The sticky liquid that was drawn off had a high sugar and alcohol content, in spite of the short time allowed for fermentation. And the wine was finally decanted into huge jars, sunk into the earth, like those used for the corn; these were well sealed and not opened until the end of the winter.

Meanwhile, immediately after the first autumn rains, the thinning out of the woodlands had begun, and also the second ploughing of the arable lands, during which the soil was loosened and the weeds turned under. The season of seed time, the last great work of the Farmer's Year, was under way.

Before beginning to sow, the ploughman would seize the plough handle, lightly touch the backs of the oxen, and address a prayer to Zeus of the underworld, and to Demeter, that they would swell the grain of the next harvest. Then he sowed the seed and buried it under a third furrow. The ploughman was followed by a slave-child who would prod the clods of earth with a hoe and complete

[1] *Iliad*, XVIII, 565–72.
[2] *Works and Days*, 609–14; *The Shield of Heracles*, 292–301.

the covering of the seeds where the plough had missed them, for the furrows were not very deep. This gave the seed better protection against marauding birds.

Winter was now come; the weather had deteriorated. The Farmer's Year was over.

### THE COMMON FISHERFOLK

Our picture of the lower classes who lived isolated from towns and manor houses would be incomplete if we did not try to describe the life of another class of working people, although indeed neither Homer nor Hesiod considered them of much account.

These were the fishermen. We may appropriately class them with the *thetes*; except that, as they owned their own tackle, boats, nets, lines and harpoons, they probably enjoyed more social and economic independence than their congeners on the land. This did not, however, make them materially any better off.

For Homer fish is a detestable food, while Hesiod does not even deign to mention it. Never is fish eaten at the Homeric repasts. The very sailors who were still recruited from the warrior class and who, even when engaged in commerce, were as much pirates as merchants, despised and disdained fish. It was food for the poverty-stricken.

When the crew of Odysseus' ship is kept for a whole month on the island of the Sun, owing to contrary winds, and not daring to touch the Sun-God's herd of heifers, they first eat up all the ship's provisions, mainly stores of flour. It is only when tortured with hunger that they condescend to use hook and line to catch fishes and sea birds.[1] We have another instance of this happening, when the crews belonging to Menelaus are in the same plight, while becalmed and ashore on the isle of Pharos.[2]

Nevertheless, there were certainly communities of fisherfolk

---

[1] This detail will not seem strange to anyone who, during the war, in the cantonments behind the lines, saw men 'fishing' with hooks for geese, ducks and even poultry of a less aquatic kind.

[2] *Odyssey*, XII, 329-32, and IV, 368-9.

along the coasts of Greece, and Homer does refer, if only incidentally, to their occupation.

Thus we know that men fished with a net, which was no doubt
trailed between two boats working in conjunction. Hook and line
were also used, as by the companions of Odysseus and Menelaus.
For the larger fish, mainly tunny, a harpoon was employed. There
is an indirect reference to this in the episode of the Laestrygonians
in Book X of the *Odyssey*, when the fleet of Odysseus, which has
taken refuge in a deep bay, is attacked by these giant savages: we
see them harpooning the sailors who have fallen into the sea, 'like
fishes'. This method is still used in the Mediterranean: the shoals
of tunny are driven into a deep bay and then harpooned with ease.

The harpoon of Homer's day is actually described in detail in
the last book of the *Iliad*.[1] The shaft was fixed into the end of an
ox-horn, filled with lead. Thus weighted, the harpoon went
swiftly through the water and sank deep into the victim's flesh.

If we have a fair knowledge of the fishermen's gear and equipment, we know very little on the other hand about their actual
way of life. We may simply hazard the guess that they were
humble folk of modest means, who were not to advance very far
until the progress of democracy and the organization of city
markets made possible and widespread the use of fish as food.

[1] *Iliad*, XXIV, 81–2.

# CHAPTER VII

# PUBLIC WORKERS AND CRAFTSMEN

H OMERIC society included a very interesting class of people who occupied a singular position: the *demiourgoi*. At the beginning of the sixth century, which was scarcely a hundred years after our time, they enjoyed a certain legal status in Athens. On the morrow of Damasias' *coup d'état*, some twelve years after Solon had ceased to be archon, it was decided to take the exceptional measure of raising the number of archons to ten; five were to be Eupatridae and three were peasant proprietors, but two seats were reserved for the *demiourgoi*.

It has been concluded, and is still generally admitted, that for the first time in Athens the lowest class of free men, those whom Homer calls *thetes*, and whose conditions of life we have just been examining, had won access to magisterial rank. This confusion arises from transposing into a very remote period of Greek life various notions respecting manual work which are markedly more recent. In Homer's world the *demiourgoi* were not *thetes* but specialists, who from generation to generation carried out genuine social duties, a right which conferred on them, at the dictate of custom, a special rank and status.

### THE NATURE AND FUNCTIONS OF THE *Demiourgos*

The Greek word *demiourgos*[1] is usually translated by 'artisan' or even 'workman', which is certainly incorrect. The real meaning is 'public worker'. And in Homer's vocabulary the word is applied to many categories other than that of the manual workers simply engaged in the manufacture of material objects.

Homer makes Eumaeus speak of the *demiourgoi* whom one

[1] *Demioergos* is the spelling in epic; but the form in ourgos is the more usual (Translator).

brings to one's home, even from abroad, in the passage beginning:

> '. . . Save he be one of those who serve the people,
> A prophet or a healer or a builder,
> Ay, or a holy minstrel who delights
> Mankind with song. . . .'[1]

He elsewhere places heralds in the same class.[2] In other words, the members of this class exercised professions which placed them in the service of the public and, *a fortiori*, in the service of the city and its chief magistrates. Most of the callings Homer cites, and notably that of minstrel, are of an intellectual order; the only manual occupation he mentions in the passage quoted above is that of the builder or carpenter. But there were other manual occupations of which the members evidently belonged to the same class — the blacksmiths, metal-workers, and potters, to name only those who were most numerous and important from the economic point of view. And one might add flute-players, acrobats and cooks, or at least those cooks who as a matter of custom and almost of obligation officiated at public and private ceremonies.

We have already noted the close connection that existed between the intellectual professions, such as those of soothsayer, physician and bard, and the practices of religious ritual. Now the fact that Homer groups the men who exercised these professions with the *demiourgoi* who were manual workers is extremely significant, because it places the social and moral situation, and the way of life, of the latter in an extremely significant light.

We shall better understand their way of life, and the part they played, if we try to reconstruct what these originally were in the oldest Indo-European communities. Thus a rapid glance of what has survived in India, where the old social classes became crystallized into castes, may be of interest in this connection.

Although class distinctions in Homeric Greece were infinitely less clear-cut than caste distinctions in the most ancient Indian

[1] *Odyssey*, XVII, 383–5, p. 307. 'Those who serve the people' is a good rendering of the word (Translator).

[2] *Odyssey*, XIX, 135, p. 337. Penelope speaking (Translator).

communities, the class of the *demiourgoi* approximates at least in part to the Indian caste of the *çudra*, which was the fourth in the social hierarchy. It included blacksmiths, potters, barbers, laundry-workers, town criers and others. In public and private ceremonies, and even in the simple performance of their professional work, all the members of this caste had an hereditary calling or were specially initiated for the performance of certain rituals, which rituals conferred great efficacy on their functions or on the products of their trade. They communicated to these employments or to the articles they fashioned, a peculiar virtue of a mystical and quasi-religious origin. Any Tom, Dick or Harry can beat a drum, but only the public crier, when he plays on the drum, knows how to ward off the devils. Only the potter who has been initiated into his craft knows how to fashion funeral urns, for example. The plates, cups and other household vessels he makes for us possess virtues that protect them from those malevolent beings who are on the watch to damage our stores or spoil our food. In much the same way, the weapons and tools forged in the workshop of a high-caste craftsman are particularly efficacious.

It was not essential for the high-class artisan to do the work himself; he could delegate the task to mere under-workmen; but he presided over and directed their labours, and from time to time added a touch of his own. He was really a master of ceremonies who guaranteed the success of the finished article.[1] The Sanscrit word *karma*, which means 'work' or 'action', applies both to the work of the craftsman and to the rites of religion.

This primitive ritualism in the field of manual work had been considerably attenuated by Homeric times, but fairly definite survivals of it may be noted.

Certain operations in ritual, for example, could be carried out only by professionals. A typical case occurs in Book III of the *Odyssey*, when Nestor is preparing to offer a sacrifice to Athena.

---

[1] Robert Knox, in *An Historical Relation of Ceylon* (London, 1911), records the case of a Singhalese blacksmith who, as late as the seventeenth century, limited his activity to sitting solemnly on a stool and holding the piece of iron while his customer did the work under his direction.

For this purpose he summons the working goldsmith, Laerkes, who is to gild the horns of the cow which Nestor intends to sacrifice. Laerkes arrives with his instruments of bronze: the anvil, hammer and pincers. He beats out the gold provided by Nestor and wraps the gold leaf artistically round the animal's horns. We know, too, from later evidence that there was a very old family in Athens, called the Praxiergidae, which, as we may judge from the name of their ancestor (signifying 'one who performs work'), must originally have been a family of craftsmen, or *demiourgoi*. Each year, at the festival of the Plynteria, this family had the duty and privilege of carrying out repairs to the statue of Athena.

Homer tells us that carpenters and in particular shipwrights work under the inspiration of this goddess. Their knowledge is derived from instruction she has given them.[1] Athena and Hephaestus are the joint instructors of goldsmiths.[2] Whenever an artist gives form to a work of art, Hephaestus is really responsible for it. This, I think, is how one should interpret the passage in Book VII of the *Odyssey* in which we read that Hephaestus has wrought 'by his cunning art' the gold and silver dogs which guard the house of Alcinous.[3] These dogs are ageless and immortal.

In this way all work produced by the *demiourgoi*, with the assistance of the gods, had its share of divine virtue. There is perhaps an unconscious stirring of this distant past in us, when we speak today of a work of art's being immortal and eternally young.

The work of the Homeric *demiourgos*, work accomplished in collaboration with the deity, possesses — like the work of the Indian potter or blacksmith — an active virtue peculiar to itself. Thus Hephaestus, the divine blacksmith, makes tripods that move about spontaneously and go where they ought to go. The golden handmaids[4] he has created to wait on him are conscious beings; they have the power of speech and, by divine grace, are able to perform their duties. This is not a miraculous exception to

---

[1] *Iliad*, V, 60–1 and XV, 411–2.
[2] *Odyssey*, VI, 232–4 and XXIII, 159–61.
[3] *Odyssey*, VII, 91–4.
[4] These were apparently a sort of robot (Translator).

the rule; only, the divine *demiourgos* possesses, as is right and fitting, powers superior to those of his human counterparts. In essence, however, his power is not different from theirs; or, if it is, the difference is one of degree and not of kind. Such is the meaning revealed by the myth.

In many ways, therefore, the *demiourgoi* were initiates. It would seem, as far as we may judge from the slight clues available to us, that this initiation consisted, at least in part, in their entering into ownership of the tools proper to their trade. Now these tools were generally the attributes of the god who protected and assisted the craftsman: the hammer and pincers, for example, in the case of Hephaestus, the set-square and line in the case of Athena Stathmia. The tool of the *demiourgos*, so far from being a passive instrument, had its own virtue and efficiency, and collaborated in the work. The goldsmith Laerkes' tools, Homer tells us in a well-nigh untranslateable expression, are things that 'complete the art', or bring it to perfection.

One is irresistibly reminded here of the curious and minutely detailed description of how Odysseus builds the raft and of how, on this occasion, Calypso helps him to initiate himself into the craft of naval carpenter. One feature is particularly striking. The goddess not only furnishes the felling axe, the double axe and the augers or drills; she brings them to the scene of his labours and 'gives' them to him. We do not at all know how or where she has obtained such tools on her lonely islet, and we cannot but ascribe to her gift of the tools to a man who has become a *demiourgos*, as it were by accident, a symbolical and even a mystical meaning.

### PUBLIC WORKERS AND CRAFTSMEN IN
### THEIR RELATION TO CIVIC LIFE

There was nothing rigid, as we have seen, in the class structure of Homeric society; and it would be virtually impossible to assign, within this structure, a definite place to each group of *demiourgoi*.

Thus certain families which still followed callings classed by Homer among the public professions had long since risen to the highest social position and even to 'royal' rank. This was the case with the Kerukes (or heralds), the Eumolpidae (descendants of Eumolpus, the singer) at Eleusis, and the Praxiergidae at Athens. Machaon and Podalirius, the military doctors at the siege of Troy, fight side by side with the army chiefs and are treated as their equals.

In the Trojan army we find the son of Tecton, the carpenter, fighting among the warriors (and, incidentally, killed by Meriones, the Cretan chief) in an inferior but a still very honourable rank. He had built the ships which Paris took when he went to abduct Helen. The social rank of this family was certainly not inferior to that of the citizen-soldiers, and was apparently much the same.

If we turn now from literary to historical tradition, we find in the early seventh century a certain Orthagoras, the first tyrant of Sicyon, who belonged to one of those families of 'cooks' who assisted in sacrifices. We suspect that even in Sparta, that most aristocratic of the Greek states, certain *demiourgoi* enjoyed a prestige perhaps as great as that accorded to the warriors. We are thinking of the flute-players who set the time for the troops when marching and also in battle. Herodotus[1] tells us that their calling, like those of cooks and heralds, was hereditary.

There were certainly grades among the public workers. One would like to know the rank assigned to those pairs of professional acrobats whom we see turning somersaults which must have been part of the ritual, for example when Menelaus is celebrating the marriages of his son and daughter;[2] or again, among the young men and girls whom Hephaestus depicts as dancing in one of the scenes on the shield of Achilles.[3]

The carpenter and builder, the blacksmith (*chalkeus*) and the potter (*kerameus*) were the most important *demiourgoi* who were manual workers.

There was a blacksmith in every little town or *komé*. The forge where he 'sat' was a meeting place for all the idlers and talkers who came there to exchange news. Hesiod advises the serious and in-

---

[1] Herodotus, VI, 60.

[2] *Odyssey*, IV, 18–9.

[3] *Iliad*, XVIII, 605–6.

dustrious man to pass by without stopping. The simple equipment was the same as that which Hephaestus disposes of in the workshop he has built on Olympus. It consisted of a hearth with bellows, which were merely skins blown up as required; an anvil, and a chest for the tools — the hammer, the short pincers and the long-handled pincers which were used for holding red-hot metal on the anvil. Here the blacksmith wore the dress traditional in his class, namely a sleeveless tunic open on the right side so as to leave exposed his shoulder and half his breast. He carried out the work, or rather organized and directed it, with the help of the customer who had brought the piece of iron or bronze which was to be fashioned, and also with the assistance of the bystanders, or of a slave or of one of his own children who was being instructed in the craft and who would ultimately succeed him. When he had finished, he wiped down his chest and arms with a sponge, as we see Hephaestus doing before he receives Thetis.

The metallurgical industries were not solely in the hands of these widely scattered workmen. The specialized branches of the trade were concentrated in certain quarters of the great cities or in certain small towns. Here the master forge-owners were associated in confraternities, as we may deduce from the collective names which they bore and which often remind us of the patronymics of the aristocratic clans. Thus in ancient Attica, at the foot of Mount Aegaleus where they could obtain supplies of charcoal, three groups of metal-workers, the Eupyridae (sons of the kindly fire), the Cropidae (sons of the sickle) and the Pelekes (men of the helmet) had become associated in a *trikomia*, or community of three villages. Further north, at the foot of Mount Parnes, lived the Aethalidae (sons of soot); and on the banks of the upper Cephisus the Hephaestidae (sons of Hephaestus) side by side with the Daedalidae (sons of Daedalus). The members of each of these confraternities were united by a common cult, into which they had been previously initiated.

Owing to the nature of their craft, the potters and also the manufacturers of tiles, even more than the metal-workers, lived in distinct quarters near to the clay pits. In Athens the potters dwelt in the suburb of the Cerameicus, north-west of the Acropolis, where there was an abundant supply of clay on the banks of the Cephisus. Here were fashioned those lovely funeral vases which have been discovered in the Dipylon cemetery. Another great centre for pottery was at Cape Colias, south of Phalerum, where there were also excellent clay deposits.

All the industries associated with fire were under the patronage of Hephaestus and Athena Ergané.

We may now try to reconstruct the kind of existence that was led by these manual workers, and first of all enquire as to how they were remunerated. The evidence is scanty, but the problem has its importance because, as we have just seen, none of the categories of public workers were tradesmen subsisting on wages for their services or on the sale of their wares. Like the priest, the 'king' or the peasant-soldier, they performed public duties.

When the goldsmith Laerkes is summoned to Nestor's manor to gild the horns of the cow that is to be sacrificed, he comes at the king's order. There is no question of remuneration for him, any more than for the bard Demodocus who is 'summoned' by order of Alcinous to sing at the banquet given to the Phaeacians; or for the bard Phemius whom the suitors compel to amuse them at their games and feasting. It would really seem that these men are called in simply to fulfil a duty for which they are qualified. They are well treated and well fed; perhaps they take some present home with them, but to this no allusion is made; and there is no mention whatever of a wage, or *misthos*.

It appears then that the *demiourgoi* were required to perform certain services at least, just as citizen-soldiers were required to furnish their own gear and equipment. For this purpose a 'lot' of land was assigned to the latter; and one wonders whether, by analogy, the families of *demiourgoi* held a grant of landed property. The thing is likely enough, and the example of India suggests that it was in fact so. The functions of the Indian *çudra*, who corresponded with the Greek public workers, were not always remunerated, but a land grant was attached to them. In seventeenth-century Ceylon, for example, the blacksmith, the potter and the laundryman held a piece of land in return for the services they rendered to the king, to the lord and to his household; and they were paid only for the work they did at the request of private individuals.

The partial glimpses afforded by Homeric poetry into the life of the *demiourgoi* lead one to imagine them as in a similar situation. As public servants, endowed with an hereditary holding, they were required to perform certain services free, for the benefit of the community, that is, of its chiefs; and their only gains were derived from the personal services they were called upon to perform on other grounds; services which, owing to their hereditary calling, they probably could not refuse to render. We must hasten to add that by the Homeric age, these latter represented the greater part of their activity.

In those cases which did not require a fixed installation or very heavy equipment, they carried out the work at their customers' houses. This was the usual practice of the carpenters and sometimes even of the blacksmiths. In the houses they visited they were received as honoured guests and shared in the life of the family. Their customers produced the wood and the ingots of copper, tin, bronze or iron, generally imported from abroad; and when he and the members of his family did not themselves assist in the work, he provided the necessary help. The craftsman was the director and counsellor; above all, he held the key to that science of divine origin which conferred a special efficacy on the work and without which the finished product was dead and useless.

Metal-smiths and potters operated mainly in their own workshops. Those who enjoyed the greatest repute and were in most demand had slaves and paid workers in their employment, workers who, though not numerous, had to be fed and in certain cases remunerated. The employer could provide all this, thanks partly to the produce of the land attached to his function and, for the rest, through the payments he received from his customers. Such payments were generally made in kind because, though money had already been invented, it was as yet scarcely used except for maritime commerce and in dealings between states.

Assistants were particularly needed in the pottery trade. It was they who dug out, sorted and refined the clay; and also saw to the production of charcoal. The master-potter modelled the vases and other vessels, and supervised the firing.

These master-craftsmen rarely worked except to order. We shall see how in the course of time they established an export trade, for example at Aegina (which came to be known as 'the saucepan-dealer'), at Chalcis, Corinth, Athens, Miletus and elsewhere. Some of them were artists who enjoyed wide celebrity. Homer mentions the name of Icmalius, the master ebony-worker who had made the *klisié* or *chaise longue*, incrusted with silver and ivory, on which Penelope reclines. The fame of certain artists spread far beyond the limits of their home country; in such instances they were invited abroad, just as were soothsayers, bards and physicians. Thus the élite of the craftsmen sometimes wandered far and wide over ancient Greece, much as their intellectual compeers who, like them, were protected by their association with a deity.[1] We read in the *Iliad* that Ajax the Locrian sent to Boeotia for Tychius, the master bronze and leather-worker, to make a shield for him. And Thucydides[2] tells us that in the closing years of the eighth century the men of Samos had recourse to Ameinocles, the master ship-wright of Corinth, to build them four war vessels.

### THE BEGINNINGS OF URBAN LIFE

Many and perhaps a majority of these craftsmen lived as part of the scattered rural communities on the plains. Some, as we have seen, were organized in confraternities and established in small towns near to the sources of supply, such as wood or clay. But a fair number, attracted by the custom of great and wealthy families, settled in the cities or in one of the industrial suburbs which were now growing up around them.

This was the beginning of urban life. If therefore we are to imagine the kind of existence that was led by craftsmen and others,

---

[1] Odysseus spares the minstrel Phemius because the latter takes care to remind him that he sings only under divine inspiration.

[2] I, 13.

we must now attempt to indicate what the Homeric town was like.

The town (*astu* or *polis*) was the political and religious capital of the 'city' or state. Here resided the 'kings' in their manors which were built round the manor of the king of the city, or of the magistrate who had replaced him. With the latter, king or magistrate, they met in council, like the twelve doges of the Phaeacians whom Odysseus finds assembled in the *megaron* of Alcinous. Nearby was the agora, or market-place, where the assembly of the people was held, that is, the assembly of those free men who were admitted to its deliberations. Here also rose the temples dedicated to the gods of the city.

Round this nucleus, which was aristocratic, were the working-class quarters. In Scheria, the modern Corcyra, the shops where they manufactured ropes, rigging, sails and oars,[1] stood near the naval dockyards round the two ports. The famous Athenian suburb of the Cerameicus stood on the plain, north-west of the Acropolis.

Some of these towns lay unprotected on the plain. Such was the capital of Ithaca, where the manor of Odysseus gave on to the open country. Such also was the town of Lacedaemon, where Telemachus and Peisistratus on their arrival found direct access to Menelaus' palace.

Most of the towns, however, had inherited the sites of ancient Achaean fortresses of the Mycenaean age, and were built round a fortified knoll which served as citadel and place of refuge. When space was sufficient the knoll was occupied by the great temples and royal manors. This is the impression Homer gives us of Troy and Pylos; and excavations have revealed the same general arrangement at Athens, Argos, Thebes and Orchomenus.

More rarely still we find a whole town including the residential district and the industrial suburbs surrounded by walls. Ilium, which had a citadel crowned with Priam's palace, was protected with a continous wall. The town of the Phaeacians was likewise guarded by a wide and lofty rampart topped by a palisade. This

---

[1] *Odyssey*, VI, 263–9.

was an obvious precaution, as both were exposed to sudden attack from the sea. The same need for security was to lead the Milesians, during the second third of the seventh century, to surround their town with a strong and continuous wall, twelve yards high and four yards thick, with towers at the angles and well-defended gates.

All these towns had a common feature: they covered an area very limited in respect of a relatively large population. This was a feature which all Greek towns were to retain throughout their long history. In the aristocratic quarters, the manorial buildings occupied a good deal of room, as Homer indicates; but, as if to compensate for such extravagance, the working-class districts were full of buildings crowded along narrow and tortuous alleys, where the visitor had to undergo the distrustful inspection of a population ill disposed to welcome strangers. That is why Odysseus, when wishing to find his way to the palace of Alcinous, needs a guide; and his guide is no other than Athena disguised as a little girl, who advises him as follows:

> '. . . I will lead —
> And look upon no man, nor question any;
> For these folk do not gladly suffer strangers,
> Nor welcome kindly comers from abroad.'[1]

If we wish to picture to ourselves the dwellings of this population, the absence of written or archaeological evidence leads us to suppose that they were like the houses of Greek artisans some two centuries later, lightly constructed of unbaked brick and wood. The floor might be paved or might simply consist of beaten earth; while the roofs were made of thatch or wattle. There would be three of four small rooms of a few square yards each. Behind the house was a little yard or garden, where the cooking was done in the open, and where there was a shed for wood and coal. The house had doors but no windows.

This was indeed a humble, possibly very humble sort of home; but one should not exaggerate its meanness. The public workers

---

[1] *Odyssey*, VII, p. 113.

and the craftsmen, when not working in the dockyards or work-shops, or jobbing, lived out of doors, gossiping in little squares or in the agora. They went indoors mainly to eat and sleep. Their only luxuries and comforts were the blue skies, the sun, the lovely weather and the clear air.

Let us now consider these folk at work.

### INDUSTRIAL WORK

Most of the work we now call industrial was still carried out in the home. Here the mistress and her servants spun the wool and flax, wove the cloth and made the garments. Eumaeus cut out and fashioned his own sandals. Hesiod tells us how, for the winter season, one should make oneself boots of ox-hide, well-fitted to the foot, tied by straps and fitted inside with felt. He advises men as to a method of fabricating a closely woven cloth, somewhat like felt, for a cloak to protect them against the cold; they are to do it themselves. Leather garments and sheepskins were also prepared in the house, the skins being steeped in oil before being stretched by hand.

All the gear and equipment for working purposes were likewise of home manufacture, from the spade to the farm cart or waggon. The latter, says Hesiod, comprised a hundred different pieces; these should be prepared and carefully assembled before one began to put them together.

The same system applied to ordinary furniture, such as tables, chairs and beds; only the manufacture of ceremonial chairs was in the hands of specialized craftsmen. Odysseus, be it noted, made his own bridal bed; better still, he built the walls of the bridal chamber, roofed it, made the door with its wooden panels and set it in place. All the less solid kinds of house, Eumaeus' cottage for example, were of domestic construction; and it was only the great assembly rooms or ceremonial chambers, like the *megaron* with its four columns, its raised terrace and lantern, that required the service of professional carpenters. Paris employed men of this kind to assist him in building his own house, beside the palace of Priam.

The manufacture of household utensils in metal was the business of the professional metal-workers. The most popular and important were called 'tripods'; they were really hemispherical cauldrons mounted on three legs. They could be set above the fire, and they also served to carry boiled meats from the kitchen to the dining-room. They were provided with handles; but the tripods that Hephaestus made for his fellow Olympians also had castors, naturally made of gold. Some of them were of splendid appearance, like the one that Achilles gave as a prize for the chariot race and which held twenty-two measures, which probably made about seventeen gallons.

The metal-workers also made every kind of vat and cauldron, funeral urns, kitchen jars and drinking cups. These were mostly of bronze or copper, but sometimes, especially in the case of drinking vessels, they were made of precious metal and highly wrought with decorative designs. Nestor's cup, which had two (if not four) handles and was adorned with doves, was the reproduction of a very old Mycenaean design.

There was no dividing line between the crafts of blacksmith and goldsmith. At Pylos, Laerkes is described indifferently by both appellations, *chalkeus* and *chrysochous*. Craftsmen of the same confraternity manufactured cauldrons as well as jewels, collars, necklets, bracelets, ornate pins, pendants, breast ornaments and diadems.

It was these artists and decorators who adorned the *megaron* of Alcinous' manor with plates of bronze, with a frieze of blue enamel along the upper margins. They lined the threshold with bronze, covered the side supports and the lintel of the door with silver-plating and the door itself with a sheet of gold. They also knew how to carve wood in the form of statues which were then covered with sheets of gold or silver; as witness the wonderful dogs that guarded the doorway of Alcinous and the golden torch-bearers who adorned his *megaron*; witness also the statue of Zeus plated with gold, which Cypselus, tyrant of Corinth, dedicated to the god towards 650 B.C., and which Strabo saw at Olympia seven hundred years later.

Most gifted of all were the experts with hammer and chisel, like those who made the famous coffer for Cypselus and the great shrine dedicated by Myron of Sicyon, after he had won the horse race at Olympia in 648. The melting down and shaping of bronze, the fitting, soldering or riveting of the separate pieces, had no secrets for such men, as the bronze industry had at that time been established for more than a millenium.

It was in the manufacture of armour and weapons, according to Homer, that the bronze-worker displayed his greatest mastery. The art of the armourer was complex and difficult, combining as it did the crafts of leather- and metal-workers. Thus a shield comprised several layers, of which the outer and inner only were of metal, the others being of leather. Achilles' buckler had five layers, while Agamemnon's breastplate contained forty-two metal bands which were probably riveted on to a core of solid leather. The helmet was certainly lined with leather, and to this were attached the neckguard and cheekpieces; the greaves also must have been so lined. The armour worn by chieftains, and especially the shields, were usually adorned with carved figures and also painted or gilded.

Hence the armourers were always specialists. There was a confraternity of helmet-makers in Attica. Especially sought after were the swords forged in the workshops of Chalcis, the breastplates and high-crested helmets of Corinth, and the shields made in Boeotia.

Bronze reigns supreme on Homer's battlefields. Nevertheless the metalsmiths had been acquainted with the use of iron for many centuries past; and excavations have revealed the fact that good iron swords had been in use since the eighth century. But bronze remained the noble metal, at least in Homer's eyes; and, although the art of tempering had been discovered, it appears that weapons of forged iron had not yet acquired the hardness, lightness and resistance to shock which were qualities of the bronze. While the supply of iron was comparatively abundant, the metal was scarcely employed as yet except for spades, axes, ploughshares and so on. The soldering of iron was only to be invented, or perhaps imported, by Glaucus of Chios at the end of the seventh century.

We know little of the technique of these crafts save from descriptions of the finished articles. The art of pottery is on the other hand more familiar to us, owing to the realistic pictures of the successive stages of manufacture which we find on the earthenware votive plaques which Corinthian potters used to hang in the temples of their quarter in order to conciliate hostile demons: these were Syntrips the breaker, Smaragus who shattered or cracked the pots, and Asbetus who coated them with soot.[1]

In the trench of the clay field which was about two yards deep we see one man attacking the wall with a pickaxe, another gathering the lumps of clay in a two-handled basket; while a third hoists them in his hands to a fourth who, leaning over the edge of the trench, brings them to the surface of the ground. The work is hard and makes the men thirsty, so an amphora is suspended over the trench high enough to catch the breeze which keeps the wine cool.

When the clay has been brought to the workshop, sifted, washed and kneaded, the master-potter takes it in hand. We see him seated in front of the wheel, which he manoeuvres with one foot, while he shapes the clay with his hand and scraper. Common household ware would simply be dried and hardened in the sun; the more valuable pieces would go into the oven.

This was a circular structure, some four and a half feet in diameter at the base, and it had to be partly rebuilt after each firing, as the upper part was destroyed in the process. The lower part was shaped like a tunnel, long enough to ensure a suitable draught; here the charcoal was set alight. The clay vessels were placed in the oven. The upper part of the structure was conical, terminating in a chimney, and this was rebuilt each time. In the wall of the oven there was a hole which could be closed or opened so as to allow the potter to observe the progress of the firing.

When this was complete there still remained the most delicate, or at least the most hazardous manoeuvre, because a clumsy move-

[1] These plaques belong to a later period than the one we are describing; but the technique they reveal was very ancient.

ment might ruin everything. To demolish the upper part of the oven, a workman, perched on a short ladder, attacked it with a sort of hook, detaching the fragments one by one, and drawing them outwards. Once the oven was laid bare, one had only to wait for the pots to grow cold.

The pottery was extremely varied and we shall not attempt to describe all the types of vessel. Some were immense. The great jars, or *pithoi*, designed to conserve wine, oil, barley and wheat, were buried, as we have seen, in the storehouses. They were large enough to hold a man. Large, too, were the funeral urns that have been found in the Dipylon cemetery. These were set above the tombs of the nobility; and as they were pierced at the base, they served to transmit libations and other offerings to the dead.

If less imposing than these, the two-handled amphorae, which usually tapered upwards, were still of respectable dimensions. They held some five gallons each, and were indispensable in the maritime trade for the transport of oil and wine. Mention may also be made of the large craters, with handles, which were used for mixing the wine and water at meal-times; the broad-bellied pitchers with three handles, two horizontal ones on the sides and one vertical handle near the neck, which were used for drawing water; the long-necked *oenochoae* which had a spout and a long vertical handle and were used to fill the wine-cups. Nor should we forget the little vases for perfume, the circular jars for toilet oil, and the *lecythae*.

These various types of vessel bear witness to a traditional gift for adaptation and even for elegance. They were frequently the work of artists who shared with the professional metal-workers a taste for decoration. Many vases, like the great funeral urns of the Dipylon cemetery, were adorned with paintings. This was the famous black-figure work; the paint was laid directly on the polished clay which often preserved its natural tint, although after a time the potters learned to colour it with oxides.

For many years and until the end of the eighth century this remained a very stylized kind of art. The style is known as geometric; the same *motifs* recurring continually, waving and twisting lines, swastikas, but sometimes also men or horses, and even such scenes as a funeral procession. The persons or objects are little more than very formal silhouettes, juxtaposed or even superimposed one over the other, without any care for perspective. The busts are represented by triangles, the thighs by inverted cones, and the legs by lengthened lozenges. Cubism does not date from the twentieth century. The total effect often reveals a fairly sound feeling for composition and decorative balance.

The end of the eighth century, however, brought an abrupt change in taste and fashion. Sargon's occupation of Cyprus opened the way for the traders of the Phoenician cities which were now vassals of the Assyrian king; and the result was a sudden irruption into vase-painting of *motifs* borrowed from Phoenician cloths and embroideries. These were painted in parallel bands on the vases: honeysuckle ornaments, twisted cords, lotus flowers, sphinxes and even ibex, the animals being flanked with floral designs. The geometric style now gave place to a style of oriental inspiration, which very soon crossed from Ionia to continental Greece, where the Corinthian potters eagerly took it up.

But this change was only one sign of a deeper transformation which was very rapidly to modify, and in certain districts almost ruin, the living conditions of the craftsmen we have been studying — men who were at once artisans, artists, public officials and agents of the deity — and whose existence was so curious and original.

## THE *Demiourgoi* IN CONFLICT WITH ARISTOCRATIC CAPITALISM

This great change arose out of the rapid development, which began in the mid-eighth century, of Greek maritime trade and colonization along the shores of the Mediterranean; and in the first instance it affected the corporation of builders and carpenters.

These men, excepting only the makers of artistic furniture, like Icmalius of Ithaca, were never really independent tradesmen, like the artisans of the forge or the pottery works. Employed mainly in the erection of private houses, public buildings and temples, they seem to have worked only under the authority of their customers who supplied the necessary materials and labour; they themselves did little more than direct the labours of others. But now, in most of the city states, these occupations were becoming more and more of secondary consideration. The master-carpenter was mainly, in the future, to be a shipbuilder.

Now the construction and possession of a ship were privileges of wealth and aristocracy which, in Homer's time, were identified one with the other.

Only the rich aristocrats were in a position to recruit from among their domestics and clients the teams of woodmen and labourers who went into the state forests to fell, prepare and transport the timber, which had then to be left to dry for at least a year in the woodyards. Book XXIII of the *Iliad* contains a picturesque description of one of these teams of woodcutters and their mules, who had gone to the slopes of Mount Ida to procure wood for the gigantic pyre on which the body of Patroclus was to be cremated.[1] Sometimes it would be necessary to fit out an expedition to a distant and still wooded region, to procure the necessary kinds of timber, such as alder, spruce and poplar;[2] after which the master-builder had to be supplied with the workmen and assistants who were indispensable.

The trade however was governed by political as well as material exigencies. Ships, in the Homeric state, belonged to the man who had had them built, but they were not his exclusively private property. Every owner of a ship was required, on a decision of the popular assembly, to put it at the disposal of the state. He was then supplied with a crew, of which he took command. The ship-owner had therefore, by virtue of his situation, the rank of a chief and a magistrate; and he could not but be a member of the aristocracy. These were the principles that governed the very ancient Athenian institution of the *naucrariae*, an organization certainly not peculiar to Athens.

It existed among the Phaeacians and in Homer's Ithaca. This

[1] *Iliad*, XXIII, 110–26.
[2] *Odyssey*, V, 239.

was why Telemachus, when he has decided to start for Pylos, is obliged to ask the popular assembly to supply him with a ship and twenty seamen. It is true that he circumvents their refusal; but he is only able to do so because of the exceptional assistance of Athena who borrows a vessel for him from the shipowner Noemon and herself recruits a crew of volunteers. But one should note that Noemon has to apologize to the suitors by explaining that he could not have rejected the request of so great a nobleman.[1]

What is certain, in any case, is that the capacity to own and equip a vessel was in general reserved to men of the highest social rank. In the maritime cities which were entering on an era of great commercial expansion, the time had now come when this class was forming a privileged aristocracy of shipowners and organizers of naval shipyards.

A consequence of this was that the ancient corporation of carpenters, once so highly honoured, was sinking progressively to the level of employees of the rising capitalists.

A similar evolution can be traced in the metallurgical industries and in the manufacture of ceramics, but it took a rather different form. The two ancient corporations were not in these instances absorbed by the new capitalism; but they had now to face the rapidly increasing competition of large and powerful enterprises engaged in mass production. The reasons for this change were commercial.

For the making of bronze the supply of raw materials was growing more and more precarious in proportion to an increasing demand. In the local copper mines, for example in Eubaea, the veins of ore were nearly worked out; and practically all the copper needed was henceforth to be imported from Cyprus, Thrace and Chalcidia. Tin had always been imported. In the tenth and ninth centuries it had come by land across Asia Minor. but the consumption of this metal was increasing. Tin was no longer employed solely as an alloy for making bronze,[2] but also for purposes of decoration. It could no longer be passively waited for; one had to

---

[1] *Odyssey*, II, 212 and IV, 649–51.

[2] The proportion of tin in Greek bronze varied from 10 to 15 per cent.

anticipate competition and go by sea, far away, to the sources of supply.

As early as the first half of the eighth century sea convoys were organized for this purpose. Some sailed for the Caucasus by way of the Hellespont, the Bosporus and the Black Sea; others went by the straits of Messina — or the routes across Southern Italy — to Etruria. We have tried elsewhere to show how the organization of these sea routes was connected with the birth of Homeric poetry.[1] The main fact to be noted here is that the supplying of raw material for the bronze trade and, incidentally, the bronze industry itself, were now become directly dependent on the shipowners of the great maritime cities.

This commercial aristocracy was at the same time growing into an industrial aristocracy. It was establishing mass production in comparatively large factories operated by slave labour; and it was engaged also in the slave trade. A large part of the production was now exported far overseas, to the new colonies and even as far as Egypt, where the first Pharaohs of the twenty-sixth dynasty were struggling against Assyrian domination with the help of mercenary troops armed and equipped in the Greek manner.

The same revolution was taking place in the pottery trade. The export of wine and oil was being organized side by side with the export of armour and other metal articles. Now this demanded a huge supply of amphorae which had to be manufactured on a large scale in workshops which only the wealthy shipowners were in a position to establish. These workshops quickly devoted themselves to the mass production of pottery for export, and the trade spread to all the markets in the Mediterranean region, from Egypt to Etruria.

We may note, by the way, that the household industry in textiles was beginning likewise to evolve in the same direction. Workshops for spinning and weaving were founded inside the manors of the aristocracy. Thus in Priam's palace we find old Hecuba managing a shop for embroidered veils where the work is

[1] *Les Poèmes homériques et l'Histoire grecque*, Vol. I, *Homère de Chios et les Routes de l'Etain.*

in the hands of a party of Sidonian slaves that Paris brought from Phoenicia.[1]

In any event, in the social and economic life of the country, the old corporations of the *demiourgoi* of the forge and the pottery works were now more and more relegated to the background. And it is no matter for surprise that towards the middle of the seventh century they ended by revolting in support of the new tyrannies of a democratic complexion whose rise had been provoked by the exorbitant power of the wealthy aristocrats. Thus in Corinth, Cypselus and his successors were to forbid the further import of slaves in order to protect the small artisans against the competition of the capitalists.

But this will bring us to the end of the Homeric age. The economic and social revolution which was to give birth to an urban and democratic society was already under way.

[1] *Iliad*, VI, 289–92.

# CHAPTER VIII

## BLOOD VENGEANCE AND THE FAMILY

IT may surprise the reader to find in a book devoted to the routine of daily life, a chapter on the repression of crimes and delinquencies. But in Homer's world the motive force behind such repressions was not, as it is in our modern communities, a matter of civic necessity, that is, of the maintenance of public order, but a private obligation; and in the most serious case, which was that of murder, an absolute and unavoidable obligation of the conscience, the duty of vengeance for blood.

One school of historians goes even further: it maintains, with regard to the earliest Greek periods, that at first affairs of justice were in principle entirely private; and that when the 'city' came to intervene more and more in such matters, this was at a relatively late period.

We have encountered this school incidentally, when speaking of the aristocratic structure of Homeric society. In the opinion of these historians the *genos*, that is, the great aristocratic clan in which property and power were transmitted in the direct line of male descent, was the social cell of the most ancient city states of the Hellenes. They regard this 'city' as a simple aggregation of patriarchal clans, a federation of *gené*, more or less loosely connected and more or less extensive. Within each clan, all the members were closely bound together in face of the other clans, and even of the city; and any injury to one member was an injury to all.

In the 'city' as thus conceived there was, almost by definition, no such thing as State Justice. Any crimes or misdemeanours committed inside the clan could only be judged by the clan; they depended on the authority of its chief, and he, assisted by the other members of the family group, judged them according to traditional forms. As to any outrage committed by a member of another clan, this automatically provoked the collective vengeance of one family upon another; such vengeance being an indefeasible duty, based on the solidarity of the family and involving a war which could only be terminated by a negotiated transaction or compromise, a genuine peace-treaty. The nascent authority of the 'city' could only intervene in a subordinate or accessory capacity — for example, to regulate any dispute that might arise regarding the execution of the agreement, or to guarantee its execution.[1]

But a number of objections are raised by this simplified and generalized conception of the oldest institutions of the Greek world, in their political, social and juridical aspects.

In the first place, as will have appeared from our previous analysis, this view clashes with the fact that the aristocratic clans did not at all constitute the whole civic community, but only one of its elements, existing side by side with the hereditary groups of military peasants, of public workers (or *demiourgoi*) intellectual and manual, and even of simple labourers. Family solidarity, if it existed, cannot therefore be presented as a simple consequence of the peculiar structure of the clans.

The most serious objection does not however lie here, at least from the point of view that interests us.

If we examine the facts without prejudice, and apart from any preconceived notions, it will indeed appear that blood vengeance — that most characteristic manifestation of justice in the Homeric world and, as we have already described it, the prime motive force behind justice — was by no means in its principle an expression of that family solidarity which is alleged to have underlain the collective action of the clan in matters of justice. Furthermore, as we shall see, the exigencies of blood vengeance might even work against that solidarity and quite disrupt it.

But, if they were not dictated by a sort of spontaneous reaction or alleged 'vital instinct' of the *genos*, the imperative obligations of

---

[1] This view of the matter has been argued with much force, and very systematically, by G. Glotz in *La Solidarité de la Famille dans le Droit criminel en Grèce*. Paris, 1904.

blood vengeance did not spring, either, from any duties imposed by the 'city'; they were indeed far superior to any such civic duties. These obligations were not in fact of a civic kind, but of a moral and private character. And that is why civic justice, even when it came to direct, control or canalize them, still remained in their service. It was only later that it was to be substituted for them. In the Homeric world, penal repressions might bring civic institutions into play; but the initiative for action was still private.

What then exactly was this obligation of blood vengeance, almost transcendent in character, a something which guided, impelled and even governed the regulations and the administration of justice? And since historians have interpreted it as an expression of family solidarity, let us at the same time enquire into its true relations with the family organization.

## BLOOD VENGEANCE WITHIN THE FAMILY ORGANIZATION

Blood vengeance was an absolute duty, because it was not a matter of social constraint, but an exigency of the victim, an unconditional claim on the part of the dead.

This was an expression of very, very ancient beliefs regarding the relations between the dead and the living. In common opinion, and therefore the most imperious — an opinion deeply rooted in the most distant past — there were very close bonds of a social, religious and even juridical character which continued to connect the souls of the dead with the world of the living, and more particularly with all those who had been united to them by ties of family, marriage or confraternity during their lifetime. Although in the underworld, in the House of Hades, the dead man led an attenuated sort of life, he still remained a redoubtable force, a powerful being — powerful to do harm — and he preserved rights over his relatives and allies, he was entitled to their trust, and he was in a position to force them to discharge their duties. Against those defaulters who might hesitate to avenge him, the haunting spectre would unleash the Erinyes, those 'enraged she-dogs' whom Aeschylus was to picture and who had been, originally, no other than the souls of the dead changed into vampires.

For the most tenacious of all the feelings of the dead was impatience over an outrage that had been suffered, and the need for reparation and vengeance. 'Blood is drunk up by the nourishing earth', says Aeschylus in the *Choephoroe*; 'but murder is ineffaceable and cries for vengeance.'

The power of a dead man was so formidable, his desire for reprisals so certain, that the murderer, whenever he could, tried at least to escape his direct intervention so as to have to answer only to his living avengers. He would therefore strive to render him powerless by mutilating his corpse. He would cut off the latter's extremities, the feet, hands, ears and nose, pass a cord through them and fasten the whole to the victim's neck by attaching the cord under the armpits. Deprived, in this way, of his sensory organs and means of movement, the victim was rendered inoffensive.

It is true that this rough and primitive way of seeing, feeling and acting, appears to be considerably toned down in certain passages of the Homeric poems. In Book XXIII of the *Iliad* and in Book XI of the *Odyssey*, it is pretty clearly insinuated that the souls of the dead, or at least of those who have been cremated, once they have been admitted to the House of Hades, finally and definitely depart from the world of the living, and that the latter has nothing further to fear from them.[1] But it seems most likely that this was just the personal opinion of a literary man, a fervent believer in cremation; in brief, of the man we have elsewhere called the second Homer, who was writing towards the middle of the seventh century. It could, in any event, only be a question of an eclipse of the popular and traditional belief, even if we admit that there was any such eclipse; because throughout the great Aeschylean Trilogy, from the *Agamemnon* to the *Eumenides*, we find this belief expressed more vividly, and even more brutally than ever. It had not ceased, even at that date, to govern men's conduct.

It commanded vengeance as an absolute duty, so absolute that

[1] On this point, cf. Chapter I of Erwin Rohde's *Psyché*, French translation. Payot, 1928.

this duty applied even within the family circle. But it also raised problems which were by no means always simple.

The Homeric family enjoyed, as a matter of tradition, an autonomy which conferred rights of internal jurisdiction on its members, and this was true both of the great patriarchal entities represented by the noble clans, and of the certainly simpler family organizations in which free men were grouped outside the *gené*.

When the infraction which had to be punished, or rather avenged, inflicted no injury on the structure of the group, there was no difficulty, and the procedure was simple. The head of the family called together all male members of the group. They feasted and palavered for several days, as the ritual required. Finally, agreement was reached, and it had to be unanimous. If the fault was recognized as obvious, or judged to be a fault, then the guilty man was condemned to expulsion, and his judges drove him out amid cries of 'Strike, hurl the spear', as though they desired his death. In reality they limited themselves to ejecting him from the family and, by the same token, from the city. By this semblance of execution, vengeance was held to be satisfied; and at the same time the absence of bloody reprisals obviated any future vengeance on the part, for example, of a child who might be still a minor, or any other interested party, such as a relative by marriage, or a companion.

Records of such sanctions are not lacking, at any rate in the epic and legendary tradition which furnishes evidence of what must have been the current practice. Thus, Peleus and Telamon are driven from Aegina by their father Aeachus in consequence of the murder of Phocus, their brother. In the same way Atreus and Thyestes are banished from Pisa by Pelops for having treacherously slain their half-brother Chrysippus. Vengeance within the family operated also in the case of accidental murder or, as we should say, manslaughter: thus Bellerophon had to flee after involuntarily killing one of his brothers. Vengeance also operated against the suicide, regarded as both victim and murderer. As murderer, his body was rejected, and buried without honours on the confines of the territory; as a victim who might turn against his family, his hand was sometimes cut off — at Athens for example — in order to paralyse his shade.

These were cases of quite uncomplicated drama; but there were others which involved, or imperilled, the very structure of the family. Consider a case in which, whether from unconcern or partiality, the head of the family neglected to set in motion the procedure for blood vengeance. It was then for another member of the family, whom his rank and degree of relationship appointed for the task, to substitute himself for the defaulter and to rise up against him. Thus when Oeneus refuses to punish his son Tydeus after the latter has, in his father's defence, killed his cousins, Oeneus' younger brother intervenes and forces Tydeus and his father to go into exile.

The head of the family might himself be the guilty man. Periander, tyrant of Corinth, killed his wife Melissa. His son, Lycophron, learned of the crime; and from that day he refused to speak a word to his father. Nothing would move him from this resolve, neither threats, nor prayers, nor exile on Corcyra. In the end it was Periander who gave way and offered himself to go to Corcyra and take his son's place there; and Melissa would have been avenged in this way, if the Corcyreans had not assassinated Lycophron in order to avoid having to receive Periander among them.

The situation which was most serious and tragic arose when, within the same *genos*, two branches of the same family, the elder and the younger, rose up one against the other in a pitiless desire for vengeance. So, in the race of the Pelopidae, we see Atreus and his descendants facing Thyestes and his descendants: Agamemnon, Aegisthus and finally Orestes, who acquires 'immense glory' by slaying his mother Clytemnestra, and Aegisthus, in order to avenge his father Agamemnon.[1]

The imperative demand for vengeance, which has been inter-

---

[1] We have tried to show (cf. *Les Poèmes homériques et l'Histoire grecque*, Vol. II, Ch. 6) how the tragedy of the Pelopidae may be interpreted as a myth concerning a disputed succession. However, even if this interpretation be accepted, it would still be true that the story unfolds and develops within the juridical framework of blood vengeance.

preted as the fundamental expression of clan-solidarity, might thus lead to the denial and destruction of the whole family organization. It could assume within the family itself a peculiarly dramatic character by starting an endless chain of murders and reprisals — endless, at least, as long as there remained a son or nephew capable of avenging an uncle or a father. Nothing could stop this, short of the extinction of the race; because, on account of the judicial autonomy of the family in respect of its own members, no social organ from outside was able to intervene in order to arrest the rain of blood. It was a very moving moral problem. Aeschylus was to treat of it as late as the fifth century, when he tried to solve it in the *Eumenides* by invoking the intervention of civic justice, a justice both human and divine, in order to put an end to the inexorable demands of the ancient Erinyes.

The fact is that the solidarity of the family was brought into play by blood vengeance only when the latter was exercised between two families. In this case again it was still the duty to exact vengeance, a private duty of the conscience, which set in motion the machinery of repression but without the need for public intervention. What is simply harder to understand is how, as soon as a vendetta between two families[1] risked imperilling civic peace within the 'city' — how, in these circumstances, the civic powers could, as has also been maintained, remain aloof from a conflict which might well raise, one against the other, two groups of armed citizens animated by such violent elemental and collective emotions. And this leads us to wonder whether, in such cases, vengeance was not restricted within narrower limits than when it operated in the framework of a single family.

### VENDETTA BETWEEN FAMILIES

However imperative the duty of vengeance may have been, it would be a mistake to imagine that it automatically let loose the whole family of the victim on the murderer's family, like a pack of hounds on a number of marauding animals.

The duty indeed rested on all members of the family, but not

[1] 'La vengeance de famille à famille.'

with the same urgency. It affected the different circles of relatives in succession, if one may so put it; it unloosed them one after the other against the offender, in the event of powerlessness or default on the part of the nearer kinsfolk.

The first wave of avengers, the only one which was called upon to act in the vast majority of cases, consisted of the male members of the family who lived under the same roof, or, in other words, those who were more closely related than cousins. Thus the duty of vengeance was incumbent, in the first instance, on the father and brothers. Eupeithes, whose son Antinous has been slain by Odysseus, cries out before the Ithacan assembly:

> '. . . for 'twill be
> A stain for even men unborn to hear of,
> If we do not take vengeance upon those
> Who slew our sons and brothers. . . .'[1]

The son naturally has the same obligations regarding his father as the father regarding his son:

> 'So good a thing it is that of the dead
> There should be left a son. . . .'[2]

says old Nestor. To this the verses of Stasinus in the *Cyprian Songs* afford a sinister echo:

> A fool that man who, having killed the sire,
> Should spare the children.

It was this limited group of near relatives who had, in the first instance, to take up the cause of the dead. The head of the family pledged himself by thrusting a spear into the tomb of the dead man who was thus armed for, and associated with, vengeance; after which he repaired to the agora and solemnly proclaimed an interdict on the supposed author of the crime. This was the *prorresis*, and it was a real declaration of war. Draco's Laws, which were enacted in Athens in the second half of the seventh century and which, in most cases, merely codified ancient custom, reserved *prorresis* to the father, the brother and the son.

[1] *Odyssey*, XXIV, 433–5, p. 433.
[2] *Odyssey*, III, 196–7, p. 41.

At the same time it was foreseen by Draco that this privileged group might, in certain instances, be assisted by other and more distant relatives who had the right, even the duty, of taking part in the prosecution of the affair. These were, first, the cousins on the male side and those on the female; because, in the matter of vengeance, there was no distinction between the *agnati* and the *cognati*. Next came such more distant kinsfolk as sons-in-law, fathers-in-law and brothers-in-law; and lastly the 'companions', *etai, phrateres*, who were linked to the dead man by the bonds of companionship. When the soothsayer Theoclymenus seeks refuge with Telemachus, he explains that, in consequence of a murder, he has had to flee from Argos in order to escape from the brothers and 'companions' of his victim.[1]

We may now enquire as to what happened when the dead man had no father, son or brother — none of those near relatives who had a clear right to pursue vengeance. In default of such, the cousins might intervene, but only after they had first established their relationship, that is, their right to exact vengeance, by a public oath.

We find an example of the dramatic ceremony of the *prorresis* in the last book of the *Odyssey*. Eupeithes, whose son has been the first of the suitors to die in the massacre, has summoned the people of Ithaca to the market-place. He gets up, utters his accusation and recalls the misdeeds of Odysseus: this man has lost all the companions he took with him to Troy, and on his return he has massacred the élite of the place — 'the very pick of Cephallenia'. Eupeithes calls on their kinsfolk to take vengeance. Let us move now, he cries,

> '. . . before this fellow gets away
> Quickly to Pylos, or to holy Elis. . . .'[2]

He knows that when the criminal has crossed the frontiers of the state, the avengers lose any right over him.

One must insist on this quite remarkable feature of the pro-

---

[1] *Odyssey*, XV, 272–6.
[2] *Odyssey*, XXIV, p. 433.

cedure in blood vengeance, that, whereas a crime involved the whole family of the dead man on his behalf, in a manner that apart from a few precautions was virtually automatic, the same solidarity did not necessarily involve the culprit's family or make it responsible for the fault of one of its members. Apart of course from an act of complicity, which was the case with Telemachus and Odysseus' servants who assisted in the execution of the suitors, no collective responsibility rested on the family of a criminal. This comes out clearly from what Odysseus says to Athena — whom he has not recognized — when, on his awakening in the isle of Ithaca, the goddess appears before him. He introduces himself as a Cretan who has been obliged to flee his native land after assassinating Orsilochus, son of king Idomeneus, in an ambush. Now he states specifically, but without the least disquiet, that he has left his family and children in Crete, in possession of considerable wealth.[1]

The collective or partial responsibility of the family of a guilty man was only involved in perfectly specific cases; as when, for example, the guilty man was the head of a family and refused to go into exile. In such an instance the family would rise up against its head and compel him to take flight. This is what happened to Tlepolemus, the murderer of Licymnius; his brothers and nephews threatened him, and forced him to take to sea and sail for Rhodes, which he reached only after sore trials.[2] It might happen, on the other hand, that the murderer was a minor, a child or a slave. In such cases the father, or the master, was responsible. The father would act by solemnly expelling his son, as Menoetius sent young Patroclus to the court of Peleus, practising thereby a form of abandonment which excluded or cut the son off from his family and freed the latter from any responsibility for his conduct. In the case of a slave, he was purely and simply handed over to his victim's relatives.

[1] *Odyssey*, XIII, 256–61. Legendary examples of a passive kind of collective responsibility only concern cases of vengeance between one city state and another.

[2] *Iliad*, II. 661–6.

Blood vengeance was not, in Homer's world, so blind and head-long a thing as it has sometimes been depicted. It operated in the framework of customary law and within narrow and clearly speci-fied limits. On the other hand it made no distinctions, it recognized no nuances, but only the fact. Circumstance and intention were not taken into account. A pure accident and a planned ambush were placed on the same level and treated in the same way. And it was only later on that legislators were to distinguish between in-voluntary homicide and premeditated murder.

The death of the guilty was, however, very far from being the necessary sanction for murder, at least in an absolute sense. It is true that blood called for blood — in principle — and that only the sacrifice of the criminal could appease the angry soul of his victim. But the very rigour of the rule was the principal obstacle to its strict application; because, since it was only the shedding of blood that was held to matter, the execution of the guilty called for vengeance on the same ground as the most sordid murder; and so it was simply one more link in the endless chain of reprisals.

It was ultimately as important to the avengers as it was to the family of the offender, and to the city as a whole, that blood ven-geance should not lead to actual bloodshed. A logic that was para-doxical, but also inescapable, required that the shedding of blood should not be inevitably requited by the shedding of blood. Hence the necessity, and the general use, of a machinery of conciliation which we come across in all so-called primitive communities, as far back as we can go, and which we naturally meet with in Homeric society.

## MODES OF COMPROMISE AND SETTLEMENT

To follow the working of this procedure let us first consider the simplest case, that in which the crime is palpable and the guilty man is not only known but acknowledges his fault and his crime. In the *Odyssey*, this is the case with Theoclymenus and also with the supposed Cretan whose imaginary but plausible story Odys-seus relates to Athena. What happens in such cases?

The head of the offended party's family repairs in great state to the market place; he is accompanied by his immediate relatives, surrounded by as many as possible of his cousins and allies, and, if he is a great lord, escorted also by his vassals. In presence of the assembled people he pronounces the *prorresis*, the formal interdict on the guilty man, who will henceforth be regarded by him and his kinsfolk as an outlaw. As a rule, however, the latter will have already fled the territory, whether of his own accord or because his family has forced him to do so.

Vengeance is now suspended. But the dead man has not obtained the vengeance he expects, his soul is unappeased and his ghost may continue to haunt and persecute the murderer. Plutarch[1] tells us the story of the Spartan Pausanias who, about the beginning of the fifth century, had killed young Kleonike at Byzantium. Every night he used to see her threatening spectre; it was in vain that he fled far from the scene of his crime. Finally, in a temple at Heracleia, he summoned the spirit of his victim and implored her forgiveness. The apparition came at his call — and simply announced that his end was near. The dead man or woman therefore continued to be menacing, while the family of the offended party remained on the alert. Were the murderer to return, he would be in peril of his life. So it was a question of negotiating the conditions under which he might return.

The exile's family applied themselves to this task, and it involved a regular ceremonial. An embassage composed of the culprit's friends waits upon the family of the dead man. The proceedings begin with a banquet, as required by tradition; then, 'when the rage of thirst and hunger is satisfied', the members of the embassage broach the subject. They come as suppliants, and they appeal to *aidos*, that is, to the obligation which every man owes to himself and his family, to other men, and to the gods and divine law. Among the duties imposed by *aidos*, the embassage invoke the duty to suppliants, to the unhappy wretches who have been victims of mental aberration or evil passions, and also to the vanquished who seek pardon and beg for mercy. They then offer, by way of compensation, magnificent gifts — gifts appropriate to

[1] *Cimon*. 6; and *Of Delays in Divine Vengeance*, 10.

the dignity of the offended party and to the wealth of the suppliant. The offended party then rises to reply. Naturally, he refuses; he cannot do otherwise, for that would be failing in regard to *aidos*, to the obligation he owes to the dead, to his relations and loyal friends, as well as to his personal dignity. He reminds his hearers of the magnitude of the offence, he eloquently exaggerates it, he explains that no compensation can be adequate, or wipe it out. This first refusal is obligatory and part of the ceremonial only; everyone knows that the resistance, which is ritual, will be finally overcome. For such is the will of men and the will of the gods.

There is an admirable description of the ceremonial in Book XI of the *Iliad*, where the Achaean leaders come as an embassage on behalf of Agamemnon to ask Achilles to forget the grave offence he has suffered from the king of kings and to offer splendid gifts as an earnest of reconciliation. Odysseus makes a skilful appeal; Achilles replies with a passionate refusal, and he persists in refusing, as is right, in spite of Phoenix's entreaties. This is not of course a question of murder; but we may suppose that the poet has scrupulously respected the ritual of this kind of ceremony, while at the same time embellishing it with his learning and eloquence.

In the end, after the death of Patroclus and in obedience to the command of Hera which Iris transmits to him in Book XVIII, Achilles naturally lays aside his resentment.

Some kind of external pressure is in fact needed, or at least a semblance of external pressure, if the obstruction of the offended party is to give way; though this will perhaps be only after the first wave of wrathful indignation has passed by and when the injured party has fully realized what dire consequences may result from continued obstinacy. Thus in the great epic we hear Achilles, after the death of his companion, of which he has been the indirect cause, cry out spontaneously:

> '... perish all debate
> From midst of gods and men! and perish hatred
> That stirs to anger e'en the wise, and tastes

> Sweeter than dripping honey, and that swells
> Like rising smoke in human breasts. . . .'[1]

The divine command completes and crowns the work of reflection and reason. In dealings between men, this order must come, or appear to come, from the city; but in reality the latter intervenes only when everything has been settled between the interested parties.

It is again the *Iliad* that furnishes us with a description of the final act. This is in the famous judicial scene on the shield of Achilles:

> . . . But the crowd
> Were gathered to the assembly, where a strife
> Between two men had risen about the price
> For some one slain: one man harangued the crowd
> And claimed to make full payment, while the other
> Refused to take a jot: and both were keen
> To get a finding from an arbiter.
> The crowd were taking sides and cheered and backed
> Their men; but heralds kept them in their place;
> And on their smooth stone seats the elders sat
> In solemn circle, holding in their hands
> Staves which the clear-toned heralds tendered them.
> And up in turn they sprang with these and gave
> Decree; and in the midst of all were lying
> Two golden talents, to be given to him
> Who should among them judge most righteously.[2]

The meaning of this scene has been much debated. What exactly is in dispute? It is possible to translate verses 499 and 500 in a different sense from the above and to interpret them as follows: 'One says he has paid everything and declares it before the assembly: the other denies having received a jot.' If we construe the lines in this way, the suit would no longer be a criminal, but a civil suit, although the consequences would obviously be serious, since the judgment might reopen the question of blood vengeance — hence the strong feelings displayed by the crowd. This interpre-

---

[1] *Iliad*, XVIII, 107–10.
[2] *Iliad*, XVIII, 497–508. Trans. Marris, p. 427.

tation has been supported by good authorities; nevertheless, it is untenable, and for this all-sufficient reason: the delivery of the ransom for blood, or *poiné* as it was called, once an arrangement had been arrived at, always took place publicly and in great ceremony. Any subsequent dispute about it would be inconceivable.

If, however, good historians have preferred the second interpretation to the one which we, with other writers,[1] offer, this is because the scene as we present it includes at first sight a very improbable-looking feature. How can a murderer who confesses his guilt — because he is offering the price of blood — how can he be present with impunity in the market-place, when he ought to have fled and when, as it is, he is risking his life? Everything, however, becomes clear if we admit that the dispute has already in fact been settled by negotiation between the litigants, and that the public scene we have witnessed is simply a show which has been designed to save the face of the injured family, the representatives of the dead. The guilty man presents himself, publicly beseeches his adversary, calls the people to witness; he is met, as is only decent, with a public refusal (though this is the last one). Meanwhile the adversaries have agreed between themselves to remit the decision to the elders 'for their finding'. 'The most righteous judgment' is known in advance; it will be an order to the avengers to accept the sum offered in settlement. The people acclaim the judgment which restores peace. And the family of the dead man may now agree to the arrangement; they are merely obeying the *demou phatis*, or voice of the people; honour has been safeguarded.

The scene on the shield of Achilles is substantially the same as the pseudojudicial mimicry which was practised up to barely seventy-five years ago in Dalmatia. The murderer faced the avenger in presence of a bench of judges. He came crawling on his hands, with his sabre at his neck. He asked three times for pardon. The avenger repelled him with his foot. The oldest of the judges then intervened and raised the suppliant's head. The latter then

[1] Sir William Marris appears to have interpreted the verses in question in the same sense as the author (Translator).

kissed the feet, the knees and the hands of his adversary, sobbing all the while, and so obtained mercy.[1]

There remained a final ceremony, that of public reconciliation. This was necessary because it had to be demonstrated that the injured family, or at least the small group of privileged avengers (father, son and brothers), had been unanimous in accepting the settlement.

The account of Achilles' reconciliation with Agamemnon in Book XIX of the *Iliad* no doubt conveys to us, heightened in the epic manner, the ceremonial procedure followed in these circumstances. The people have gathered in the place of assembly, in presence of the elders, that is, the leaders of the Achaean army. Achilles rises to his feet and makes a short speech, in the course of which come the ritual phrases:

> '. . . Ah well, let be
> What is past and done with now, for all our pain,
> Curbing the heart within us, as we must.
> Lo, hereby I forgo my wrath. . . .'[2]

Agamemnon speaks in his turn. He pleads not guilty, and throws the blame on Zeus, on Destiny and on the dark Erinyes, who have misled him. But, he adds:

> 'But since I was made blind, and robbed of sense
> By Zeus, I do desire to make amends
> And pay huge reparations. . . .'[3]

For the *poiné*, or price of blood, was neither more nor less than the ransom of the guilty man. In the present instance the ransom has been brought to the place of assembly: it consists of seven tripods, twenty cauldrons, twelve horses, seven women and ten gold talents. The pact is sealed by the sacrifice of a young boar, on which the contracting parties bind themselves by oath and whose body is then thrown into the sea, as was usual with all victims

---

[1] 'Les Jugements de sang dans la circonscription de Cattaro,' in the *Bulletin de la Société de Législation comparée* (1881).

[2] Trans. Marris, p. 434.

[3] Ibid., p. 437.

devoted to the infernal gods and on which an oath has been taken. After this, Achilles is invited in the name of Agamemnon to take part in the banquet of reconciliation.

We note that the epic imparts a few twists to the ritual, owing to the romantic character of the narrative. Thus it is only Aga-memnon who swears that he has respected Briseis; and also Achilles declines to attend the banquet as he is in mourning for the death of Patroclus. But the general procedure has been scrupu-lously respected and described. This was, in fact, how people made peace.

### THE ACCESSORY INTERVENTION OF THE CITY: THE JUDICIAL DUEL

It is perfectly clear from the evidence we have cited that any case of murder was from beginning to end a private matter, and that proceedings were initiated, conducted and concluded by the inter-ested parties even when, for reasons of prestige, the latter appeared to have recourse to the arbitration of the people and of the elders.

This was at least the case as long as no dispute arose regarding the guilt of the accused. But we must now ask what happened if the latter denied his guilt and was, quite naturally, supported by his family in this denial. In such a contingency, a third party — and here it was first of all a question of the civic authorities — could not fail to intervene.

We can reconstitute the principal phases of the procedure, al-though indeed Homer does not speak of them. All we need is to refer to the steps in procedure, of an obviously archaic character, which were consigned to writing in subsequent legal systems, and notably in Draco's Athenian Laws which, thanks to the Attic orators, are the best known. But we must make it clear that this procedure was not a public act initiated by the representatives of the city, and that it did not conclude with a condemnation. We are still only in presence of an act of private origin, and the sole object of this act was to settle a question of fact. Was the accused, or was he not, the author of the crime imputed to him?

The representatives of the dead publicly charged the accused in the ordinary forms of the *prorresis*; but, as the representatives of the accused protested his innocence, the king, or the magistrate who replaced him, now intervened. He in his turn promulgated an interdict, but this was limited to excluding the accused from the *agora* and the sacred precincts while the case was being investigated and prior to his appearance to face the charge. During this period the accused was covered by a genuine immunity and placed in some sort under the protection of the gods.

We have an extremely precious document that describes the nature of this guarantee: an Elean decree which has been preserved in an inscription at Olympia and which dates from perhaps the end of the seventh century. It guarantees that the accused and his family shall be inviolate, it forbids any material action's being taken against him, orders the magistrates and kings to see that this immunity is respected, and it specifies the fines which, in case of violation, are to be paid into the sacred treasury of Olympian Zeus. No doubt the decree limits itself to sanctioning and specifying very old rules of customary law.[1] But we should note that fines are to be paid into the treasury of the god: this shows that any violation of the immunity which has been promised to the accused is regarded as sacrilege.

Let us now return to the procedure initiated by the king in consequence of the accusation which has been brought by the relatives of the victim.

The king opened an enquiry and proceeded to an investigation: this involved three sessions held at intervals of a month. At these sessions no doubt the representatives of the families interested simply confronted each other; if the injured party maintained the accusation and if the accused persisted in denial, then the king referred them both to the Council of Elders over which, as a matter of fact, he himself presided.

In Athens this council was the court of the Areopagus which

---

[1] See the excellent commentary on this decree in G. Glotz's *La Solidarité de la Famille*, pp. 247–59. We do not however believe, as the author does, that this involved an innovation of a revolutionary kind, a sort of forerunner of the Declaration of the Rights of Man.

sat on the hill of Ares, the god of murder and violence, above the cave in which stood an altar to the Erinyes, the *Semnai*, the Eumenides.

On the day of the public appearance, the accuser and the accused were made to stand face to face, each with a foot on an unhewn stone. That of the accuser was called the 'stone of implacable resentment'; that of the accused, the 'stone of outrage'. The proceedings began with the taking of solemn oaths. The accuser swore first in order to confirm his right to prosecute; secondly, he swore to the guilt of his adversary. The accused swore he was innocent. Each party had the right to speak twice. After the first speech for the prosecution, the accused might still evade the accusation by flight, which was equivalent to a confession of guilt. We now ask how the council settled the question of guilt, which was the only question within its competence. Was this on the testimony of neutral witnesses? It was certainly not, and for this reason: that, if a member of any family, except the families of the contending parties, bore witness in such an affair, he would be taking sides in a quarrel which concerned neither himself nor his relatives, a quarrel to which his own family had to remain completely foreign, and that under pain of reprisals.

The only witnesses present on these occasions were the members of the two families who came to support their relatives on oath. They were the cojurors, or *homomotai*. The taking together of an oath in this way was in fact the only kind of proof admitted, and one may even say that it was the only possible proof. Now many vestiges of the procedure involved are to be found in the classical age. Aristotle[1] quotes a law of Cymé in Aeolis, a 'quite naïve law' which he classes with the oldest — 'very simple and barbarous ones'. This law states that if, in questions of murder, the accuser produces a certain number of witnesses, that is, of jurors chosen from among his relatives, the accused is declared guilty. An adage that was current at Gortyn in Crete ran as follows: 'The winning party is the one for which a majority of persons have taken the oath.' We must remember, if we are to under-

---

[1] *Politics*, II, 5, 11, 12.

stand these rules and customs, that a man who swore to a false-hood was devoting himself to the infernal gods.

In fact, therefore, neither the elders nor the king undertook any objective enquiry, but confined themselves merely to counting the number of cojurors. After which the king rose to his feet and in the name of the council proclaimed, not the sentence but the decision. If the accused was proclaimed innocent, he repaired to the altar of the Erinyes and offered a sacrifice of thanksgiving. If on the other hand he was declared guilty, he in theory fell into the hands of his adversaries. The latter could treat him as they wished; they could put him to death or hold him to ransom. In fact, they were morally obliged to kill him because no compromise had been arrived at between the two families. Now this was an extremely grave action, since it would automatically give rise to reprisals. And it must be added that the guilty man might, with the support of his kinsfolk, resist being arrested; and that the civic authorities, having no further competence in the matter, were not required to intervene.

To obviate a sequel which would involve everyone in great peril, one fortunately could have recourse to a final arbitrament: this was the judicial duel. It was preceded by a convention solemnly concluded between the contending parties and providing that this combat should finally and definitely put an end to the quarrel. It stood in place of an act of execution. It was not a means of discovering the truth or bringing the just cause to the light of day. In the ancient world the judicial duel was not regarded as involving a divine judgment: it was a practical method of limiting bloodshed between hostile families, and then of stopping it without either side's incurring the stigma of dishonour.

The mock-heroic duel between Paris and Menelaus which is treated in humorous vein in Book III of the *Iliad* is a document of great value, because it furnishes minute information regarding the procedure in such combats.

When Menelaus advances on foot in order to get 'his vengeance on the adulterer',[1] that is, on Paris, the latter shrinks back 'to cover

[1] *Iliad*, III, 28, p. 55.

among his friends, avoiding death'; but Hector spurns and insults him:

> 'No, but the men of Troy are very timorous,
> Else thou hadst worn a shirt of stone ere this
> For all thy evil deeds.'[1]

This means that they would have stoned him — a remarkable point, because stoning or a mimicry of stoning was the ceremony by which a family expelled one of its members and declared that the guilty man who refused to go into exile had no more lot or part in the life of the family. In face of this threat, Paris offers to submit to the ordeal of the duel. Hector then advances between the lines, that is, between the contending parties:

> Then Hector spake to both
> The hosts: 'O armoured Greeks and Trojans, hear
> From me what Alexander says, through whom
> The strife arose. He bids the other Trojans
> And all the Achaeans lay their goodly arms
> Here on the fertile earth, while in the midst
> He and brave Menelaus fight it out
> Alone for Helen, ay, and all she hath.
> . . . But let us swear,
> We others all, friendship and faithful oaths.'[2]

The technical, juridical details in this speech are perfect. Instead of having recourse to his family's aid, Paris, the guilty party, agrees to measure himself against the avenger. If vanquished, he will pay a *poiné*, in this instance Helen with all her wealth. Observe that the avenger will owe nothing, even if he is beaten. Lastly, both parties agree to conclude a solemn pact of friendship (*philotes* is the technical term) which will put an end to the dispute.

The pact is concluded before the fight. Three lambs are to be sacrificed, two of them being furnished by the friends of the guilty man. And it is the head of the avenging family — Agamemnon in this case — who performs the sacrifice. He first distributes to the participants some hair that has been cut from the heads of the lambs, pronounces a curse by which the gods are made witnesses

[1] Ibid., 56–7, p. 56.    [2] Ibid., 86–94, p. 57.

and guarantors of the pact, and finally he slays the victims. Priam then takes away the bodies, and these are to be buried or thrown into the sea, which was the rule for all sacrifices accompanied by a solemn oath.

It now only remains to set the two champions face to face. Odysseus and Hector measure out the ground and fix the boundaries, because this is to be a strictly regulated fight in a closed field. Each combatant disposes of only one spear. Lots are cast to decide which of the two shall first hurl the javelin. The lot favours Paris, and the fight begins. The champions glower furiously at each other, and there is great excitement among the onlookers. Paris casts his spear, but its point is bent and blunted against Menelaus' shield. Then the latter throws: Paris, bending sideways, evades the blow. Menelaus now draws his sword, rushes on his adversary and strikes the crest of his helmet: the sword breaks in three or four pieces; and Menelaus then seizes the helmet by the horsehair plume and begins to drag Paris along the ground. The chinstrap, however, breaks; Menelaus hurls the empty helmet into the ranks of the Achaeans who seize it as a trophy; while Aphrodite spirits Paris away to a place of safety. The gods do not wish the beaten man to die.

The description is ironical. Homer is no dupe and is obviously amusing himself. Like his hearers, he is aware that these judicial combats are usually only sham fights, conducted with spears that are easily blunted and cracked swords that readily splinter; they are ritual manifestations designed to save the face of the guilty man's family (which has decided on an honourable capitulation) and also of the family of the injured party, which has agreed to put an honourable end to hostilities: on condition, of course, that a ransom or blood-money shall be paid, of an amount befitting the means and dignity of the contending clans.

## SPECIAL CASES OF BLOOD VENGEANCE:
### ORDEAL AND SUICIDE

Blood vengeance, we must repeat, was an absolute duty. To set it in motion, it was not necessary for the murderer to be a man;

if the guilty thing was an animal or even an inanimate object which had caused an accidental death, vengeance was just as imperative.

An animal-murderer had to perish. If it were a wild animal, one had to hunt it down under pain of dishonour: the simplest way was to offer a reward to anyone who should kill it.[1] If it were a domestic animal, the owner was responsible; but all he had to do, to free himself, was to hand over the animal to the family of the injured party. In this case, however, one precaution was necessary. In order that the owner should be definitely freed from responsibility, the guilt of the animal had to be publicly proved and certified. Even in the classical era, in Athens, the animal was brought into the presence of the 'king', assisted by the 'kings' of the tribes,[2] sitting in the Prytaneum: and here, after a semblance of procedure, it was declared guilty and handed over to the offended party.

In the case of an inanimate object, the procedure was similar. The avenger brought the object to the king in the Prytaneum. The instrument of death, whether a beam for example, or a stone, or a tool, was declared guilty; then it was exiled, which meant it was thrown out of the territory, or into the sea.

This is what happened when the offender was not a man. But we have not yet finished with the technique of vengeance, and we have now to enquire as to the procedure when the injured party was not a man whose cause his own family was under the obligation of defending, but a divine being or — what amounted to the same thing — a being consecrated to the deity.

In this connection we must describe the traditional Athenian ceremony of the *Bouphonia*, if only on account of its archaic and picturesque character.

On the altar of Zeus Polieus, on the Acropolis, the Athenians used to place cakes, wheat and barley, the first fruits of the last

---

[1] Pausanias, I, 43, 3.

[2] Presumably the king-archon and the heads of the noble families. In the fifth century, monarchy as a political institution had long since disappeared, but the names survived (Translator).

harvest. Some oxen were then brought near to the altar. The first of them who touched the offerings was immediately struck down with an axe by a priest known as the 'ox-slayer'. Now this act was traditionally regarded as a murder — and the murder of a divine being — because the ox by devouring the first fruits consecrated to the deity had himself been assimilated to the deity, the Spirit of Corn or even Zeus Polieus himself. The priest therefore threw the axe far away and fled from the spot.

The machinery of vengeance was at once set in motion. The persons designated for this duty presented themselves to the king in the Prytaneum and proceeded to a semblance of enquiry; after which the king proclaimed the axe guilty and the axe was solemnly thrown outside Attic territory.

Vengeance was in fact required for any attack or injury inflicted on the gods, especially on the gods of the city, which meant their property, their houses, their priests and servants; or again for any serious failure to carry out ritual ordinances or to fulfil an oath for which their names had been invoked. The god often began by avenging himself, as does Apollo at the beginning of the *Iliad* when, in his wrath over the insult offered by Agamemnon to the priest Chryses, he sends a plague upon the camp of the Achaeans. In such instances an act of redemption was necessary, to stay the course of divine vengeance. Thus Agamemnon, after consulting the soothsayer Calchas, is reconciled with the god by the sacrifice of a splendid hecatomb.

This great king is clearly a privileged person, on account of his eminent dignity, perhaps. The general rule was very much more severe; indeed the current practice was to hand over the guilty man to the will of the god. This was the practice of the 'ordeal'. Monsieur G. Glotz[1] sees clearly that the ancient 'ordeal' was not an ordeal in our sense of the term, it was not a judgment of God, but an offering up of the individual who was placed at the disposal of the offended deity. The latter did what he liked with this being; he might let him perish, he might also save him, if that suited his purpose. It was this power which gradually, with

[1] *L'Ordalie dans la Grèce primitive.* Paris, 1904.

the evolution of moral ideas, gave rise to the belief in a judgment of God.

In primitive Greece, the 'ordeal', or offering up, appears to have been a fairly current practice in the execution of family judgments. A father who did not wish to shed his own blood would prefer to abandon to the gods the guilty child he had had to condemn, particularly a daughter who had borne an infant outside wedlock. Thus such heroines of legend as Danaë, Auge, Semele and Rhoio were placed with their children in a chest or coffer, and thrown into the sea. When Tenes, the son of Cycnus (Kuknos), king of Colonae in the Troad, was accused by his stepmother of attempting to violate her, his father had him placed in a chest and consigned to the waves. In Rome parricides were confined in a leathern sack and thrown into the water; and the same fate was meted out to those guilty of sacrilege.

The ordeal was the normal procedure in taking vengeance for a crime against the gods. Its agents were the representatives of the god, whether magistrates, priests or even, if an oath had been violated simple witnesses; because in this case vengeance still preserved its fundamentally private character.

There were two principal ways of executing it. In certain instances the guilty person was hurled from a lofty crag or thrown into a quarry or excavation — a 'mouth of Hades' as it was called. This mode of execution was still practised in the classical era in holy cities such as Olympia and Delphi. A law of Elis prescribed, for example, that any woman who crossed the Alpheus to witness the Olympic games should be thrown from the top of mount Typhaion. When Aesop was accused of sacrilege at Delphi, they hurled him from the Hyampeian rock, one of the summits of Parnassus. And during the second Sacred War, Philomelus, the leader of those guilty of sacrilege, was forced to leap down a precipice.

Generally, however, the place of sacrifice appears to have been a sea cliff. Ancient Greece was familiar with a number of such crags, like the Scironian cliff at Megara and the cliff of Thoricus in Attica. By far the most celebrated of these 'leaps' was that from the Leucadian rock, rendered famous by the memory of Sappho. The *Odyssey* contains a description of an ordeal which concerns this very spot.[1]

Odysseus, disguised as a beggar, is conversing with Eumaeus. He has taken Zeus and the other gods to witness in swearing to his sceptical host that Odysseus will soon be back home and will wreak vengeance on the suitors. To confirm the oath which, if he has lied, will devote him to divine vengeance, the hero makes the following proposal to his companion:

> '... But come now,
> Let's make a bargain; and in season due
> The gods who hold Olympus shall bear witness
> For both of us. If to this house thy lord
> Returns, then give me raiment, cloak and tunic,
> And send me onward to Dulichium
> Where I desire to be. But if the lord
> Comes not as I declare he will, then set
> The slaves to hurl me down some mighty cliff,
> To warn another beggar 'gainst deception.'[2]

What in short Odysseus is proposing is to undergo the ordeal to which all who offended the gods by taking a false oath rendered themselves liable. Eumaeus, of course, has no power of life or death over anyone; but, as he has been witness to Odysseus' oath, he is henceforth qualified to become the eventual agent of divine vengeance. As a matter of fact he refuses the pact or bargain, because he does not wish to fail in the duties of hospitality.

This 'devotion', if one may so call it, of the culprit to the gods was therefore the normal procedure in executing vengeance on those who had offended them. It was unavoidable; an absolute duty but also a fearful one, like that of vengeance between families. For, once again, whether it were a question of gods or men, there was risk of an endless chain of reprisals. In the case of vengeance executed in the name of the gods, one could and had to fear the

[1] That is, if, as we have tried to prove after Dörpfeld, Homer's Ithaca is to be identified with the isle of Leucadia. (Cf. *Les Poèmes homériques et l'Histoire grecque*, Vol. II, Ch. 3).

[2] *Odyssey*, XIV, 393–400. Trans. Marris, p. 250. The verb used by Odysseus at the end — *eperopeuein* — means 'to lie when under oath'. (Cf. the *Hymn to Hermes.* 274–82).

consequences arising from the posthumous hatred of the victim, who might unleash the Erinyes against the ministers of vengeance and even against the city itself.

This fear, quite natural and legitimate as it was, explains the remarkable, and at first sight paradoxical, precautions that were taken when executing the victim of an 'ordeal'.

We learn, for example, from narratives of legendary 'ordeals' that on the occasion of 'the leap from the rock', the victims were often saved by a net; and we know, in any case, that, in connection with the Leucadian leap, birds were attached to the victim, birds whose flight and wing-beats were designed to soften the fall; and that, at the foot of the cliff, a number of boats waited in a circle in order to row to the aid of the victim after the inevitable plunge into the sea. There is nothing surprising in this ceremonial, because a fall that was not fatal might indeed signify that the divine wrath was appeased; and then no one needed any more to fear the subsequent reprisals of the victim.[1]

This observation leads us to conclude our review of special or singular cases of vengeance.

The leap from the rock was not always designed to deliver an offender to the god with the object of appeasing him. The act might be one of deliberate choice, and in that case it was simply a form of vengeance by suicide, a procedure we find in most primitive civilizations.

There were instances in which the injured party saw no hope of obtaining satisfaction from his enemy, and in which he decided to die in order to let loose on the latter, after a last and supreme curse, his own powerful and avenging spectre. Thus, in Sophocles' tragedy, Ajax, before he falls on his sword, calls down upon the Atridae and the whole army the vengeance of the Erinyes.

---

[1] Among other artifices designed to prevent or attenuate the posthumous reprisals of executed persons, one must mention the stoning of the fugitive and also walling up [of which the confinement of Antigone was presumably an example — Translator]. In the former case, which was often merely a pretence, responsibility was divided between a large number of 'executioners'. The latter kind of execution isolated the culprit without involving any direct attack on his body or his life.

Plutarch relates several stories of avenging suicides, like the episode of the orphan Charila at Delphi who, when ill-treated by the king, hanged herself and so brought famine and plague upon the land; and like that of the daughters of Scedasus at Leuctra who, after being violated by the Spartans, called down curses on Lacedaemonia and then killed themselves; which explained why, long afterwards, Sparta was defeated on this very spot. Another such episode was that of the Argive Melissus who had sought reparation from Corinth for the murder of his son; when his entreaties met with no response, he implored the aid of the gods and threw himself from a lofty cliff. A number of legendary death-leaps, such as that of Britomartis in Crete and of Ino-Leucothea at Megara, have sometimes been interpreted as avenging suicides, provoked by persecution.

This desperate mode of avenging oneself brings fully to light the meaning of the whole procedure of blood vengeance. The procedure was determined by the will of the dead man or woman, now divinized, and ultimately by the will of the gods themselves; for it was their will which demanded and guided what was done. The living executants could only obey; it is true that on occasion they did not refrain from dodging or cheating: the maintenance of peace and public order required them to do so — a fact which explains the increasingly urgent intervention of the state.

Now the progress of moral and religious thought was, in its turn, to justify this intervention. In the *Eumenides* we see Aeschylus placing it under the auspices of Apollo and Athena. Homer's gods, on the other hand, were scarcely ready to play such a part. They were only just beginning to acquire a vocation as justicers in the mind of Hesiod, who represents Zeus as wedding Themis, who is Equity, mother of Discipline, Justice and Peace.[1]

## OF THE PROSECUTION OF CERTAIN OFFENCES
### UNDER THE SYSTEM OF PRIVATE JUSTICE

If in Homeric times, in spite of the occasional and incidental intervention of the state, the punishment for murder remained a

[1] *Theogony* 901-2.

private affair, one might suppose that simple offences would constitute no exception to the rule. The prosecution of persons guilty of minor offences did not, to be sure, arouse those passions of a specifically family nature which were inspired by the cult — and the fear — of the dead; but such prosecutions did not for that reason fall within the public jurisdiction.

There were nevertheless two offences of a peculiarly private character which seem to have occupied the attention of the most ancient legislators. These were adultery and rape. Lawgivers took pains to fix, and adjust in some detail to the social position of the interested parties, the scale of reparations which were to be made by those guilty of such offences. This was done at Gortyn, for example, in the fifth century. And we may therefore ask whether, in Homeric times, the authorities had any jurisdiction in such matters.

We have no authority for supposing so. On the contrary, at least as regards adultery, we learn from a very definite text that the procedure was entirely private. This, as the reader will have guessed, is the story of Hephaestus' conjugal misfortune when he is flouted by his spouse Aphrodite in collaboration with Ares.[1]

In such cases, the first and essential thing was to surprise the accomplice of the adulteress in the very act, and especially to arrest him. When the divine Blacksmith is warned of his misfortune by the Sun (for the Sun sees everything), he stretches above and around the nuptial couch a net of fine wire mesh so contrived as automatically to fall upon and trap the guilty pair. And this in fact happens.

Hephaestus has made as if to start on a far journey; but, being advised by the Sun who has been keeping watch that the trap has worked, he suddenly returns home. His first care is to summon the neighbours so that they may take cognizance of the flagrant

---

[1] *Odyssey*, VIII, 266–306. [Some ancient authorities appear to have looked askance at this passage, and simply omitted it from the text — Translator]. The procedure in the matter of rape must have been rather similar, at any rate when the offender was taken *in flagrante delicto*.

misdeed that establishes his claim; he therefore cries out to all the male gods who live near him on Olympus. They speedily arrive; nor do they refrain from jests and laughter, while poor Hephaestus is choking with rage. Poseidon alone preserves a grave demeanour; he knows that the matter is a serious one. When the adulterer is caught in the act, and imprisoned, he becomes the property of the injured husband.

Poseidon therefore at once opens the negotiations which the case demands. In this instance he occupies the position of the culprit's relatives. 'Release him,' he tells Hephaestus; 'I promise thee he shall pay, at thy command, all that the rules require in the eyes of the immortal gods.' The husband does not refuse; but he wants security, and his response is sarcastic. 'What recourse shall I have against thee, in the eyes of the immortals, if he takes to flight and so escapes his debt?' — 'In that case,' says Poseidon, 'it is I who will pay thee.' — 'I cannot, I will not, doubt thy word,' concludes Hephaestus. The culprit has now found a surety, and is released.

It will be seen that everything takes place in private. The essential thing is to lay hands on the culprit in the presence of witnesses. But two other points deserve mention.

First, there is no discussion as to the amount of the reparation payment, that is, of the ransom of the culprit who has fallen into the power of his adversary. It would seem therefore that when this passage was written (and for our part we date it from about the middle of the seventh century), there already existed a customary scale of payments for misdemeanours of the sort, a scale which subsequent legislators no doubt simply codified.

A second circumstance to be noted is the intervention of neighbours who are urgently called in as witnesses. This means that they were to be the eventual aids and assistants of the injured party. Whereas in cases of blood vengeance the solidarity of the family was first of all and even exclusively involved, it seems clear that in the matter of less serious offences, an agreement on the part of the neighbours took precedence over the solidarity of the family and was even substituted for it.

This in any event was the practice in cases of theft, which were also naturally dependent on private justice. It sometimes went a very long way. Heracleides of Pontus[1] tells us, for example, that at Cymé in Eolis the neighbours of a man who had been robbed co-operated in all the measures he took and, in the event of failure, clubbed together to compensate him. Heracleides comments on this custom by recalling a verse of Hesiod's:

> Not an oxen even will perish if thy neighbour be not bad,[2]

a passage that should be read in conjunction with two verses that come just before it:

> For if aught untoward happen in the township, the neighbours come ungirt. . . .[3]

that is, in the state of undress, if one may so put it, that was obligatory for men in pursuit of a thief.

We must now examine the customary procedure in dealing with theft. In a clear case where the thief has been caught red-handed and fallen into the hands of the man he was robbing, the latter had a discretionary right over him. In other words he had the right to demand a ransom, just as an injured husband had in respect of an adulterer. Like the injured husband, and for the same reason, the victim of a robbery immediately raised the alarm among his neighbours.

If the thief were unknown the injured party, assisted by his neighbours, would set out in pursuit. As it was nearly always a question of cattle which, at least in country districts, were the sole ordinary form of moveable wealth, one simply had to look for and follow a trail; and in such tracking peasants and shepherds were naturally very skilful.

We possess a humorous and picturesque account of one of these investigations, in the *Hymn to Hermes*. The child Hermes has stolen Apollo's heifers under cover of night. To throw pursuers off the scent, he has taken all the precautions which a good thief

---

[1] Fragment XI, 4 (*F. H. G.*, II, p. 216).

[2] *Works and Days*, 348, p. 13.

[3] Ibid., 344–5, p. 13. He adds: 'the kinsmen gird themselves' — which suggests that they may have assisted, though less urgently (Translator).

usually takes. He has made the animals walk backwards, and to conceal his own tracks has tied on his feet a sort of wicker sandals made of interwoven withes of myrtle and tamarisk. When, by ill chance, he encounters an old man, he takes care to lecture him: 'Thou art blind to what thou seest, and deaf to what thou hearest: keep silence.' And before regaining his cave, he has hidden the beasts in a byre some distance away.

Apollo meanwhile has set out in search of the heifers. He has picked up the trail, questioned the old man who had witnessed the theft, and realized that the thief is Hermes. In the early morning he reaches the cave where the infant god has climbed back into his cradle. Now when the victim of theft had followed a trail to the threshold of someone's dwelling, he had the right to proceed at once to a search; and the master was required to offer every facility for the purpose. If he refused, he was held to be the thief. So Apollo enters Hermes' cave, explores all its recesses, seizes the key and opens the store-rooms which contain provisions of nectar and ambrosia, as well as reserves of gold and silver and clothing. Finding nothing there, he furiously threatens to hurl the suspected culprit into Tartarus.

Hermes on his side has naturally offered no obstacle to the search. But as he is already very learned in common law, he will before long tax Apollo with having committed two grave faults: those of threatening the owner, and of coming without witnesses. Plato, in the *Laws*, tells us of the fundamental rule which governed a house-search. The victim of a theft was required to appear with his neighbours who would assist him unarmed and clad simply in short tunics without a belt.

Apollo meanwhile has not recovered his cattle. He will not however abandon the search, believing as he does that he has collected enough clues for a formal accusation. He therefore takes little Hermes and brings him before Zeus, that is to say, before the king or the magistrate who replaces him. The procedure is similar to the one followed when, in a case of murder, the accused declares himself innocent. The judge, or rather the arbiter, before whom the plaintiff and the defendant appear, is still only required to settle a question of fact. Is the accused innocent or guilty? If innocent, he remains free; if guilty, he falls into the power of the injured party.

So Apollo and Hermes appear before Zeus. The former relates the facts, and how he has followed the trail of the heifers; he cites the old man's statement and the denials of the young rascal. Hermes very astutely replies that Apollo came to his cave without a witness, and also that he threatened him: circumstances which are evidently not in favour of the plaintiff. To complete his defence, Hermes takes an oath which is quite unassailable, because he merely swears that he has never brought any heifers into his dwelling.

This ambiguous oath completes Zeus' enlightenment. He pronounces no judgment — he has not been asked to — but merely orders Hermes to conduct Apollo to the spot where he has hidden the cattle. This Hermes does. Covered with confusion, he finally redeems himself by presenting Apollo with a cithara he has made out of the shell of a tortoise — a marvellous new instrument.

The procedure is over. Initiated by the private action of the injured party, with the customary assistance of the neighbours, it concludes with an equally private settlement agreed to by plaintiff and defendant. The public authority has never, either as guardian of order or in defence of law, intervened of its own accord. It has been called in as arbiter by one of the parties to the dispute when the facts, but only the facts, have left room for doubt; when the evidence is clear or when the accused has been caught in the act, the arbiter has nothing further to do. The victim executes judgment for himself, while, as a matter of fact, respecting customs which have been consecrated by tradition and by public opinion.[1]

This private justice of the Homeric age, if rough and ready, was not for that reason an arbitrary justice. It operated in the

---

[1] Theoretically, the victim of theft having become master of the thief, had the right to kill him; in practice he was content with a ransom. Draco's Legislation at Athens, which seemed so severe to later generations, naturally preserved this theoretical right of life and death in cases of theft; but it certainly made no change in traditional practice.

general framework of that Themis, or Equity, a natural feeling in the heart of man, a feeling of which Hesiod is the warm and eloquent advocate. And we could find no better conclusion for this chapter than by citing the following verses[1] of the poet of Ascra.

Also there is the maiden Justice, the daughter of Zeus, glorious and worshipful among the gods who hold Olympus. And whenever one injureth her with crooked reviling, straightway she sitteth by Zeus the Father, the Son of Kronos, and telleth of the unrighteous mind of men. . . .[2]

[1] *Works and Days*, 256–60. Trans. Mair, p. 10.

[2] The reader should not conclude from this chapter that there was no public jurisdiction in Homeric Greece. The elders or 'kings', sitting in presence of the assembled people, constituted a regular tribunal. This exercised disciplinary powers: it could inflict fines on individuals who, for example, neglected to fulfil their military obligations, or who gave public offence to the 'kings' (*Iliad*, XIII, 663–70; *Odyssey*, II, 192). As a court of arbitration, it also settled civil disputes between individuals; as witness the suit between Hesiod and his brother Perses. In such cases the parties concerned remunerated the judges with 'presents' — hence the epithet 'bribe-devouring' which Hesiod bestows on the 'kings'. Before the appearance of written laws in the second half of the seventh century, these 'kings' were the guardians of custom and precedent.

# CHAPTER IX

# HOMER'S WOMEN

WOMEN occupy a place of honour in Homer's work. The old poet is obviously very sensitive to their charm and beauty. He is generally full of admiration for them, or of kindly indulgence, or a pity sometimes tinged with irony.

And what an admirable gallery of feminine portraits he gives us, varied and subtly differentiated! Nausicaa, that unmatched type of the young maiden, radiant with modest grace and spontaneity and youthful simplicity; Areté the accomplished mistress of a great house, affable and dignified, full of native authority, the beloved and respected counsellor of her husband; Penelope, a symbol of anxious and rather tearful fidelity, living a life of memories and hopes, wily, passive, patient, unshakeable, instinctively distrustful of the happiness of which she has a glimpse and which she at last recovers; Helen, that mystery of femininity whose halo of beauty and native nobility preserve her from any meanness whether in the tumult of passion or in the calm of the home she returns to; Andromache, the loving wife, flushed with admiration and fear for her hero; and lastly, the old stewardess Eurycleia, all affection and grumpy devotion. In this attractive array of the women of the heroic age, there is one monstrous exception — the terrible Clytemnestra.

We must not forget the goddesses whom Homer, as if to redress the balance, treats with a certain flippancy: Athena, marvellously faithful to her elect, full of intelligence, biased also and imperious, implacable and utterly devoid of sensibility; Hera, the jealous wife, acrimonious and cross-grained, but fascinating on occasion and even desirable when she cares to take the trouble; and Aphrodite, an epitome of every physical charm, but cowardly, malicious, licentious and stupid into the bargain. Among the divine heroines of his epic, Homer would seem to have reserved a portion of the favour he lavishes readily enough on mortals, for the deities of the second rank such as the maternal Thetis or the amiable Charis, Hephaestus' second wife, who contrives for her ill-favoured and unfortunate spouse, on the margin of Olympian society, a sort of cosy, bourgeois happiness.

In striking contrast with Homer's sympathy is the harsh misogyny of Hesiod, the devout but rough peasant-poet of Ascra.

Hesiod declares bluntly that woman is a calamitous present of the gods. Full of allurements, and all the more dangerous for that reason, he sees woman as Pandora, the dispenser of evils. In both his poems he harps insistently and ponderously on her history and on the part she plays:

> Yea, of her is the deadly race and the tribes of women.
> A great bane are they to dwell among mortal men. . . .[1]

There is certainly nothing original about his grievances. He especially reproaches women with their taste for expenditure. 'Who putteth his trust in a woman putteth his trust in a deceiver.' But he also dreads their frivolity and licentiousness. He advises an intending husband as follows: 'Marry a neighbour best of all, with care and circumspection, lest thy marriage be a joy to thy neighbours.' Elsewhere he is more precise: 'Get a house first and a woman and a plowing ox — a slave-woman — not a wife.'[2]

These two attitudes, the benevolent and the critical, show in any case that no one, whether admirer or detractor, regarded woman as an indifferent being, and that, in the minds of poets at least, she held a privileged position. We shall see now that she played a very honourable part in Homeric society.

### THE WOMAN IN THE HOUSE

In the first place she was in no way confined to the house. The gynaeceum, in which woman at one time lived as a semi-recluse,

---

[1] *Theogony*, vv. 591–2. Trans. Mair, p. 53.

[2] *Works and Days*, vv. 375, 701, 405. (See ed. Mair, pp. 14. 25 and 15 respectively).

is not a Homeric word or conception. Hesiod is tempted rather to reproach the 'regiment of women' with an excessive freedom of movement.

Homer's women also move about freely. Helen, when warned by Iris, quickly leaves her house and climbs to the city walls, where the old men are assembled, to witness the duel between her two husbands. Andromache, on hearing that the Trojan army is drawing back, rushes like a mad thing to the Scaean Gate, bringing with her the nurse and little Astyanax. When Hector falls under the blows of Achilles, his mother Hecuba is on the walls, surrounded by Trojan women to whom she gives the signal for lamentation. Areté, we are told, moves freely about the town and everyone salutes her as though she were a goddess. The girls do much the same. Nausicaa goes alone with the servants to wash the palace linen, some way from the town. One should simply note that women of quality were normally accompanied by female attendants.

Women certainly knew nothing of the rules of conduct which were later to be set down in a treatise on feminine behaviour, a work of Pythagorean inspiration, which admitted only three motives for an honest woman to go out: to attend a festival, to make purchases, or to fulfil religious obligations.[1]

While women were fairly free outside, their existence in the house was subject to certain restrictions. These were doubtless an attenuated survival of very ancient taboos of a magical or religious nature.

The women's apartments were separate from the men's. The marriage chamber belonged to the husband: here he invited the wife, but also, on occasion, some concubine. In Odysseus' manor, this room was on the ground floor. Penelope's *thalamos* was on the terrace above the *megaron*, or hall of honour, with which it communicated by a staircase. The rooms of the boys, who left the women's apartments at the age of seven, were built round the court. The girls' rooms were in the inner part of the house, near the mother's apartment;[2] among the wealthy classes, the doors of

[1] Jeanmaire, *Dionysos*, p. 168.    [2] Hesiod, *Works and Days*, v. 520.

these rooms were guarded at night by chambermaids. The women were debarred from the bathroom which was on the ground floor in the servants' quarter and was provided with stone bath-tubs. It appears that by washing in the same bath as the women, a man exposed himself to painful though temporary effects.[1] For the women there were portable bath-tubs of metal which they used in their own rooms. During his stay at Thebes in Egypt, Menelaus received two silver baths of this kind from his host Polybus. The women's rooms were provided with a hearth where a fire was lit at night, even in summer, in order to furnish a little light.[2] For the women who remained in the house, the best defence against cold in winter was not a fire but anointing with olive oil, well rubbed in.[3]

The women, then, lived apart. They also took their meals in their own rooms. They shared neither in the men's meals nor in the banquets for guests in the *megaron*. Herodotus tells us that at Miletus, even as late as the fifth century, the women never took their meals with their husbands and even refrained from pronouncing their names if they wished to call them. The legendary explanation of these customs given at that time was that the first Ionian colonists who founded the city had killed the relatives of their Carian wives.[4] Now the first custom appears to have been the general rule in the Homeric age; there is, however, no trace in the poems of the second prohibition.

But once again it must be pointed out that women did not lead a cloistered life. When the men had finished eating and banqueting, the women joined them; even more, they presided over the gathering and directed the conversation. This is what Areté does when present, in the evening, at the Council of the Phaeacian doges and when, next day, she presides over the assembly that listens to Odysseus' narrative; Helen of Sparta also, when she

---

[1] Ibid., vv. 753-5. Hesiod says in the same 'water'; but he does not explain what these 'inconvénients' were (Translator).

[2] *Odyssey*, IV, vv. 125-8; VII, vv. 7-8.

[3] *Works and Days*, vv. 522-3.

[4] Herodotus, Book I, paragraph 146.

appears in the *megaron* after Telemachus and Peisistratus have finished their meal, takes up a position on her chaise longue, plies her husband with questions about the visitors and, like the perfect society-woman she is, soon begins to recall those of her souvenirs which are to the honour of Telemachus' father.

The ladies received and paid visits. The *Iliad* shows us a visit of this kind, in Book XVIII, where Thetis goes to the house of Hephaestus to request him to forge new weapons for her son, in great urgency. This is a piquant genre-picture. Of course it is a question of deities; but life among the gods is, in Homer, only a transposition of human life.

So Thetis presents herself at the house of the divine Blacksmith, who is at work in his forge. Charis sees her and rushes to receive her. Following the usual ceremonial, she takes her hand and addresses her by her names and titles:

> 'Why, long-robed Thetis, wherefore art thou come
> Unto our house, a dear and honoured guest?
> Before, thou wert not wont to visit us.
> But come thou in with me that I may set
> Before thee entertainment.'

After which she leads Thetis in, seats her on a silver-studded chair, places a footstool at her feet, and calls her husband:

> 'Come here, Hephaestus; Thetis needeth thee.'[1]

This is how ladies received each other on Olympus and in the mansions of the nobility.

All these heroines of epic poetry, even the queens, are home-loving women. They all spin, weave and embroider. When they are at the head of a large household they direct the work of the servants, with the help of one or two stewardesses, supervise the making, cleaning and mending of the clothes for the whole family, men and women, see that guests are hospitably received and that a comfortable bed is set up for them in the vestibule. One depart-

---

[1] *Iliad*. XVIII, vv. 369 et seq., p. 423.

ment, however, was outside their control, at least in part, and this was the kitchen. The preparation of meat, especially roasts, was a man's business and gentlemen of the highest class did not disdain to take a hand in it. To the women fell only the making of bread, girdle cakes, porridge or pudding, of which the domestic staff at least ate great quantities; perhaps also — but this is less certain — the cooking of vegetables, that is, mainly chick-peas, beans and lentils, an important item of food for the middle and lower ranks of the peasant-class, together with cheese and dried figs.

Between the higher and lower ranks of society, the feminine way of life naturally varied a great deal. Hesiod might have given us a vivid picture of the peasant-women of Ascra. But he had an aversion for womankind and preferred not to talk about them, except to denounce their coquetry, their love of dainty food and the lightness of their morals. He agreed however that nothing is better than a good wife; but what a rare godsend — something that can only be compared to a fine stroke of business! Thanks to Homer, we can form a less sketchy idea of how the women of the aristocracy lived.

Through him we know that their toilet was an important affair. They gave minute attention to it, but modestly and discreetly, in the privacy of their own rooms.

When Hera wishes to adorn herself with every physical charm before she goes to visit Zeus — whom she intends to allure for her own purposes — on the summit of Mount Ida, she shuts herself up in her room which is defended by a secret lock:

> First with ambrosia from her lovely body
> She cleansed all blemish, and anointed her
> With oil, ambrosial, soft and scented for her,
> So sweet that shaken in the house of Zeus
> With its bronze floor, the fragrance would go forth
> To earth and heaven as well. This oil she rubbed
> On her fair skin, and combed and twined her hair
> In lovely gleaming coils ambrosial
> On her immortal head. Then she put on
> A heavenly robe, fine-finished, which Athene
> Had wrought for her with much embroidery,

And pinned it on her breast with golden brooches;
And girt a hundred-tasselled zone around
Her waist, and in the piercings of her ears
Put ear-rings with a cluster of three drops
That flashed deliciously. Then over all
The radiant goddess draped her in a veil,
A fine new veil — bright as the sun it was —
And tied fair sandals on her glowing feet. . . .[1]

Here we have an idealized description of the toilet of a great lady. Confident no doubt in her natural charms, the consort of Zeus is discreet as to the artifices of adornment. Her only jewels are the golden brooches, and earrings. The jewel-box of a lady of quality was generally better supplied, as appears from the gifts which the suitors make Penelope, in Book XVIII of the *Odyssey*. Apart from a long embroidered *peplos* which had 'twelve golden brooches with bent teeth', we are told there was 'an amber-beaded chain of quaint gold setting', like the one which the Phoenician traders had offered the mother of Eumaeus when he was a child, in Syros, earrings identical with Hera's, and a necklace, 'a lovely jewel'.

If Hera's jewels were discreet, her clothes on the other hand were of exceptional quality. The *eanos* was in fact a splendid robe, long and ample and generously draped and pleated: it was reserved for ladies and girls of rank. On the walls of Troy Helen wears an *eanos*, and so do the three daughters of king Celeus in the hymn to Demeter. It was a formal dress for great occasions, festivals or ceremonies.

The everyday dress was simpler. It included a straight tunic, the *chiton*, more or less long according to age and rank; and it was worn by both sexes. This tunic was sometimes lined, sometimes replaced by an ampler garment, the *peplos*, a still rather vague term which might serve to describe a simple length of soft material, embroidered to serve any purpose, even as a table-spread. Another piece of material, equally ample but of finer texture, was thrown round the shoulders: this was the *pharos*, which was

[1] *Iliad.* XIV. vv. 170–86 (pp. 311–12).

draped round the waist and drawn in with a girdle; it served as a mantle. A veil covered the head. The feet were shod with sandals, simple leather soles which were attached with straps knotted round the ankle and more or less artistically wrought.

It seems at first glance that in Homeric Greece, women's dress was designed to veil rather than emphasize the lines of the body. Elegance was less a matter of the cut than of the fine quality, pliancy or lightness of the woollen or linen garments. But one must not forget the resources of feminine coquetry. Hesiod puts his brother on guard against the woman whose clothes display her form too distinctly, in his opinion.

## WOMAN AND FAMILY LIFE

The contemporary of Homer or Hesiod might have one or several concubines, slaves or captives of war. He had only one wife, the woman with whom he had contracted marriage. Contrary to what may have been written, marriage was in no sense an act of purchase; it was simply accompanied by a ceremonial exchange of presents. The misogynist Hesiod, as we know, recommends having a slave-woman rather than a wife.

The wife was in no way, as is still repeated by certain writers, the property or thing of her husband. He was her master; he could punish or repudiate her, if she seriously compromised the interests of his house; he could even kill her in case of adultery, though he took care not to do so, for he would otherwise incur the vengeance which was obligatory on her family. The wife nevertheless possessed vague but unquestionable rights. She remained above all under the protection of her paternal family. For having killed his wife Melissa, Periander was involved in armed conflict with Procles, the tyrant of Epidaurus.

A marriage, especially between great families, had all the features of a solemn treaty, concluded according to a strict ceremonial. It conferred on the legitimate wife a place apart in the house or manor of the husband, a position of eminent dignity which Athena defines very well when describing to Odysseus the position of Areté at the side of Alcinous:

... Her
Alcinous made his wife, and honoured her
As no one else is honoured on the earth
Of all the wives who nowadays keep house
Under their lords; so hath she been and is
Heartily honoured of Alcinous
And her own sons and folk, who look on her
As goddess, and salute her when she goes
About the city: yea, for she herself
Doth not lack judgment, and she ends the feuds
E'en of the men-folk of her women friends.[1]

Areté is the ideal wife of a great lord; and, besides, she has a perfect husband. Penelope enjoys less authority and independence, despite her exceptional moral bearing. She sometimes allows herself to be snubbed by her son Telemachus who reminds her that, now he is of age, he replaces the master; she listens without wincing to the story of Odysseus' amorous adventures which he confides to her without the least embarrassment on the very evening of the day she recognizes him. These infidelities were certainly frequent, even under the family roof; and easy, because the master's room, as we know, was in the middle of the women's quarters, and the wife's in another part of the building.

They might even sometimes be a matter of family policy. It was not wise to have many legitimate sons, if one wished to avoid a division of the patrimony; it was better to have bastards who had no title to a share of the lands but who might replace the legitimate heir in the event of his disappearing.

Such infidelities might even be necessary when the wife was incapable of giving her lord a male heir. Thus the divine Helen herself, to whom the gods have refused any issue after the birth of her daughter Hermione, has, after her sensational adventure with Paris, to agree to Menelaus' asking a son of a slave-woman: this son was the 'strong Megapenthes' at whose marriage Helen herself presides at the beginning of Book IV of the *Odyssey*.

It must not be supposed, however, that all wives willingly accepted the amorous escapades of their lord. Odysseus' mother,

---

[1] *Odyssey*, VII, vv. 66–74, p. 114.

for example, Anticleia, seems to have been a woman of strong character with a firm hold on the reins of authority. Her husband Laertes had been very fond of the young and attractive Eurycleia, who in the *Odyssey* figures as the old and devoted stewardess. As she came of a good family of freemen, he had paid a good price for her, twenty oxen.[1] But he never lay with her. He dreaded the scenes his wife would make, Homer tells us.[2]

Things did not always proceed so happily. Witness the adventure of Phoenix which is related in Book IX of the *Iliad*. His father Amyntor had been enamoured of a young slave and had neglected his wife, Phoenix's mother. The latter begged her son to seduce the favourite. Phoenix obeyed and succeeded. Fury of the father who cursed his son, invoking the vengeance of the Erinyes and of Hades and Persephone. The young man wondered for a moment whether he should not kill his father; finally he decided to flee the country. He took refuge with Peleus who made him governor of the young Achilles.

These revolts of a wife who has been insulted and is supported by her sons cannot have been rare. But there was another class of dramas, which were provoked by a conflict between the mistress of the manor who had become a widow but was still jealous of her authority, and her son who was now her lord and master. The story of Meleager at war with the Curetes is a case in point. His mother Althaea was a Curete. Now her brothers having been killed in the war, Althaea cursed Meleager and prayed to Hades and Persephone for his death. Thus, in the manor which she continued to occupy, she took part with her own family against her son.

To understand this tale, which is legendary but very significant, we must not forget what has been mentioned above, namely that the mother's family was the guarantor of the respect due to

---

[1] Homer says that he gave the *value*, or *worth*, of twenty oxen. This probably means that he handed over certain precious or useful objects, such as metal utensils, or textiles, equivalent in value to twenty oxen. (See M. I. Finley, *The World of Odysseus*, London, 1956, pp. 71–2. — Translator).

[2] *Odyssey*, I, 429–33.

her as wife and mother, and also, when the case arose, of her authority. One should also recall what Odysseus said to Penelope when he was setting out for the Trojan war and envisaging the possibility of his never returning. He gives her charge of the inheritance and of his own relatives, adding

> '. . . and when thou seest
> Thy son a bearded man, wed whom thou wilt,
> And leave thy house.'[1]

The widow, while her son was a minor, was thus in certain respects in the position of the daughter *epicleros*,[2] whose office it was to transmit the heritage to the next male heir. But during her son's minority, she was mistress of the patrimony; circumstances and custom had placed her in the first rank, and it was then sometimes very hard to abdicate.

The eminent position of a wife, when her husband was head of the family, might be paradoxically strengthened, even in respect of her lord and master, by the privileged situation of an eldest son and even by reason of the unequal and sometimes precarious situation of his younger brothers.[3] When the latter were not able to set up house for themselves, they often continued to live under the paternal roof. This might lead to a promiscuity that lent itself to intrigues and transgressions. Hesiod stigmatizes them with horror:[4] this means that they were not rare. In Sparta where the absolute indivisibility of the patrimony remained the rule over a long period, the custom was finally established in a number of cases for the wife of the eldest son to be also the wife of all his brothers. This *de facto* polyandry changed her automatically into

[1] *Odyssey*, XVIII, 259–70, p. 325.

[2] The word 'epikleros' ( *feminine*) is usually translated as 'heiress', though she was not an heiress exactly in the modern sense (Translator).

[3] The French in this passage is not absolutely clear. It seems to be a question of the wife of a man whose younger brothers are, some of them at least, married and living in their brother's house. The 'transgressions' referred to by Hesiod were apparently intrigues between these brothers and their sisters-in-law (Translator).

[4] *Works and Days*, 328–9.

mistress of the patrimony and really head of the family, the more
so as the men had no right to the possession of precious metals.
Thus the greater part of Spartan wealth was to pass progressively
into the hands of women.

## MARRIAGES, BETROTHALS AND BIRTHS

It was by virtue of a fairly complex series of minutely regulated
ceremonies that a woman acquired the title of 'legitimate wife'
(*couridiè alochos*), which invested her with a peerless status in the
home.

According to Hesiod, men should marry about the age of
thirty. A woman should be four years beyond the age of puberty:
she should therefore be marriageable when she is about sixteen.

When a father decided to marry off his daughter, he publicly announced the fact and invited possible suitors to become candidates. The latter then visited the future father-in-law, who lodged
them, received them as his guests and junketed with them. They
had naturally not come empty-handed; they had brought food for
the master of the house and personal gifts for the intended fiancée:
clothes, veils and jewels. The quality and number of the gifts and
the festivities that went along with them varied, of course, with
the social position of the parties concerned. Penelope reminds her
suitors of all this, in some detail:

> 'Men who set out to win a worthy lady,
> A rich man's daughter, vying with each other,
> Bring with them cattle of their own unasked
> And goodly flocks, to feast the lady's friends;
> They make her splendid gifts. . . .'[1]

These preliminary merrymakings in the house of a girl's father
were not simply manifestations of courtesy or a means of making
acquaintance. They were also the occasion of a veritable competition among the suitors: the latter speechified, or sang, or danced,
or defied each other; they competed in games or trials of strength
and skill.

In spite of its mythical character and although it took place in

[1] *Odyssey*, XVIII, 276–9, p. 326.

obviously exceptional circumstances, the gathering of the suitors for the hand of Penelope, in Odysseus' manor house, did not materially differ from this ceremonial.

A gorgeous, if not ostentatious, example of such a gathering is described complacently and perhaps even embellished by Herodotus. It occurred some three-quarters of a century after the period we are dealing with, at the beginning of the sixth century; but it evidently perpetuated and reproduced very ancient traditions.

When Cleisthenes, tyrant of Sicyon, was victor in the four-horse chariot race at Olympia, he caused a herald to proclaim that all the young men who deemed themselves worthy to marry his daughter Agaristé would be received at his court six days later. Herodotus gives us the names of thirteen suitors, the flower of young Greek manhood. Cleisthenes entertained them for close on a year. He prepared an arena for hand-to-hand contests and races. He questioned them, observed their behaviour, 'especially at table', put their valour, their character, their morals and their education to trial, and, for the rest, treated them with magnificent hospitality. At the end of a year he was still hesitating between two noble Athenians, Megacles and Hippocleides, with a preference for the latter.

The day came when the final choice had to be made. Cleisthenes offered up a hecatomb and gave a splendid banquet for the suitors and the men of Sicyon. After the wine had gone round, they began to discuss music and dancing. Hippocleides, who was the object of general curiosity, began to dance to the sound of the flute. Feeling bolder every moment he got on to a table, took up various positions in imitation of the Spartans and then of the Athenians, and at last, making a sort of bridge with his body, while his head was resting on the table, he began to gesticulate with his legs in the air.

'By dancing like that,' cried Cleisthenes indignantly, 'you have just missed your marriage.'

'Hippocleides doesn't care a rap,' haughtily replied the rejected suitor.

Cleisthenes then called for silence. He delivered a little speech in which he thanked the suitors, regretted that he was obliged to make a choice, announced that the unsuccessful candidates would each receive a silver talent, and lastly proclaimed that he was giving his daughter to the Athenian Megacles. The latter, as we know, was to be the father of the Athenian Cleisthenes, the democratic reformer, and great-grandfather of Pericles.[1]

But to return to the age of Homer. When the father of the fiancée had chosen his future son-in-law, the latter offered him presents. These were called *hedna*. The father-in-law responded, at the time of the marriage, by giving his daughter a dowry, known as the *meilia*, or gratifications, which had to be returned in the event of repudiation. Telemachus does not neglect to recall this fact to the suitors, who are asking him to send his mother back to her father Icarius. It was this exchange of presents, which in most primitive cultures was a matter of ritual when a solemn agreement was being made, that has led to the belief that a man purchased his wife.

The marriage ceremony itself consisted, in the main, of the solemn transfer of the bride from her father's house to her husband's. This transfer was preceded by a joyous banquet which has a special name in the Homeric vocabulary: it was the *eilapinè*, and was given by the bride's father. When evening came the bride — at least in the case of wealthy families — was conveyed in a chariot by torchlight and accompanied by a procession as befitted the rank of the contracting parties. Hephaestus portrayed a number of these processions in one of the scenes he wrought on the shield of Achilles; which leads us to suppose that marriages must have been celebrated simultaneously on those days of the month that were considered particularly favourable:[2]

> On it he made two towns of mortal men,
> Most lovely. In the one were wedding feasts
> And bridals; and by light of blazing torches

[1] Herodotus, Book VI, paragraphs 126–31.

[2] Hesiod advises that the transfer be made preferably on the fourth day, after one has consulted the birds (*Works and Days*, 800–1) [that is, the omens indicated by the appearance or flight of certain birds — Translator].

Out from their bowers and through the city they led
The brides, and loud arose the marriage song.
Lads danced in circles, and among them flutes
And lyres made music; and the women stood
Each at her porch and marvelled.[1]

The final rite to be accomplished was the consummation of the marriage in the husband's bridal chamber. To evoke it may cause a smile; but for long ages it was a serious affair and not free of peril, at least for the husband.

It was a belief common to all primitive peoples and all those who held a mystic conception of the world, that a primal interdict of a divine or demoniacal character rested upon every new being or new thing. This ban could only be raised by a sacrifice which paid its due share to the deity. Hence the founders' sacrifices, like that of the first-born son, which were so widespread in ancient times on the shores of the Mediterranean; hence, too, the offering of first fruits; and again, among other peoples, the belief that the first being who entered a new house or a city that had just been founded, was dedicated to the 'daemon' or the god, that is, to death. So, when Remus was the first to cross the boundary lines of Rome, he was immediately put to death by Romulus. In certain districts of southern Germany, in quite recent times, people took care to make a cock, a cat or a dog first cross the threshold of a new house, so as to turn aside the curse upon itself. Our official ceremonies of inauguration are simply a survival of these age-old rites.

A woman's virginity was also naturally subject to a ban of this kind and the inaugurator consequently exposed himself to formidable reprisals. In the story of Tobit, the virginity of Sara is defended by Asmodeus, a peculiarly jealous and evil demon who has caused the death of her first seven husbands as soon as they came near her. One method of raising the ban which was currently employed in the East was for the woman to consecrate her virginity to the god by virtue of a simple act of sacred prostitution,

---

[1] *Iliad*, XVIII, 490–6, p. 427. Keats in his famous ode presumably recalled this and other scenes on the shield (Translator).

the material profit of which went into the temple treasury. There
were other ways, for one may well suppose that people very soon
applied their ingenuity to solving a problem as frequent and as
urgent as this.

Does the primitive Greek world afford a trace of such problems
and of the concern they aroused? The clues are certainly very slight
but they are not entirely absent.

In Athens, for example, even in the classical age, young girls
were assigned to officiate, on a temporary basis, in the service of
the Artemis of Brauron. The service was carried out 'for the redemption of their virginity and to forestall the reprisals of the
goddess'. These young officiators were then simply the delegates
and representatives of their generation, on behalf of which they
proceeded to a sort of symbolical and collective redemption. It is
highly probable that, in more ancient times, the obligation of redemption had been strict and general before becoming the pretext for a purely honorary office which was reserved to the
daughters of the best families.

Amid the wealth of legends that ancient Greece brought forth,
one should perhaps consider the story of Protesilas in this connection.

Protesilas was the Thessalian hero who, when the Achaeans
landed on the plains of Troy, was the first to set foot on shore —
in spite of an oracle full of menace for whoever should commit
that act — and was immediately killed. Protesilas, therefore,
whose name is revealing because it can be interpreted as 'the first'
or 'the inaugurator', met with the fate reserved for him who opens
a new way by violating an interdict.

But he was not only the hero of this warlike adventure; he was
also the protagonist of a curious matrimonial legend which, in
principle, was probably identical with the other legend, although
unfortunately 'contaminated' by it. We can try to disengage
this.

Protesilas had set out for Troy the day after his marriage. In his
absence (the legend says it was after his death) his wife, Laodamia,
had made a waxen image of him and was passionately embracing

it in her room when she was surprised by her father who had the statue thrown into the fire. Her husband, however, had been restored to life; he came back and found her, though only for a short time, after which Laodamia followed him into the next world. The legend, which Euripides was to treat in one of his lost tragedies, had thus become the story of the inconsolable widow who ends by rejoining her beloved in the house of Hades. Now it is maybe possible to discern, beneath these romantic trappings, the primitive and significant story, the story of the husband who disappears the day after his marriage night, in order to escape the consequences of having violated the interdict, or, to speak more exactly, of having 'inaugurated' a virgin; after which he is sacrificed in effigy and so dies, in a symbolical sense. He finally returns, symbolically resuscitated, and takes his place beside his wife, the deity having been now satisfied by means of a ritual sacrifice of substitution.[1]

Our conjecture is doubtless not susceptible of proof; but it acquires a certain likelihood when we compare it with the ritual of the Spartan weddingnight. The latter offers all the characteristics of a sort of comedy contrived to outwit the perils incurred by the consummation of marriage and to dupe the jealous deity. Here are the details on the subject which we find in Plutarch.[2]

The matron who, in this circumstance, acted the part of mistress of the ceremonies, used to shave the head of the bride, after the latter had been transferred to her husband's house. She then dressed her as a man, laid her on a mattress serving as a bed and left her in darkness. The husband, who had taken his meal as usual at the common table, then arrived in secret, unloosed the wife's girdle and carried her to another bed. Having performed his office, he soon retired decently to go and sleep as usual with his comrades in their tent. He continued the same procedure for a fair period of

---

[1] Cf. the study of the literary fortune of 'La Legende de Protesilas' by Louis Séchant in *Lettres d'Humanite*, XII, supplement to the *Bulletin de l'Association Guillaume Budé*, December 1953. [English readers will recall Wordsworth's treatment of the legend — Translator].

[2] *Lycurgus*, 15.

time. It appears that many even had a child at a time when they had only lain secretly with their wives at night.

The authors of the classical age naturally considered this procedure as a consequence of the strict military discipline of the Spartans. This is obviously an inadequate interpretation, for it explains neither the masculine disguise of the bride nor her clandestine transfer in the dark from one bed to another, before the consummation of marriage. For our own part we see in all this much rather the survival of very ancient ritual wiles or stratagems designed to deceive the vigilance of those jealous powers which were guardians of virginity, and to protect the ravisher from the consequences of his action. It is not surprising to find these survivals in Sparta which was the most conservative city in Greece.

If this interpretation, and the interpretation we outlined of the legend of Protesilas the 'inaugurator', be accepted, then it will be admitted that in primitive Greece the consummation of marriage, for the husband at least in theory, was not always a safe business.

The first and principal duty of the wife was to assure the perpetuity of the family by producing legitimate children, preferably sons.

The entry of a child into the family was not a simple business, either. It was accompanied by a certain number of ritual acts of which the purpose was to ensure in the presence of eyewitnesses, his incorporation into the family and his accession to the domestic cult.

His birth had in the first place to be effected according to traditional forms. What these were we know from the hymn to the Delian Apollo which describes the birth of Apollo. On the isle of Delos Leto has been overtaken with the pains of labour. The goddesses who surround her, ready to help, can do nothing without the assistance of Ilithya who presides over child-bearing. Iris is therefore sent to fetch her. She arrives in secret.[1] The delivery is effected and those present greet the arrival of the babe with ritual wailings. When their hands have been purified, they take

[1] Ilithya was no doubt replaced by an initiated matron for the delivery of mortal women.

charge of the child and wash him: this was a rite of purification, since child-bearing was a pollution from which the mother — at least if she were a mortal — would in turn have to be freed by a sacrifice to the gods of the nether world. When the child has been washed he is wrapped in new white linen, surrounded with swaddling clothes and laid in a cradle shaped in the form of a winnowing-basket, like newly harvested grain.

We may note in passing that according to Hesiod certain days of the month were more particularly favourable for births: the 6th, 10th, 16th and 19th for boys, and the 14th and 19th for girls.

The new-born child was then presented to the father who could reject him on account of a physical defect, because certain infirmities rendered a man unfit to exercise the domestic cult. In Sparta, he was also presented to the elders of the tribe, who had the same right. If rejected, he was exposed in some wild and lonely spot, that is, he was consecrated to the gods. One wonders whether this rite of exposure, which became optional and probably rare, was not the last vestige of an ancient sacrifice of the first-born.

Once accepted, however, the child had not yet become a member of the family. At Athens in the classical age, this step was taken in the ceremony of the *Amphidromia*, which generally took place on the fifth day after the birth. The father then carried the child at a run round the domestic altar, in presence of relatives and connections who brought gifts. We find no mention of this ceremony in the Homeric texts; but this does not mean that it did not take place.

On the tenth day there was another festival, more gifts and a fresh banquet. The child now received his name. We find a mention of this ceremony in the *Odyssey*.[1] Autolycus, Laertes' father-in-law, had come to Ithaca on the occasion of his grandson's birth. After the banquet his daughter Anticleia placed the child on his knees and asked him to give it a name. In this way the son of Laertes received the name of Odysseus and made his official and final entry into the family and the city; with the promise of splendid gifts from his grandfather who had become also his godfather.

[1] *Odyssey*, XIX, 399–412.

### RELIGION AND MYSTERY CULTS

Women naturally took part in the religious life and cults of both family and state. In a number of sanctuaries, primarily those of feminine deities, they even occupied eminent positions such as that of the high priestess of Hera at Argos, or of the eponymous priestess at Eleusis. At Ilium the priestess of Athena was the pretty Theano, Antenor's wife. They had a place even in the cult of masculine gods: as for example the Pythia at Delphi, and the wife of the king-archon at Athens, whose union with Dionysus was celebrated every year at the feast of the Anthesteria. On many occasions societies of women took part in the service of the deity, like the college of the *Melissai* in the temple of Artemis at Ephesus, or that of the *Arrhephoroi* at Athens. The girls who belonged to the latter were confined for a period of four years, during which time they worked in pairs at making and embroidering the *peplos* which was to adorn the antique effigy of Athena. There were also the 'temple-servants' of Aphrodite at Corinth, whose particular trade contributed greatly to enrich the sanctuary.

This participation in civic cults requires no special comment. Women took their place, in such circumstances, with the rest of the population. They figured, by reason of their sex, in particular places and performed certain specific tasks or fulfilled certain offices, but on the whole their collaboration was not different from that of the other members of the social group interested in the particular rite or ceremony.

Recent studies on Greek religion and its primitive forms and institutions lead one, however, to ask whether there did not exist in archaic Greece, that is in the Hellas whose daily life we are trying to reconstruct, ceremonies personal to women, rites in which they alone participated as women, secret in certain respects, conducted out of sight of the menfolk, even when they took place in the open — rites so strictly exclusive that any masculine curiosity would expose its author to a savage pursuit which might end in his death or laceration.

It has therefore been conjectured,[1] and with much likelihood in our opinion, that there existed in primitive Greece a society of women whose members advanced through successive initiations. The latter were connected with the cult of the great female deities: Hera, Artemis, Athena and Demeter, all more or less heiresses of the Great Goddess of the Aegean world, the deity of trees and vegetation, of wild beasts and wild nature. These cults were to be progressively monopolized by the cult of Dionysus and assimilated to it.

They were accompanied by frantic dances, conducted to the sound of the flute, which before long threw the dancers into a state of trance or ecstasy: the mouth was open, the neck bent and the whole body thrown back stiffly in attitudes that remind one of a regular crisis of hysteria. They included wild races in procession, by torchlight, across wooded and hilly country. On such occasions the senior initiates, at least in the cult of Dionysus, no doubt wore the *nebris*, the skin of a fawn which had been sacrificed on their behalf during an earlier initiation: this generally involved a laceration. It is likely that certain of these initiations, such as the one that took place at the age of puberty, required a sometimes fairly long period of retreat, during which the future initiates were subjected to ordeals and lived hidden, in small companies, in wild and lonely places. In other instances, such as the initiation preparatory to marriage, the retreat might take the form of a period of service devoted to the deity; which, of course, by no means excluded ritual dances. Thus in Athens the girls who, prior to their marriage, had been placed in the service of Artemis, had to have 'done the she-bear', that is, danced a bear-dance in honour of the Artemis of Brauron.

We can therefore imagine what these feminine mysteries were like in the Homeric age and before the great vogue of the cult of Dionysus. This last was to popularize the words 'maenad' and 'thyad' which designated the participants in these feminine 'orgies'. The word 'maenad', however, already occurs in the

[1] Cf. in H. Jeanmaire's *Dionysos* the chapters relating to divine *mania* and to maenadism.

*Iliad*[1] where Andromache, who has a presentiment of Hector's death, rushes along 'like a maenad'. It is found a little later in the *Hymn to Demeter*, which was composed towards the end of the seventh century: 'she bounded along', we read in verse 386, 'like a maenad who is rushing down a wooded mountain side'. The allusion to the nocturnal careerings through forested mountains, which were characteristic of the feminine mysteries, could not be more specific.

Nor should we be misled by the silence of Homer and Hesiod in respect of these mysteries, a silence due perhaps to reverence and truly very natural, because it was a question of secret ceremonies from which men were rigorously excluded and which it was wise to ignore, so as not to draw down on oneself the vengeance of these sororities, and also — what amounted to the same thing — the fearful reprisals of the offended deity.

We must therefore admit that, from time to time, and probably every two or four years following the rhythm of the great Hellenic festivals, and that is, on dates established by ritual, both the young girls and the women of Homeric society freed themselves roughly and simultaneously from the constraints of family life and abandoned themselves to the frenzies of a collective religious madness; or, if you like, to the influence of divine possession.

If we forget this, we should probably be ignoring an essential aspect of their psychological life.

### THE SERVANTS OF APHRODITE

Historical accuracy requires us to add at least a few words about that small fraction which engaged in the very personal trade that certain misogynists have irreverently called the oldest profession in the world.

This trade was, as we know, currently practised within the precincts of the sanctuaries of Aphrodite. The 'temple-servants' of the goddess at Corinth were already well known in very ancient times. In the second half of the seventh century the tyrants of the

[1] Book XXII, verse 460.

Cypselid dynasty even claimed to give them a legal monopoly; though history does not tell us whether they succeeded in suppressing the clandestine market.

Did there after all exist a free commerce, outside the regulated one? On *a priori* grounds this seems likely enough, and a passage in Hesiod allows us to suppose so. He speaks,[1] certainly without indulgence, of those women who dress so as to make their shape conspicuous, who cause men to lose their senses by flattering speeches which merely 'aim at their barn' — because remuneration for service was then made in kind — and whom he compares to thieves.

But why dwell on these human and social infirmities which belong to every age and every country and which in Homer's time seem to have presented no original feature?

[1] *Works and Days*, 373–5.

## CHAPTER X

# POPULAR FESTIVALS: FUNERAL RITES: PUBLIC GAMES

THE religion of Homeric Greece, of all ancient Greece for that matter, was essentially official. Each city had its gods. It selected them as a rule from the Pantheon of great deities common to the Hellenic world; but it frequently also had secondary gods of its own. It was bound to these divine beings by a sort of pact which created reciprocal obligations. These deities were in truth members of the city. They had their dwellings there, they had land — a *temenos*, which was a veritable concession, granted by the state — and they maintained servants. By reason of the services they rendered the community, they had a right to a collective tax, or grant, in the form of sacrifices and ceremonies.

These official forms of religion are not strictly to our purpose. But just as in some of our modern cults there exist, side by side with the great and solemn celebrations, a number of minor festivals, familiar and unofficial, sometimes even family affairs, such as Patron Saints' Days, or local or anniversary festivals — Corpus Christi, the Rogation Days, Mid-Lent, Candlemas, and in certain aspects the great festival of Christmas — so there always existed in Greece, especially perhaps in the early centuries of the historical period, a succession of popular rites and rejoicings of which the regular return furnished a rhythm for daily life.

### RUSTIC, SEASONAL AND POPULAR FESTIVALS

In all rural cultures each of the principal actions of the farmer's year, seed time, harvest, threshing, grape harvest, has been and sometimes still is accompanied by festivities which are designed to favour those natural forces that promote fertility, to celebrate their metamorphoses, their seasonal death and resurrection, to ward off hostile influences and raise the ban that weighs on every new creation.

These festivals usually permitted of dancing, music and songs, the magic virtue of which was universally recognized. The Homeric poems tell us very little of them; but there is a revealing picture of grape harvest in the description of the shield of Achilles. The grapes are gathered by young men and girls. In the midst of them a boy is playing the cithara and in a reedy voice singing a *linos*, or funeral lament. The others strike the earth in cadence and accompany him with cries and dances. There is no doubt that we have here a case of agrarian magic, a harvest ritual, which normally includes a lament for the god's death. Some few centuries later Theocritus[1] tells us how once, on the isle of Cos, he took part in the Thalysia, a rural ceremony in which, at the time of threshing, one offered the first fruits to Demeter. The celebrants lay on a bed of freshly plucked rushes singing alternate songs in honour of an effigy of the goddess. This was adorned with stalks of wheat and poppies and stood on the threshing-floor beside a pile of yellow wheat in which a threshing-shovel had been planted. One may take account of this recent text because it certainly describes a very ancient ceremonial.

The present writer has conjectured and tried to show that the various episodes of Odysseus' sojourn among the Phaeacians represent a transposition, on to the plane of myth, of the successive rites of a Springtime festival of rebirth. This, like many ceremonies that have survived into our own day, began with a 'quest' for the spirit of the Tree, or of Vegetation, a spirit drowsy and overwhelmed by winter; it ended, after a victorious ordeal, with the revelation of the god rejuvenated or resuscitated, with a recitation of his trials, and the expulsion, on a boat by night, of a person who played the part of a scapegoat.

A certain number of these popular festivals of a rural character took place during the winter months. The enforced leisure and an abundance of provisions were at that time favourable to festivities. Winter was related to the world of night, and also the reign of the

[1] *Idyll*, VII.

subterranean and infernal powers, permanent sources of fertility and dispensers of wealth. And, finally, winter was the season of the dead, when they once more came in contact with the living who evoked them in masquerades and displayed their presence in processions of masks.

Of these winter festivals we are fairly well acquainted with those that were celebrated in Athens and which at an early date were placed under the patronage of Dionysus.

The 'Rustic Dionysia' took place at the end of our autumn and the beginning of winter. They were village festivals strung out through the course of the month Poseideon and consisting mainly of a procession which carried a large phallus and was no doubt designed to promote fertile harvests. The procession was accompanied with sacrifices, songs and games. The most popular contest consisted in balancing oneself on a wine-skin oiled for the purpose, and the young man who contrived to stand on it longest without slipping carried off the skin and the wine. There were also gay processions, marching to the sound of the flute, of young men wearing masks and disguises; in the course of these diversions, two of the youths came to grips in a grotesque sort of combat. These processions, interspersed with comic episodes[1] — the *comoi* — later gave birth to Comedy.

During the months that followed, but this time outside the city itself, a similar festival was celebrated. This was the Lenaean Festival, of which we know little except that the Lenaea included a procession.

On the 11th, 12th and 13th of the month Anthesterion which roughly corresponds to our February, came the *Anthesteria*, a festival both joyous and funereal as was customary for most of the rustic ceremonies devoted to the cult of fertility. The first day was marked by 'the opening of the *pithoi*', or wine-casks. Each vintner brought a *pithos* of wine to the sanctuary of Dionysus 'in the Marsh', the oldest sanctuary in Athens, opened it, poured a libation and tasted the wine. This was a day of family rejoicings and drinking-bouts in which all the servants were associated.

[1] They may have been something like student 'rags' (Translator).

The object of this opening of the *pithoi* was to raise the ban on the last vintage which could now be consumed without sacrilege. To consecrate the event, the second day, which was known as the day of 'Pitchers', was devoted to a drinking contest at which the king himself presided. Each competitor provided himself with a pitcher of wine. At the signal of the trumpet, he had to swallow the contents as quickly as possible. The victor received a crown of foliage and a leather bottle full of wine.

On the same day the god made his solemn entry into the city. Dionysus, who was supposed to have come by sea, was borne on a 'naval chariot' at the head of the procession. The prow of this boat on wheels was formed by a pig's head, the stern rose in the form of a swan's neck. Accompanied perhaps by mummers, the god went to fetch the queen, who, in the historical period, was the wife of the king-archon. They then formed a kind of wedding procession which repaired to the old royal palace of the *Boucoleion*, and here was consummated the union of the god and the queen, a symbol and pledge of fertility.

Meanwhile, precautions were taken throughout the city to ward off the malignant influence of the souls of the dead who, that day, emerged from the depths of the earth. People decked themselves with hawthorn and smeared their doors with pitch; and all the sanctuaries were closed and surrounded with a rope, save only the temple of Dionysus in the Marsh.

The third day of the Anthesteria was devoted to the souls of the departed. For their benefit the citizens prepared a pudding of mixed grains, in earthenware saucepans — a pledge of abundance — which had to be consumed before nightfall. This was the day of 'Saucepans'. When it was over, one took leave of the infernal powers amid cries of: 'Out go the Keres: the Anthesteria are over.'[1]

A number of ceremonies of the same order, beneficent or purifying, gay or funereal, sometimes even tragic, were performed in similar circumstances and in many another city. We conjecture that variants of the Anthesteria were celebrated in the Ionian cities

[1] For details of these ceremonies, see H. Jeanmaire, *Dionysos*. Paris, 1951, Ch. I.

of Asia Minor. Memories of most of these rites have been but sparsely preserved in later texts. But the most widespread of them appear to have related to the practice of the scapegoat, which consisted in removing the sins, misfortunes or sufferings of the whole people by transferring them to a victim who was then expelled or sacrificed.

A few echoes of them have reached us. At Chaeronaea, for example, each head of a family, and also the chief magistrate in the Prytanaeum, practised 'the expulsion of Hunger'. A slave was beaten with rods and driven away amid cries of: 'Begone, Hunger; enter, Health and Wealth!' On the sixth of the month Thargelion (May) in Athens, the people led out of the city two human victims, one wearing a collar of white figs, the other a collar of purple figs, and then stoned them. On the following day, after this rite of collective purification, an offering was made of the first fruits. At Abdera a citizen was excommunicated every year 'in order that he alone should bear the burden of all the sins of the people'. Six days later he was stoned by the whole population. There was also a very ancient custom still surviving in the sixth century before our era in the cities of Asia Minor: in order to banish plague or famine, they chose an ugly or deformed person, took him to an appropriate spot, made him eat dry figs, a barley loaf and cheese, and then, while the flute was being played, whipped him on the genital organs with branches of a forest tree. Finally he was burned on a pyre of wood cut from the forest and his ashes were then thrown into the sea.

These cruel and joyous festivals were essentially collective. If they were to be efficacious, the whole population had to take part, at least indirectly. It was a common belief in the archaic period that life was born of death.

## FUNERALS

Hence the place and importance of funerals in family life. For the great families a funeral was the occasion for a public demonstration in which they displayed their wealth and power, and the extent of their clientèle.

The first and imperative duty of the living was to bury the dead

'. . . Hector, whom I loved the best
Of all my husband's brothers. . . .'[1]

The end of each couplet is followed by a long wail from the mourners.

The exposure of the body did not usually last long, but the time varied. In the classical period it was often limited by law. The shade of Patroclus asks for it to be short. Hector's body on the other hand was exposed for nine days, and Achilles' for seventeen. In this case the body had to be roughly embalmed. The kings of Sparta continued to be embalmed. A sacrifice was then offered to the dead. The blood of animals was poured from cups round the body, and the flesh was consumed in a copious repast.[2]

The second act was represented by the funeral procession. The body was carried to the place of burial on a four-wheeled carriage, accompanied by a sometimes splendid train of women-mourners on foot and men in chariots.

The supreme ceremony of burial was reserved for the close relatives of the departed, who, after dismissing the procession, proceeded alone to this duty. In the case of cremation, those nearest and dearest to the dead man themselves raised the pyre. The body was placed on the summit. Victims were then offered in sacrifice: their fat served to cover the corpse, while their bodies were laid round about, with jars of honey and oil. In addition to all this, Achilles sacrificed four mares on the pyre of Patroclus and two of the dead man's favourite dogs.[3] When the whole pyre had been consumed, wine was scattered over the ashes to extinguish them; then the bones were gathered together and after being wrapped in a double layer of fat were placed in an urn. This was wrapped in a cloth and set in a grave covered with large flagstones. Earth was piled up on it to form a 'tomb', on which a 'stele' or vertical stone was sometimes planted.

When the burial was a matter of simple inhumation, the body

[1] *Iliad*, XXIV, pp. 564–5.

[2] *Iliad*, XXIII, vv. 29–34.

[3] Not to speak of the twelve Trojan prisoners who were slain to appease the soul of Patroclus. (See Book XXIII. Trans. Marris, pp. 511, 512).

was laid in a rectangular grave about a yard deep. Beside the dead
man they placed, for his use or diversion, his weapons, his jewels
and an assortment of vases and household utensils. Finally, on the
flagstone that covered the grave, they sometimes set a large
sepulchral urn, open at the bottom, as a means of transmitting to
the departed the family offerings, such as libations of wine, oil
and honey. The funeral ceremony itself was often depicted on
these painted vases.

On returning home, the members of the family purified themselves and partook of the funeral banquet. The soul of the dead
man was supposed to be present at this, a fact which forbade
anyone's saying a word that was not in his praise. On the third
and again on the ninth day after the funeral, another repast was
offered on the tomb to the dead man himself. This was the end of
the period of mourning; in other words, it was held that from that
moment the departed had finally taken his place in the world
beyond.

## FUNERAL GAMES AND PUBLIC GAMES

It is obvious that the public for whom the Homeric poems were
written was extremely fond of games, athletic contests, chariot-
races, and also of artistic competitions in singing, dancing and
poetry.

The greater part of Book XXIII of the *Iliad*, which is one of the
longest in the poem, is devoted to an extraordinarily vivid and
picturesque description of the games given by Achilles on the
occasion of Patroclus' funeral; while a long passage in Book VIII
of the *Odyssey* shows us the public games, mingled with dance
and song, that were celebrated in Phaeacia in presence of Odysseus.

The games given in honour of a hero's funeral are represented
in the Homeric poems as a current practice: as witness what the
shade of Agamemnon says to the shade of Achilles as they stand
in the fields of pale asphodel:

'... Thou in thy day
Hast seen the funeral games of many heroes,
When young men gird themselves and make them ready

To struggle for the prize, at some king's death;
But at that sight thou wouldst have marvelled most;
Such glorious prizes did the goddess offer,
Thetis the silver-footed, in thy honour. . . .'[1]

The games celebrated in honour of Achilles are not the only ones
to be so described. The talkative old Nestor does not fail to recall
his own triumphs at the games which, when he was a young man,
had been held in honour of Amarynceus, king of the Epeians.[2]
And the same book of the *Iliad* contains an allusion to the games
celebrated at Thebes after the death of Oedipus.[3]

That the holding of these contests, which were not always exclusively athletic, persisted to a late period and even to the end of
the Homeric age, among the great royal and aristocratic families,
is proved by reference to Hesiod. He recalls how he once went to
Chalcis to take part in the funeral games in honour of the valiant
Amphidamas. The dead man's sons offered a great quantity of
prizes, and Hesiod himself won a prize for his hymn, a two-
handled tripod which, on his return home, he dedicated to the
Muses of Helicon.[4]

These contests and the prizes that crowned them were simply a
survival of old customs or rather very ancient institutions the
meaning of which has long been lost. There was in fact a time
when funeral games were not games, but veritable combats, fights
for the succession which often had a tragic issue, and in which the
competitors disputed among themselves the offices, honours and
property of the departed; sometimes also his wife or daughter,
pledges or vehicles of legitimacy. The ultimate victor was the
elect of heaven. It was held that he owed his triumph less to skill,
strength and intelligence than to the protection and assistance of
the deity. And we find very clear traces of this conception not
only in the ancient tradition relative to the games but also,
naturally, in the Homeric texts.

Thus the chariot race, which was the main feature of the funeral
games for Patroclus, was really only a contest between Apollo

---

[1] *Odyssey*, XXIV, vv. 87–9, p. 421.     [2] *Iliad*, XXIII, vv. 630 et seq.
[3] *Ibid.*, vv. 679–80.          [4] Hesiod, *Works and Days*, ed. Mair, p. 24.

and Athena. The former who is protecting Eumelus, son of Admetus, causes the whip to fall from Diomed's hand at the most dramatic point in the race. Athena restores the whip to her favourite and breaks the yoke of Eumelus' team which is hurled to the ground, opening a way for his rival. In the foot race Athena makes the son of Oileus slip in the dung of the sacrificed oxen, in order to assure Odysseus' victory. But in the contest with the bow it is Apollo's turn to secure the triumph of Meriones.

However that may be, it is evident that the funeral games described by Homer and Hesiod served then only to honour the memory of the dead and to permit his descendants to display their power, wealth and magnificence.

According to the legendary tradition, the public games and, specifically, those which became the great Panhellenic contests — the Olympic, the Isthmian, the Nemean and the Pythian — were in principle no other than funeral games held near the tomb of an ancient hero or tutelary genius, the tomb of Pelops at Olympia, of Melicertus at Corinth, of Opheltes at Nemea and of Pytho at Delphi. It seems difficult, however, to reconcile this identification with the regular renewal of these celebrations from generation to generation, and with their periodical character. Was it not the peculiar feature of funeral games that they were held by the family once for all? If in the first instance they had been a means of establishing the succession, they ceased to have any reason when it was once established.

But when this has been said, we must admit that the identification of public games with the funeral games of the family is not, in certain respects, entirely unjustified, and that it at least deserves attention.

The public games held at regular intervals were very probably designed to promote the renewal of those subterranean energies which perpetuated life and presided over its annual restoration. Now according to primitive notions this vital energy was normally incarnated in the king. He had therefore to be put to trial at fixed intervals. In a certain number of Greek cities the normal duration of a reign appears originally to have been limited to eight years. Homer tells us that Minos caused his power to be renewed every ninth year by Zeus.[1] In the historic period the ephors could suspend the powers of the kings of Sparta after they had reigned eight years. In primitive times the public games were doubtless only a means of periodically testing the vital energy of the reigning king — every eight years perhaps. If victorious, he commenced a new reign; if beaten he yielded up his place, and also his wife or daughter, to the victor.

The public games therefore, like those which followed a funeral, were also in principle designed to regulate a succession or inheritance: hence certain of their funereal aspects. The presidents at the Nemean games were dressed in mourning garb.

We have already remarked how, in our opinion, the games held in Phaeacia at the time of Odysseus' return were doubtless simply an episode in a number of renewal rites. In these games the man who represents the spirit of the Tree, the incarnation of vegetable life — and this happens to be Odysseus — is victorious. It is even worth noting that his success is immediately followed by a song of Demodocus who, amid an accompaniment of dances, describes in a sprightly vein the union of Aphrodite and Ares. That this should be a coincidence is by no means certain. It was normal and frequent for a marriage in heaven to be evoked, and even celebrated, on the occasion of ceremonies of which the purpose was to honour the forces of generation and life, as witness the union of Dionysus with the queen at the festival of the Anthesteria in Athens.

In any event, what appears certain is that the poet who described the Phaeacian games in the *Odyssey*, and the games that followed the funeral of Patroclus in the *Iliad*, was familiar with the celebration of the great Panhellenic games, notably those at Olympia which were the most ancient. This is the only explanation for the place of honour given in the *Iliad* to the chariot race which was certainly not a normal contest in the family funeral games. This race is described with such minuteness and precision that the narrative can only have come from an *habitué* of the racecourses, and that he is perhaps even alluding to an historical event,

[1] *Odyssey*, XIX, vv. 178-9.

namely the victory at Olympia in 648 B.C. of the team belonging to Myron of Sicyon, brother of the tyrant Orthagoras.[1]

After the parade of competitors and horses we first hear a number of recommendations which Nestor makes to his son Antilochus, a kind of lesson on the art of driving and, more especially, on the way of handling the team at the turning-post.

> '. . . Drive close to it,
> And bear thy car and horses hard upon it,
> Throwing thy weight upon the well-laced car
> A little to their left; and then call on
> The off horse, voice and whip as well, and give him
> The rein, and let the near horse hug the post
> So tightly that the nave of thy stout wheel
> Appears to graze it; but beware of hitting
> The stone, for fear of smashing up the car
> And injuring the horses. . . .'[2]

A judge is needed, to stand by the turning-post. Achilles appoints Phoenix. Then the signal for the start is given.

There follow in succession all the unexpected turns and incidents of a fine race: the breaking of the harness on Eumelus' team and his fall; the jostling in a narrow passage between Menelaus and Antilochus who, by irregular and alarming procedure, compels his rival to yield him the passage; the cries and arguments between the betters, between Ajax and Idomeneus on the lawn near the finishing-post; and lastly, after the race, Menelaus' complaint against the unfair manoeuvre of Nestor's son. Things must have happened like this on the race course at Olympia; we must remember, too, that the chariot race was only the most spectacular and aristocratic of the contests.

Homer also mentions the boxing-match in which the combatants wore thongs of hide on their fists; the foot race; the fight in armour; throwing the discus; the archery contest; hurling the javelin; and also songs and dances.

In imagining the scene at Olympia, we can picture the crowd of pilgrims and other men — for married women were excluded on

---

[1] Cf. *Les Poèmes homériques et l'Histoire grecque*, Vol. II, Ch. VIII.
[2] *Iliad*, XXIII, p. 518.

pain of death — who have flocked to the ancient sanctuary from every part of Hellas, under the protection of the sacred truce. Over the little plain swept by a singularly gentle and restful breeze, unique in Hellas, there reigns the atmosphere of a kermesse. People are eagerly awaiting victories that will confer lustre on the cities of the champions, and all amid the tumult of a fairground and place of pilgrimage.

It was a tireless and insatiable public, in any case, an admirable public for the bards who had come to seek glory and profit by reciting to the multitude their latest works, which had probably been enjoyed in the first instance by the courts of the nobility.

Perhaps, indeed, it was for this public that the *Iliad* and *Odyssey* were written.

# CHAPTER XI

# WANDERERS AND EXPATRIATES

HOMERIC poetry is the poetry of adventure in far countries. The first of these miraculous masterpieces, which were to fix the destiny of Greek epic as a whole, were probably in the first instance, towards the end of the eighth century, addressed to a public of sailors and pioneers who were preparing to set sail for the conquest of barbarian coast-lands.[1] Two privileged ports of call had been chosen as the scenes of their fabulous and varied stories, both on the margin of the Greek world properly so-called: the entry to the Hellespont which gave access to the north-eastern seas, and on the other hand the two ports of Corcyra, in the isle of the Phaeacians, which was on the threshold of western navigation. The choice was significant and is no doubt revealing.

All or nearly all the heroes of these poems themselves figure as wanderers and even expatriates. At the point where the *Iliad* opens, it has been nearly ten years since the heroes, at the head of their followers, have left hearth and home; and after the final victory, Odysseus wanders over the seas for another ten years and returns to Ithaca only to set out on another adventure, at the bidding of Tiresias. Menelaus, whose ships had been thrown on to the coast of Crete, embarks on a new expedition, this time to Egypt and Phoenicia, and only returns to Sparta seven years later. How unsettled and mobile were all these heroes! Agamemnon, Menelaus, Aegisthus, Diomed, Ajax, Achilles and Alcinous are all grandchildren of exiles. Patroclus and Phoenix had been compelled to flee their country and take refuge with Peleus, as Theo-

[1] See Emile Mireaux, *Les Poèmes homériques et l'Histoire grecque*, Vol. I, *Homère de Chios et les Routes de l'Etain* [the trade routes for the supply of tin].

clymenus does with Telemachus in the *Odyssey*. The next generation, moreover, had to leave their native land, in their turn, under
the violent pressure of the 'return of the Heracleidae'. It was they
who went to colonize the islands and the coasts of Asia Minor,
and plant new dynasties descended from Nestor and Agamemnon.

In this way the heroic world of the epics appears in our eyes as
something mobile, effervescent and tumultuous. We must certainly make an allowance for dramatic imagination; nevertheless,
the reading of the poems warns us that we should be taking a great
risk if we supposed that here is an incorrect and distorted picture
of the actual life of the times when the poems were written, and if
we ignored the fact that Homeric society, no doubt like all
human societies, comprised a mobile element, a contingent that
was wandering and itinerant, often by profession, but also from a
taste for change, a desire for gain, a love of risk, and sometimes
from necessity. On the margin of the established routine of the
community, there was a picturesque and unexpected fringe, which
perhaps represented only the inevitable reaction of liberty, chance,
and individual initiative to the quieter virtues.

### THE SEAFARERS

We must naturally place seafarers in the front rank of those whom
we see leading an adventurous life.

In Homeric society the sailors do not represent a social category
or a clearly-defined profession, and this is a most original feature.
They have in this respect nothing in common with the *demiourgoi*
who occupy as such a well-marked social position and prefer to
exercise certain activities in the service of the public. On the other
hand a 'king', a landowner, or again the son of a 'king' or landowner, may apply himself to seafaring even as his principal occupation, as Menelaus does during his seven years of enterprise in
Egypt and Phoenicia. He none the less remains, socially speaking,
a sailor by chance, a temporary and in some sort an accidental
seaman. Or perhaps it would be truer to say that, if no one was
specifically a sailor in Greece, everyone was more or less a sailor,
at least in the seabord towns, and that is nearly everywhere.

There was therefore no naval 'demiourgia', or class of specialized navigators. This was so true that the cities were obliged to organize, for the service of the state, a kind of maritime conscription.[1] We discover from the Homeric texts that such in fact existed in Phaeacia and at Ithaca;[2] but we know most about it from the very ancient Athenian institution of the naucrary,[3] which there has already been occasion to cite.[4] In each of the forty-eight naucraries in Athens, among which the citizens were distributed, one great family was required to equip and maintain a ship which the head of the family as *naucraros* would eventually command; the other members of the naucrary had to furnish the rigging and the crew. But this was an official organization designed to operate only in the event of mobilization or when it was a question of providing overseas transport.

It is not, save by exception, in the ranks of the officially enrolled that we should look for the promoters of maritime enterprise or adventure, or for those who took part in them; and among these men all were not of the same rank nor did all possess the same capacity.

In a passage of the *Works and Days* which Hesiod devotes to navigation, he introduces us to the humblest of such men, those who aspired only to a modest profit at the cost of a limited risk. When Hesiod's father was living at Cymé, in Eolis, he had gone in for seafaring, the poet tells us, in the delusive hope of making a fortune; but in the end, and to avoid penury, he had crossed the Aegean on 'a black ship' and taken refuge at Ascra in the heart of Boeotian territory. Hesiod confesses that he himself has no leaning for sea life. Perhaps his brother Perses had inherited the paternal vocation; however that may be, the poet is lavish of counsel, a counsel of prudence. He first recommends him to choose a broad-beamed vessel to carry his merchandise, and not a light one;[5]

---

[1] 'Inscription maritime': as in France where the seafaring population are registered and can be called up for service in war.

[2] See Chapter VII above, and *Odyssey*, II, 212 and IV, 649–51.

[3] Greek 'naucraria' (Translator).

[4] See Chapter VII above.

[5] See A. W. Mair, *Hesiod, the Poems and Fragments*, pp. 23–4 (Translator).

which shows that Perses did not himself own a ship. For a lands-man it would not have been normal to do so.

These details throw light, indirectly, on some of the forms of maritime trading. The latter must have been carried on, in part, by means of boats which were rented from the shipowners on the coast; we are here concerned only with the question of coastal trading or short crossings. Indeed in Hesiod's view, the season for navigation lasted only for fifty days after the summer solstice, when the winds were regular and the sea without peril. There was another good season at the beginning of spring, but it was very short and rather uncertain. Such periods, in any case, did not al-low of long expeditions, and those who engaged in trading under these conditions had not ceased to be landsmen, and, as Hesiod recommends, they would hasten to pull the ship up on the beach before the first equinoctial rains set in. They would then surround it with heavy stones to prevent its being overturned by the winter storms. They would open the bung-hole in the hold so that the vessel should not fill with rain-water, which would rot the boards; they would carry the rigging and sails up to the house and hang the rudder in the smoke above the hearth.

But there were on the high seas men of a different character and of another stamp.

In the story he invents for the benefit of Eumaeus, Odysseus poses as a Cretan bastard of good family. On the death of his father, he had been allotted the small portion due to him by the legitimate sons, but he had then married a rich heiress. He was great in war, he says,

> 'But labour in the fields I never loved,
> Nor household thrift, that nurse of goodly children:
> But ever to my taste were ships of oars,
> And war, and polished spears and darts — grim things
> Whereat most others shudder. Well, no doubt
> I loved the things the gods put in my heart.'[1]

Nine times, at the head of a fleet and a company of gallants, he had sought fortune in foreign lands; by which we understand

[1] *Odyssey*, XIV, vv. 222–7.

that he had taken part in nine expeditions of rapine and piracy.

Maritime ventures of a commercial kind were not yet materially distinguishable from piratical incursions. Opportunity created the robber. Piracy was moreover a very honourable occupation and one readily boasted of it, as does Odysseus who does not hesitate to pose as a former pirate. When Polyphemus finds Odysseus and his companions in his cavern, he asks them quite simply: 'Are you not pirates?' The question was natural. Pirates went in for trade; they had to, in order to convert the value of their takings. Merchant seamen, on the other hand, dabbled in piracy when occasion offered. They were armed, if only to defend themselves against pirates; and being equipped for violence, they were naturally ready to take advantage of every good opportunity for pillage, like all men of pluck. In the course of a fairly long cruise, was it not necessary to pillage here and there in order to obtain the necessary provisions as cheaply as possible?

In any event, we learn from Odysseus' narrative in Book XIV of the *Odyssey*, how a maritime venture was organized, what sort of men the crew were, and how they were recruited. In the circumstances in question the promoter is the illegitimate son of a great noble who has only received a paltry share of the estate and who, after marrying a rich young woman, has tried to make his fortune outside the ordinary or traditional walks of life. Our man has decided to try cruising along the coast of Egypt. He begins by securing the assistance of some 'godlike comrades', that is, men of noble birth but in a social and moral position similar to his own. They are to be the officers under him, and this enables them to fit out nine vessels. It was easy to collect the crews. The narrative tells us that the sailors were recruited from among the 'warriors', that is from the class of peasant-soldiers which must also have counted in its ranks a number of younger sons ready for adventure. The men 'come in quickly', we are told. For six days they are entertained and they carouse with the commander; on the seventh they embark and sail for Egypt, where they arrive after a crossing of five days. The enterprise, in point of fact, goes very much amiss owing to the indiscipline of the men and their excessive thirst for pillage. There is no question of dividing the booty, which was usually done by allotting equal portions to the men after the leader of the expedition had first received 'what liked him best'.[1]

Commercial ventures to distant lands were planned in much the same way. The ships had to sail as a fleet and on a semi-military basis, if they wished to avoid unpleasant surprises at sea, and especially when moored at anchor, even in Greek waters and, *a fortiori*, on barbarian coasts.

The composition of a commercial convoy was a complex affair. The Homeric texts and the contemporary paintings or drawings which have survived acquaint us with three kinds of ship. There were two sorts of 'hollow' and 'swift' boats, with keels. The lighter one carried a crew of twenty-two men: the captain, the pilot who managed the rudder, and twenty rowers. The more powerful was manned by fifty-two men, of whom fifty were rowers. This was the *pentecontoros*, a warship as much as a trader, and often armed with a ram. Finally, there was the *phortis*, broad in the beam and flat-bottomed: this was the trader par excellence. All three were navigated by oar and sail. The sail was a large sheet of square or rectangular canvas which was fastened to a horizontal yard and attached to the deck-planks. Handling it was difficult and awkward. It could scarcely be raised except in the open where it was easy to catch the wind. The oars were invariably used to bring the ship in and out of port.

A commercial convoy almost necessarily comprised these three kinds of ship. The 'swift' ships served as scouts and defended the others in case of need; but their capacity for lading was poor. A passage-way or half-deck ran from end to end of them, and there was practically no space for cargo except under this half-deck or

[1] *Odyssey*, XIV, vv. 231-3. As a matter of fact (or rather fiction!) the men were all killed or enslaved by the infuriated natives. Odysseus, however, conceived the brilliant device of throwing himself on the mercy of the king, who took pity on him and spared his life. Odysseus then stayed seven years in Egypt and came away loaded with gifts. Further hair-raising adventures followed. All this, needless to say, is a wonderful romance invented by Odysseus for the entertainment of the unsuspecting swineherd (Translator).

under the rowers' benches. It was therefore only the presence of some real trading ships that allowed of profitable transport. Unfortunately these were slow and hard to manoeuvre. If the weather were ever so slightly uncertain, one had to land and wait for the sky to clear completely. So the convoy would trail from anchorage to anchorage, the daily stages in calm weather not exceeding fifty sea miles. One never sailed by night, because navigation near the coasts was always dangerous in the dark, even for a lone ship. For a convoy it was impossible.

No doubt Telemachus sails by night on his journey from Ithaca to Pylos and back; but it is a question of escaping the attention of the suitors; and, besides, he is under the special protection of Athena, both ways. Eurylochus roughly reminds Odysseus of the sound rule when the latter refuses to stop at nightfall off the Island of the Sun. 'The nights beget fierce winds, the bane of ships,' he says. One should stop towards sunset, go ashore and prepare supper near the vessel; and only put to sea next morning.[1]

The best landing place was a deep cove, with a good beach on which the ships could be pulled up. Failing that, one might take refuge in a bay hemmed in with cliffs, provided it were deep and well protected, sheltered from the waves and from wind-squalls. The ships would then be moored side by side and roped to jutting rocks: this is how Odysseus' fleet proceeded when they stopped at the 'fair haven' of the Laestrygonians.[2]

The first precaution, immediately on landing, was to send scouts to the nearest look-out place so as to raise the alarm in case of danger. Hence the favourite landing places were on small islands, deserted or thinly inhabited, just off the mainland: these offered the maximum of security. On such an islet Odysseus hauled up his boats, facing the land of the Cyclops. This was the site of the islet of Ortygia at the entrance to the bay of Syracuse: it was a very ancient resting place for the seamen of Chalcis and Corinth.

When one had to cruise for several weeks along barbarian shores, such improvised halts in hostile or unknown territory

---

[1] *Odyssey*, XII, vv. 279–93.
[2] *Odyssey*, X, vv. 87–94.

were inadequate for a convoy. It needed organized stopping places where the men could obtain some rest, take in stores and carry out repairs. From the last third of the eighth century onwards, this need was to be supplied by the colonies that had been regularly founded all along the coastlands of southern Italy and Sicily, and on the shores of the Black Sea. These colonies were like organized swarms of bees; they had been sent out by the mother-city to hold a strategic point or provide a safety-valve for the turbulence of a surplus population. Built in accordance with ancient rites and with the offering of 'splendid hecatombs' to the gods, they were established by a founder who belonged to one of the holy families of the home city, and who brought with him some of the soil of the motherland and fire taken from the civic hearth. At the beginning of Book VI of the *Odyssey* we learn that the city of the Phaeacians had been founded in this way by Nausithous.

These official colonies, however, were not planted at hazard. We know that in many places they had been preceded by the trading posts of adventurers, like that of the Eretrians on Corcyra or of the Chalcidians at Syracuse, prior to the foundation of the Corinthian colonies. These settlements were not real 'cities'; because, as Fustel de Coulanges says, 'a band of adventurers could never found a city.' They were mere fortified camps, places of refuge for sea convoys, and held by a little group of sedentary traders. We can imagine what they were like from the picture in the *Iliad* of the 'camp of the Achaeans' which had been pitched on the shore near the entrance to the Hellespont. Now in the bay of the Scamander, at this important stage in the sea route to the north-east, an encampment of this kind must have preceded the foundation of the Greek Ilium, which took place about 700 B.C. This early settlement perhaps served as a model for the author of the older poem on *The Wrath of Achilles*. Protected by a ditch and a 'wall' which was only a strong palisade, and built by a stream which supplied drinking water, it covered a landing place for the ships that were drawn up on the beach and included a group of huts and a place for public meetings, where also cases were judged by the tribunal, and where there were altars to the gods. The author of the *Iliad*, however, takes great care to inform us in Book XII that his camp had been built 'in despite of the immortal gods' and without the sacrifice of those 'splendid hecatombs' which accompanied the foundation of every true city.

We must suppose the existence, at least at the outset, of a whole series of similar settlements, half counting-houses, half refuges, along the two great sea routes that led to the sources of supply for the trade in tin, that rare metal indispensable for the making of bronze. These were the Caucasus in one direction and Etruria in the other. In Book I of the *Odyssey* it was the latter route that Athena, disguised as Mentor, Prince of the Taphians, pretended to be following when she, or rather perhaps he, said he was carrying a cargo of iron to be exchanged for bronze at Temesa, on the shores of the Tyrrhenian Sea.

How long might these distant cruises last? The convoys that left the various ports on the Aegean Sea assembled some at Corcyra, others at the entrance to the Hellespont where they awaited the definite return of good weather, which was at the summer solstice. From those places they needed twenty or thirty days if the former were to reach Cumae in Campania, the oldest of the Greek colonies, or the coasts of Etruria; and if the latter were to reach the further shores of the Black Sea and the land of Colchis. If there were no accidents or serious delays, they might in theory be back home just before the autumnal equinox, which put an end to navigation. In fact, the business of discharging cargo, bartering and reloading must have taken a fairly long time. The return voyage was, as a general rule, only made in the following year.

Maritime ventures to Egypt, which became frequent after the expulsion of the Assyrians and the establishment, in the second third of the seventh century, of the Twenty-Sixth Dynasty, followed a somewhat different pattern. Only bold sailors ventured to contemplate such a voyage. From Crete to Egypt one had to reckon with a crossing of at least five days and five nights, a terrifying venture for such poor navigators as were the Greeks of Homer's time, men who would not readily lose sight of land.

The crossing was only possible in summer, thanks to the Etesian winds which then blew steadily from the north. No one dreamed of crossing in the opposite direction in winter, when the winds were blowing from the south. The return voyage was effected in spring by following the shores of Phoenicia,[1] of Cyprus and of southern Asia Minor. Egypt was not a country where one was satisfied with simply landing in order to take on cargo and set off again. One stayed there for months, even years; one traded; one made a fortune. The Greek merchants lived in concessions, of which the most important was to be Naucratis. Menelaus stayed in Egypt for six years.

## COMMERCE AND COINAGE

The only passage where Homer depicts merchant seamen does not concern Greeks but Phoenicians. In Book XV of the *Odyssey*, Eumaeus relates how he has been kidnapped, as a small child, with the complicity of a slave from Sidon, by the crew of one of their ships which had come to trade at the isle of Syros. He naturally speaks of them without indulgence:

> 'Thither Phoenicians, famous seamen, came,
> Rapacious rascals, bringing countless trinkets
> In their black ship. . . .'[2]

These merchants hauled their ship up on the beach, camped near-by and went from house to house until they had disposed of all their junk, glass trinkets, jewels, textiles, embroidered veils and so on. Homer describes them in the *megaron* of a 'fine house' offering to the mistress surrounded by her maids a necklace of gold and amber; the jewel is weighed and examined; they bargain. While this is going on, the servant, who is in league with the Phoenicians, picks up three gold cups, takes little Eumaeus by the hand, and escapes to the ship.

Prior to this the merchants, as they sold their stock, had been making up a new cargo by purchasing local products which they

---

[1] Eumaeus' nurse was a slave of Sidonian origin who had been carried off by Taphian pirates.

[2] Book XV, pp. 270–1.

would go and sell elsewhere. These operations, systematically recorded by an accountant on the ship,[1] had been going on for a year. When the hold is full again and good weather has returned, they put out to sea, in secret, because they have taken advantage of the last few days to enrich themselves by theft.[2]

This realistic description no doubt reveals to us what the general pattern of maritime trading was like.

What now, we may ask, did Greek commerce deal in, during the age of Homer?

It handled, as regards exports, the products of Greek industry, which was now rapidly expanding: pottery, weapons, woollen goods and linen, but also and perhaps especially wine. This was not what we call wine, which would have occupied an exorbitant amount of room in the diminutive boats of the eighth century, but a thick black juicy liquid which could only be drunk after being copiously diluted with water and which, being transported in well-stoppered *amphorae* (wine-jars) was not excessively cumbersome. The sailors of Chios had at an early date become specialists in the wine trade.

A first priority in the import trade was placed on the metals that were lacking in the Aegean basin, especially tin. Egypt supplied salt, soda, alum, alabaster, certain medicinal specialties celebrated in the *Odyssey*,[3] corn also, and what was perhaps essential in the history of civilization — papyrus. The northern seas provided corn, slaves and timber, which as Greece became progressively deforested was more and more indispensable.

The transport of timber by sea set an even more difficult problem than that of wine. The ships of the eighth and seventh cen-

---

[1] *Odyssey*, VIII, vv. 162–4.

[2] Listeners to the *Odyssey* must have been gratified — and edified — to learn that later on, during a tempest, the wicked servant who had kidnapped Eumaeus was smitten by the thunderbolt of Zeus and thrown overboard. Eumaeus was sold to Laertes. After listening to this true story of the swineherd's early life, Odysseus rather smugly congratulates him on having fallen into the hands of so 'thoughtful' a master (Translator).

[3] Book IV, vv. 229–32.

turies were scarcely capable of taking any considerable cargoes of wood, which was cumbersome and hard to stow away. Fortunately the sixth book of the *Odyssey* informs us that Greek navigators possessed a highly advanced technique for the construction of rafts, which were formed of a score of well-dried tree-trunks, grouped in an oval like the bottom of a flat boat and well ballasted to resist wind and wave. Herein perhaps lay the secret of the oldest sea commerce in timber.

There is no doubt whatever that barter was still the principal instrument in the technique of exchange. The operation involved no major difficulty. By reason of the comparatively small number of categories of merchandise, it cannot have been hard to establish a ready-reckoner of their relative values. Immense progress, however, in the form of an invention that was greatly to facilitate the expansion of overseas trade, had been made at the very beginning of the Homeric era. This was the appearance of coinage.

Historians have hotly debated, and will continue to argue, about how money was invented. Who were the people or the ruler who first had the notion of circulating little stamped ingots of gold, silver or electron (a mixture of gold and silver), coins of a specified weight and a value guaranteed by the imprint of the place of origin? If we are to believe Herodotus,[1] it was the Lydians, and therefore Gyges their first king, who first struck a coinage in gold and silver. This testimony has lost much of its value since the discovery of a deposit of coins in the foundations of the first temple in Ephesus, which certainly antedated the accession of Gyges. It seems in fact that money was invented fairly early in the eighth century by the Greek cities in Asia Minor and that the use of it spread into continental Greece quite quickly, thanks to Pheidon of Argos.

Homer was certainly acquainted with money. His affected archaism, natural in a poet who was depicting the heroes of very ancient times, merely prevented his mentioning as a standard of value, apart from the ox, anything but the golden talent. But this

[1] Herodotus, Book I, paragraph 94. In 687 B.C. Gyges the Lydian overthrew the old Maeonian dynasty of the Heracleidae.

clearly figures as a unit of value of a fixed but inconsiderable
weight. In Book XXIII of the *Iliad*, the second prize in the foot
race is an ox, the third a half-talent of gold; in the chariot race the
third prize is a cauldron of four measures, the fourth, two gold
talents. We may recall here that in the treasure which was discovered in Aegina and which dates from about the beginning of
the eighth century, the excavators discovered five gold rings without ornamentation, four of which weighed about 132·7 grains,[1]
that is, half the weight of the Babylonian shekel which had been
adopted by Phocaea as a unit of value, and which was also, in the
future, to be the weight of the Athenian gold stater. It was perhaps
the prototype of the Homeric talent.

In this field, as elsewhere, there was decidedly nothing primitive about Homeric civilization.

### THE STRANGE LIFE OF BEGGARS

Among the host of wanderers in the Homeric world, a place apart
should be reserved for the beggars. Not that the profession — for
it was a real profession that men adopted either from necessity or a
sense of vocation — was in principle a vagabond's occupation.
But strangers who had been or seemed to have been particularly
unlucky adopted it readily enough: as witness Odysseus. It was, as
we shall see, a genuine function which one sometimes had to gain,
and also defend, with all one's might. If one lost it, one risked
having to go, once again perhaps, into exile.

However surprising it may appear at first glance, we must accept
the evidence. Homer, and after him Hesiod, count beggars among
the *demiourgoi*, that is, the servants of the community or 'public
workers'.[2] There is no ambiguity in the texts. When Eumaeus
enumerates the *demiourgoi* who were sometimes sought out among
foreigners, he mentions prophets, healers, carpenters and bards;
but, he adds, 'none would call a beggar in'.[3] So the latter is in-

---

[1] '8·6 grams.'

[2] Or perhaps, as Sir William Marris renders the word, 'those who serve the
people' (Translator).

[3] *Odyssey*, XVII, vv. 382–7. See translation cited, p. 306.

cluded among the genuine *demiourgoi*. And we find the same in-
clusion in Hesiod, who inserts the beggar in a list of men who
were unquestionably such:

> So potter with potter contendeth: the hewer of wood with the hewer of
> wood: the beggar is jealous of the beggar, the minstrel jealous of the
> minstrel.[1]

What then was this strange 'service' that an official beggar performed?

At the beginning of Book XVIII of the *Odyssey*, Homer describes the life, appearance and manner of the 'official' or 'public'
beggar who collects alms all over the city of Ithaca. He is an insatiable eater and drinker; tall, young and of fine appearance. The
young fellows call him Irus because, like Iris, he carries their messages. He inspires no pity. Although well fed, he wears the uniform of his profession: clad in rags, with only a stick and a wallet,
for the dress and the attitude of a beggar are a matter of ritual. The
beggar sits in the doorway, with his back to the doorpost against
which he 'rubs his shoulders'.[2] Here he waits until someone brings
him his portion of bread and meat or, if a banquet is proceeding,
until he is invited to go from table to table, collecting. His
response is to beg Zeus to fulfil the desires of the master of the
house.

In respect of a stranger newly arrived, who presents himself as a
beggar, as Odysseus does, and who may be one of those gods
who go from city to city sounding the hearts of men, feelings of
humanity and a consciousness of the duties of hospitality may
well play a part;[3] they would obviously not be felt for a professional beggar like this Irus, who is healthy and prosperous. The
part he plays and the reception reserved for him must have been
due to other causes and admit of another meaning, connected no
doubt with his paradoxical function as a *demiourgos*.

A probable clue is afforded by the word *apolymanter* which was
applied to beggars as a natural epithet, in an expression usually

---

[1] *Works and Days*, vv. 25–6; pp. 1–2.

[2] *Odyssey*, XVII, vv. 220–1.

[3] *Odyssey*, XVII, vv. 484–7.

translated by 'scourge of banquets' or 'kill-joy'.[1] This term is
derived straight from a Greek verb which belongs to the Homeric
vocabulary and admits of only one precise meaning: 'to purify by
eliminating pollutions'. It can in our opinion only mean 'purifier'.
On the occasion of meals or banquets, the beggar plays the part of
one who takes pollutions upon himself in order to remove them.

On the plane of daily life, this was the function of the scapegoat. We have elsewhere[2] studied its manifestations in public life,
where it had a solemn and collective character. That the part
should be played by a ragged beggar was perfectly natural. It was
not unusual for the scapegoat, when he figured in official ceremonies, to be represented by a man ridiculously clad in old tog-
gery. The attitude of the public toward the scapegoat was dual: on
the one hand he was loaded with gifts and at the same time with
blows and insults. Those were two ways of transferring pollutions
in a rite of purification. Now beggars were received at banquets in
exactly the same manner; for the insults and blows, and notably
the hurling of a stool, were traditional, at least in the same degree
as the gifts of food. When Eumaeus is bringing Odysseus disguised as a beggar to his own manor house, Melantheus the goatherd predicts as much; and the prediction was a sound one, and it
was fulfilled, because while one section of the suitors treated
Odysseus well, the others insulted him; Antinous and Eurymachus hurling stools at him while Ctesippus aimed a leg of beef
at his head.

By his presence and behaviour as a daily purifier, the beggar is
in fact a source and guarantee of prosperity. He begins, moreover,
by praying Zeus to grant prosperity to those who receive him; and
he is himself the living image of prosperity. This is why the beggar is, and professionally must be, a heavy eater and great drinker,
a yawning gulf for food and wine. It explains the allusions to the
demands of his stomach of which Odysseus, disguised as a beggar
but knowing the trade, is so lavish in his addresses; allusions

[1] *Odyssey*, XVII, vv. 220-1.
[2] *Les Poèmes homériques et l'Histoire grecque*, Vol. I, Ch. IX, and Vol. II,
Ch. VI. See above, Chapter X.

which he repeats, and which have surprised and shocked many commentators who have wanted to exclude them from the text. Such an exclusion would remove from the work a good part of its meaning.

The beggar is, in fine, the ragged bringer of good luck; an office he has not even today entirely ceased from filling in popular belief.

As a symbol and pledge of prosperity, he must naturally be a worthy representative of it. He must be the best man, at least in that branch of mendicancy which has fallen to his lot. This means that, when a competitor arrives, he must defend his position. This misadventure is exactly what befalls Irus, the official beggar, when he finds Odysseus seated at the very door which is Irus' domain. The question must first be settled by a regular bout at fisticuffs. Iros is vanquished and dragged by one leg out of the palace. But this is not the end of his misfortunes. Fallen as he has from the dignity of public beggar, he is to be expelled from Ithaca and landed on the mainland, in the domains of king Echetus who, it appears, gives a very rough reception to newcomers of this kind. So he is now, at the very least, condemned to the wandering life which his competitor Odysseus is supposed to have been leading prior to his arrival in Ithaca; and these wanderings will end only when he wins by main force a new position as a mendicant *demiourgos*.

### EXILES AND MERCENARIES

The exiles, men of all classes who had lost their homes, were to go on increasing as social and political conflict became more exasperated. The man who had been banished owing to civil strife was to become a familiar type during the classical age.

We see him appear with the advent of the tyrannies in the second third of the seventh century. Cypselus, the first tyrant of Corinth, banished a great number of his adversaries and confiscated their property. The Bacchiads, an aristocratic family who had ruled the city for nearly a century, took refuge, some in Thebes, some in Sparta, others in Corcyra, in Sicily, and even in Etruria where, according to a legend, Demaratus, the father of

Tarquin the Old, found a dwelling place. A few years later Theagenes in his turn drove the noble families from Megara.

But in any event, before the era of political exiles, large contingents of men had, during the Homeric age, fled their homeland after being conquered by some enemy. Thus the men of Asiné in Argolis who had been driven out by the Argives, wandered about for years before finding a refuge in a new Asiné which was conceded to them by their Spartan friends after the conquest of Messenia. In the reverse direction, the Messenians, who had just been heroically resisting the Spartans, made their way to Argos, to Sicyon, and the friendly cities of Arcadia.

To the number of these expatriates must be added all those who, in consequence of an act of vengeance, a crime, or a sometimes accidental homicide, had been forced to leave hearth and home and seek, often for good, the hospitality of a land that might be far distant. For when the guilty fugitive was only a bastard or even a younger son, there were not many families disposed to assume the burden of a fine in order to relieve a member who, as a general rule, was himself only an additional burden on the family patrimony.

However varied their origin, all these refugees lived for long periods in the shadow of the great aristocratic families; and here, under the traditional shelter of hospitality, they generally became integrated into the feudal system, thanks to the bond of 'companionship'. There was nothing of the romantic rebel about these outcasts and outlaws. A new development was, however, taking shape; new openings for such men were appearing, outside the patriarchal system and even beyond those maritime ventures which might attract a certain number of them.

On the edges of the Greek world and yet in close relations with it, new forces were arising and becoming centres of attraction, powers born of conflict and maintaining themselves by conflict. Such, in Asia Minor, was the monarchy of the Mermnadae which had overthrown the old dynasty of the Heracleidae at Sardis, and founded the great Lydian power; such too, in Egypt, the Twenty-Sixth Dynasty which recovered national independence from Assyrian rule. Gyges the Lydian and Psammetichus the Egyptian were moreover allies, and both were attracted by Greek civilization. Both also had recourse to the military technique of Greece which was now asserting its superiority under the influence of the armourers of Chalcis, Corinth and Boeotia, and of the Spartan tacticians.

The era of the Greek mercenary, which was to reach its zenith three hundred years later with the expedition of the Ten Thousand, had begun. At Sardis Gyges surrounded himself with a Greek bodyguard. In Egypt, Psammetichus sent to the Aegean to recruit an army of Greek and Carian mercenaries; to these men he allotted lands, and he posted them on the desert frontiers. In both cases the soldiers were hoplites, or heavy-armed infantry. Clad in the panoply of helmet, breastplate, buckler and greaves, this armoured infantry with its discipline and its serried ranks was a formidable adversary for the light-armed Asiatics who were generally provided only with helmet and buckler.

Even in Greece itself the new tyrants were before long to recruit personal bodyguards. Some of the cities also would be organizing troops of mercenaries to send as punitive expeditions into barbarian territory, with a veiw to covering the foundation of colonies. It was in one of these that the poet Archilochus enlisted, after he had lost his money. It was a question of punishing a Thracian tribe. Archilochus himself records this adventure in the verses where he tells how he had thrown away his shield when beating a hasty retreat.

Thus it was that, to ensure means of subsistence, the individual no longer needed to be inside the traditional social framework. Adventure ceased to be a matter of collective effort: it was individual, and at the same time the field of action was growing markedly wider. At the beginning of the sixth century the brother of the poet Alcaeus was to take service in the armies of Nebuchadnezzar.

The Greek world was moving towards individualism, democracy and cosmopolitanism.

# CHAPTER XII

## HOMER'S MESSAGE

A DESCRIPTION does not permit of a conclusion. We would simply point out that if we have completed our review of life in Homer's world with a picture of the movements of adventurers, of lonely or banished men, and even of reprobates, this has not been unintentional. Like all societies of men, the society we discover in Homer contained its own contradictions.

It was still — and we have many times insisted on the fact — essentially patriarchal and even feudal. It was still linked in many ways with its remotest sources, with the traditions of the Mediterranean and Aegean world, and also with those of the wandering Indo-European tribes who had been the last to reach the Greek lands. Homeric life was still impregnated with reminiscences of this immemorial past, which we can sometimes only reconstruct by induction.

This society was, on the other hand, deeply rooted in the soil. It was the possession of land that formed the social classes, regulated their distribution and controlled their relationships. It even in a large measure governed the structure of the family. Like all landholding communities, Homeric society was fundamentally traditional and traditionalistic.

All this is true; and perhaps the reading of the present work will often have conveyed the impression of a remarkably stable social order, a way of life almost unchangeable in its semi-ritual organization. Such an impression would be erroneous; yet it is the inevitable consequence of the genre, which requires a synthetic description to suggest a feeling of immobility.

The reading and study of the Homeric poems awaken, on the contrary, a very clear notion that the old social structures still reigning, the old feudal framework, were being visibly shaken by new tremors, by a fever of rejuvenation which was tending to deny and destroy them.

The best and most authentic representatives of this new ferment were, we would suggest, the pioneers of adventure whose mode of existence we have just pictured. Though still exceptional in their lives, they were none the less perhaps the most representative bearers of the typically Homeric message — a message of the creative, the unexpected and the heroic, sounding amid the inevitable monotony of daily life.

They were the leaven that leavened the whole. And in this they doubtless played the same life-giving part that was played by Homeric poetry itself in respect of the venerable tradition of liturgical and sacerdotal hymns. In our opinion, at least, one risks forming a very incorrect notion of this poetry, which conjures up so brilliant an image of the world we have been trying to reconstruct, if one imagines it as an end or conclusion, as the mere repertory of a poetical and historic past which was already dead. On the contrary, the more we study it, the more it appears to us as looking to the future. It reflects the hopes and impulses of a still young or rejuvenated people who could see opening before it the horizons of adventure, and wealth, and expansion.

The poetry is made in the likeness of the society it depicts, still archaic in form and structure, but shaken with impatience for that new life which is soon to expand in the freedom of art and thought and humanity.

The picture we have outlined in the preceding chapters must be regarded as the back-cloth, lit up by two masterpieces and before which are enacted the first scenes of that prodigious history which was to culminate in the Greek miracle.

# INDEX

## Date Due

| DEC 3 '99 | | | |
|---|---|---|---|
| NOV - 3 '61 | MAY 0 4 2002 | | |
| NOV 17 '92 | | | |
| JUN 17 '71 | | | |
| SEP 24 '84 | | | |
| OCT 9 '84 | | | |
| OCT 25 '84 | | | |
| | | | |
| MAY 02 '90 | | | |
| SEP 1 1 1990 | honors | | |
| | | | |
| | | | |
| | | | |
| | | | |
| | | | |
| | | | |
| | | | |
|  | PRINTED | IN U. S. A. | |